D0946375

CONFESSIONS

CONFESSIONS

A Life of Failed Promises

by

A. N. WILSON

BLOOMSBURY CONTINUUM
LONDON · OXFORD · NEW YORK · NEW DELHI · SYDNEY

BLOOMSBURY CONTINUUM
Bloomsbury Publishing Plc
50 Bedford Square, London, WC1B 3DP, UK
29 Earlsfort Terrace, Dublin 2, Ireland

BLOOMSBURY, BLOOMSBURY CONTINUUM and the Diana logo are trademarks of
Bloomsbury Publishing Plc

First published in Great Britain 2022

A catalogue record for this book is available from the British Library

Library of Congress Cataloguing-in-Publication data has been applied for

ISBN: HB: 978-1-4729-9480-6; eBook: 978-1-4729-9479-0; ePDF: 978-1-4729-9478-3

2 4 6 8 10 9 7 5 3 1

Typeset by Deanta Global Publishing Services, Chennai, India
Printed and bound in Great Britain by CPI Group (UK) Ltd, Croydon CR0 4YY

To find out more about our authors and books visit www.bloomsbury.com and
sign up for our newsletters

Contents

Introduction 1

1. Ungentle A. N. 7

2. Remind Me 14

3. Sorrowful Lay 19

4. Living up to the Blue China 21

5. Best of Young British 23

6. Masks 26

7. Norman Wilson's Son 34

8. Leaving Germany 47

9. The Works 54

10. Frail Travelling 58

11. Andrew Woods 63

12. Contrasts 72

13. Warfare Accomplished 80

14. Miscarriages 85

15. What is my Name? 91

16. Convent Thoughts   94

17. Newcastle Road   106

18. When I Get There, I'll Be Glad   116

19. Put Your Cap On, I Should   124

20. Notes for Boys   128

21. Little Bryan   140

22. Acqua Non Fizzimento   148

23. Journalistic Debut   157

24. A Bit of a Ruin   164

25. Mme de Liencourt, Mr Lowry and Others   168

26. Galsworthy Scholar   188

27. Kibbutznik   199

28. Lost Causes   207

29. Angel Fluffs   215

30. "Are they twa sweethearts?"   219

31. St Trinian's   234

32. Superficial Journey   250

33. St Andrew's by the Northern Sea   265

34. Prosaic and Drivelling   271

35. Clare   282

36. The Green Stick   295

Index   306

There is hardly a single action we perform in that phase [adolescence, early manhood] which we would not give anything, in later life, to be able to annul.

Marcel Proust, *Within a Budding Grove*

Introduction

All my life I have been a writer. Long before I first published a book, in my early twenties, I had formed the habit of putting experiences into written words – 'trying to learn to use words', as T. S. Eliot calls this strange activity. Those who have been kind enough, over the years, to tell me that they have enjoyed one of my novels, or something I wrote in a newspaper, or a biography, would probably be surprised that the finished product was a result – to quote from the same poem ('East Coker') of 'the intolerable wrestle / With words and meanings'. Fans and hostile critics alike have always spoken to, and of, me as one who was too fluent, who wrote with too much ease. Over fifty books published, and probably millions of words in the newspapers.

A young sub on an English newspaper once guilelessly asked his legendarily terrifying editor, 'Why are we giving so much money to that A. N. Wilson for something he's obviously just dashed off in half an hour?' The reply, flattering to me, was 'Because he CAN dash off the f**king article in half an hour something that would take others the whole f**king day.'

Inevitably, this facility has led me to write what has sometimes been deemed 'too much'. My difficulty with writing, with the business of 'trying to learn to use words', has not been in the act itself. I have never suffered from 'writer's block'. Rather, my problem has been trying to match the words to the truth of experience, whether I was composing a fiction, writing a work of history or biography, or keeping up my highly addictive work in the newspapers. (At one point, in the 1990s, I was writing three regular newspaper columns a week, as well as writing some of my longest historical works, such as *The Victorians* and its sequels, and publishing a novel every other year.)

To read the great writers is to be hit, in any number of ways, by their authenticity: they have recreated a scene, a character, in the perfect form of words for that purpose. They've scored a bullseye. This is what one is aiming for. Most printed words that we scan from week to week, or year to year, fail to hit the mark. They are newspaper articles that utterly fail to describe an event; they are slipshod biographies or unsuccessful novels. Then you come across the great writers, and you have struck gold.

Reading has always been a bigger part of my life than writing, and what I owe to the great writers of the past will sometimes be mentioned in this book. Our relationship with our favourite writers is deeper than many of our friendships with living people. For some reason, I have always been lucky enough to have time to read. So many of those I know either read for half an hour at the end of the day or reserve reading for long flights. I read constantly, and to deprive me of books would be the worst possible torture.

Through all the frantic rush of my own writing life I have had at the back of my mind the high standards set by my favourite writers, and the awareness that I was failing, over and over again, to live up to such standards. Jane Austen spoke, on her final birthday (her forty-first), of her work as 'the little bit (two Inches wide) of Ivory on which I work with so fine a Brush'. But, although I revere her this side of idolatry, that has never been the kind of writer I aspired to be, or could have been.

This book takes me up to the point where I had decided that I wanted, in my mid-thirties, to write the biography of Tolstoy. Of course, I am not worthy to lick the boots of either Jane Austen or Tolstoy, but I suppose that whatever I might have achieved as a writer would have been on the large canvas, and not the small piece of ivory. Writing the life of Tolstoy coincided with other events in life – my being sacked from an editorial post at the *Spectator* magazine, the unravelling of my first marriage and the death of my father. It seems a natural caesura in my catalogue of experiences.

So it is with the death of my father, and my visit to Tolstoy's grave, that this book ends.

———

The mind of the older person (I was born in 1950) inevitably moves back to the past, and, since I have the habit of wishing to put things into written form, it was inevitable that I should one day want to put memories of my childhood and early manhood into a book. I have called the book *Confessions*, not because I think of myself as the St Augustine, or the Rousseau, of our day, but because, without too morbid a sense of unworthiness, I am inevitably made aware of failure, both as a writer and as a human being, as a husband, a parent, a son, a friend.

All perspectives change with time, and nothing has changed more, in my last few decades, than my interior relationship with my parents. Like most people, I carry my mother and father in my head all the time, think of them every day and sometimes, years after their deaths, forget that they are not at the end of a telephone. I meet someone, or have some amusing experience, which makes me think, 'This evening, when I ring them up, I shall tell them that.' This happens often, even though well over a decade has passed since my mother died, and Norman Wilson, my potter father, died in the mid-1980s. One of my recurrent dreams is of spending time with my father, and being aware, as one is often unaware in waking life, of the pleasure his company gave me. Then someone in the dream, sometimes my older sister, says, 'But you will have to tell him.' 'Tell him what?' 'Tell him that he can't stay forever. He's …' As I wake, I realize the truth of the missing word: *dead*.

In my late adolescence I was most often conscious of irritation in the presence of my mother and father, an irritation which was combined with a sense of shock that, in most of the time I knew them, they did not do anything. Their Chekhovian existence in a remote village in Wales imposed limitations on my adolescent self which, being an adolescent, I saw entirely from my own point of view. It never occurred to me at the time to wonder how they ended up as they did, much of the time unhappy and friendless, and far from anyone who might have understood them. This book is intended, in part, as a resurrection, not only of my earlier selves but of theirs. If, in the following pages, they sometimes seem absurd, it is not because I want to satirize them. They both retained, and passed on to me, a sense of life being comic and tragic in equal doses. Their journey led to my journey, so much of the early part of my memoir will concern their lives, even before I came on the scene.

Twenty years after my mother gave birth to me, I married, so inevitably, the fifteen years as Katherine's husband were the background of all my early adult experiences. I was a married man at the age of twenty, and a father of two children by the time I was twenty-four. My wife, Katherine Duncan-Jones, was an academic: a Fellow of Somerville College, Oxford, and one of the most distinguished experts in sixteenth-century literature of her generation. The unravelling of our relationship was probably inevitable. For much of my early married life I was consumed with self-pity and rage, at having been, as I saw it, 'trapped' in this relationship. What was more remarkable, years after the story told in these pages, was the reconciliation that took place between us, no longer as man and wife but as soulmates and friends. The book begins with K in her tragic decline, when dementia laid waste to what was the most playful, sharp and retentive of intellects.

Until you have watched someone you love fall to bits, mentally, before your horrified eyes, you tend to hold on to some idea of 'self' or 'soul' which suggests our identity to be a fixed entity. Whether we are viewing ourselves as a novelist might create a 'character', a 'personality', or whether we are seeing ourselves as a 'soul', this person is *there*.

The cruel expression in the past for those who suffered from mental disturbance was that they were 'not all there'. The demented person is certainly not 'all there'. More and more of their brain has simply ceased to exist. Katherine and I used to discuss how far a sense of 'self' was natural and how far it had developed artificially in the days of the Romantic poets with their cult of 'the egotistical sublime'. K used to say that she had very little sense of herself, and I am sure she told the truth. My sense of myself is of a multiple personality – which is one of the reasons, perhaps, I wrote so many novels, trying on the guises of different *personae*. (The word means 'masks'.) It also explains to me why I can entertain quite contradictory opinions, sometimes feeling intensely reactionary and conservative and, at one and the same moment, quite the opposite; at times feeling as intensely religious as the Wordsworth who wrote *The Prelude* and at others, mocking it all, with Edward Gibbon or George Bernard Shaw.

I shared, and share, K's sense that self-awareness can be distinguished from self-obsession. We both used to like the sentence in the novel of one of our friends, Iris Murdoch, that 'the chief requirement of the good life is to live without any image of oneself'. We had both watched, with incredulous dismay, as Iris slowly lost her wits, neither of us having any conception that it would be the fate of Katherine too. When a person loses not merely memory but any bit of what made them 'themselves', in what sense can they still be said to be 'them'? And if that is the case, what happens to the idea of 'soul' or self – upon which so much of poetry and religion would appear to depend? Lifelong devotees of Tennyson's *In Memoriam*, K and I would sometimes talk about life after death, in which we both intermittently believed. Would we meet again with the juvenile selves of our friends, or with them in old age, or with them as babies? When we had these conversations, we were always imagining that the people we would meet would in some sense still cohere. They would be recognizable as their 'old selves'. What dementia does is to gouge out a person's very self, destroy it, throw out memories, desire, affections, loves, like so many confused bits of trash. It is hard to see how you can still believe in a 'soul' when you have seen unravelling on that pitiless scale.

Probably the cruel wrenching out of Katherine's memories has spurred me on to record at least some of my own. When periods of introspection force a writer to ask the reason for pursuing this profession of letters, one answer must always be – as a bulwark against death, against the inevitable consequence of being forgotten. Of course, one knows this exercise to be a vain one. To visit any library is to walk past a graveyard of the forgotten: row upon row of book spines bearing the names of those who might once have been well known but who are now unread and unheard of. Of course, as the hymn so often sung at funerals reminds us:

Time, like an ever-rolling stream
Bears all its sons away.
They fly forgotten as a dream
Dies at the opening day.

The pages that follow contain a few of the dreams that will, soon enough, have vanished before the merciless light of dawn.

1. Ungentle A. N.

Only a couple of years ago, when K was still living in her own house in Oxford, we were still having that conversation which began over half a century ago, with all its shorthand allusions to books or friends both loved, its shared quotations, which, when they were young, our two children found so annoying. ('*Why* speak in quotations all the time? Why not use your *own words?*') Yes, there had been a 'change', creeping up on her for a number of years. She had grown repetitive. Nominal aphasia was acute, but the laughter still continued. This distinctive, sparkling mind was still married to my own, though for thirty years we had been legally severed. For some years she had been working on Elizabethan clowns. In the light of what befell her, when the unravelling accelerated, it is so poignant as to be intolerable to recall: one of our last sustained, rational conversations had been about the Fool in *King Lear*.

The stage history of the play had always obsessed her, but now, having unearthed so much new material about the actors who worked with Shakespeare's theatre companies, she felt able to reconstruct the actual casting of the plays in the reign of James I. Perhaps some of her conclusions were fanciful. Twenty years ago, when we were much cagier with one another – *much* – she had published her book *Ungentle Shakespeare*. She seemed to have succumbed to that occupational hazard of Shakespeare biographers, an unconscious drift into autobiography. In K's book Ann Hathaway, admittedly only a Stratford housewife and not a Fellow of Somerville, marries an aggressively ambitious, much younger literary man, by whom she has children – considerably less than nine months after their wedding. He abandons her while pursuing his selfish career in 'literary London'. He is unfaithful to her in bed, word and heart. At a certain stage of the book, however, A. N. Shakespeare morphed into an overweight, witty homosexual who appeared to have much in common with our friend Jeremy Catto.

How she had mocked our old friend A. L. Rowse when he believed he'd 'discovered' the Dark Lady of Shakespeare's sonnets! In *Ungentle Shakespeare* she seemed to have fallen into a comparable quagmire. About the time we split up she abandoned what had appeared to be a lifelong preoccupation with Sir Philip Sidney and his circle, and strode into the more questionable area of Shakespeare biography. The finest fruits of her work here were the editions of *The Poems* (with Henry Woudhuysen) and *The Sonnets*. Before this phase of life, however, she had derided the very idea that one could know much about the author of *Hamlet* and *Lear*. (John Bayley – who introduced us to one another – liked to quote Yeats's line about Hamlet and Lear being gay, adding that, while it was obviously untrue about Hamlet, it would explain a great deal about the family difficulties of King Lear.) Was K now, as she advanced into old age, 'doing an A. L. Rowse' as she imagined Shakespeare in the role of Kent, Will Kempe as the Fool, Burbage as the King?

Maybe. But, with what exactitude she would recall and recite the scene on the heath; with what brio, what bursts of laughter, what tears springing from her clever, blue Welsh eyes, eyes with which I was once so in love! As she spoke of the scene, her words were entirely convincing. Edgar, sane, but pretending to be the mad Poor Tom; Kent, solidly loyal to his master; Lear, believing himself to be in control, but by now mad, demented, deranged; the Fool, making his bizarre commentary on the heart-ripping scene, as the storm rages. For my sixty-sixth birthday my second wife, Ruth Guilding, took me to the Old Vic to see

Glenda Jackson play Lear. It seemed then, as it seems now, the best interpretation of the role I had ever experienced. But was I actually watching Glenda through my tears, or was the old woman on stage revealing herself to me as the mad person that K was about to become?

K's expositions of those heath scenes were among the most brilliant things she ever said, and if only I had been an Eckermann or a Boswell and written them down! Within the year following, the unravelling was shockingly quick. Often, an expression of fear would cross her features. She could feel the mental powers draining away, like blood loss. She heroically tried to deny that anything was amiss. A sign that an End had been reached was when she lost her Bodleian Library card and told me it no longer mattered. She would not be going to the Bodleian again.

When, in the spring of 1971, we found ourselves planning a hasty wedding – the thirty-year-old Fellow of Somerville and I, a twenty-year-old student – Hugo Dyson, a Fellow of Merton, took us out for champagne cocktails at the Bear Hotel in Woodstock.

'There's something you must know about Katherine Duncan-Jones,' boomed this legendary figure from Oxford's yesteryear, before settling into one of his anecdotes, of drinking ale with Lawrence of Arabia at the Jolly Farmers in St Ebbe's or, together with Tolkien, converting C. S. Lewis to Christianity one moonlit night in Addison's Walk.

'Katherine Duncan-Jones can *never* be happy if she is further than a mile from the Bodleian Library.'

The noise of Hugo's voice, and the enforced jollity of manner, had once prompted Maurice Bowra to bark out, 'Here comes Dyson, the Life and Death of the Party.'

About K's need for the Bodleian, however, Dyson was right. When we were married, and children came, summer holidays would be planned less around school dates than around the dates

Four good friends – Allan Maclean of Dochgarroch, Katherine Duncan-Jones, Alexandra Artley and me. It is 1983 and we had just returned from a celebration of the 150th anniversary of the Oxford Movement – a huge rally in the University Parks.

when the Bodleian was closed. Then, it was safe to be away from Oxford. Hardly a weekday passed, in fifty-five years of adult life, when she was not seen, chaining a battered bike to the railings near the Clarendon Building in Broad Street and lurching with that sideways walk (one hip always wonky) through the quadrangle and up the shallow, wooden stairs to Duke Humfrey's Library.

For her to forsake Bodley was a signal: oh, how chilling that a vital part of her inmost being – her *haecceitas*, to use one of her favourite words – was already dead. Not long afterwards she stopped going into her college for lunch, presumably still conscious that a change had come upon her. She was afraid of being caught out. Life became ever more limited. She went almost daily to the cinema in Walton Street. It no longer mattered that she had seen a film three times already in the same week, or whether she had enjoyed it. By the time she turned up to watch it again next day, all memory of it had vanished.

What else is there to do, if you feel your powers failing, but to numb the unbearable knowledge? The strange sideways limp was now a slow crawl, three or four times daily, to the Co-Op for another bottle of plonk.

During the previous decade we'd had lunch together about once a week. In any marriage that has ended in divorce there are many unspoken resentments on both sides. My desertion of her and of our two daughters was never mentioned, but it continued to cause anger and pain.

From my side, while never losing the sense that we had a marriage of minds, and continuing to feel incalculable debts to her, there was also a boiling anger. How could a woman of that age make someone who was little more than a teenager adopt the responsibilities of a husband and father, particularly as she admitted, only a few months into the marriage, that she was still in love with someone else, and that the someone else had been her lover concurrently with me? After some of our jolly lunches in late middle age, always on the surface harmonious and joke-filled, I would come away and be filled with uncontrollable rage. She had stolen my youth, my experience of student life, my chance of developing an emotional spectrum, with several girlfriends, before settling on the Right Moment to marry? How could she, when my unfortunate parents had protested, have written such intolerable letters?

But now she had begun her terrible descent, now that she was hobbling towards eighty and I towards seventy, that changed. Little by little. Anxiety for her well-being found me catching the train from London, where I have lived since our break-up – several times a week, eventually daily, dreading what I should find. I'd ring an hour before my arrival to warn her to stay in. Then half an hour before, to remind her I was on my way. Then ten minutes before the appointment. There was always a look of surprise on her face when I arrived. It was a happy look. And sometimes, of course, she had forgotten, and was out. One would find her ambling, at an inebriated snail's pace, the leper's-bell plastic Co-Op bag clinking at her side. Sometimes I found her tottering beside the canal; her ravaged features and crazy eyes registered a baffled fear. I'd take

an arm and lead her 'home', back to the house now shared with
a live-in carer, who had been specifically engaged to prevent such
wanderings.

I was certainly no faithful Kent, then or on any occasion in our
fifty years untogether. I broke every vow and promise I ever made
to this woman. No Kent, I. Maybe the Fool, though? Unfaithful
in sickness and in health, maybe I could still provide something?
Friendship? A shared dottiness, though I wasn't demented (yet)?

> LEAR: We'll go to supper in the morning.
> FOOL: And I'll go to bed at noon.

Alcohol-numbed dementia brings many such confusions. Turning
up at her house to escort her to the Jericho Café for breakfast at
nine, one would find her already far advanced into the first bottle
of South African Chardonnay, a Co-Op prawn sandwich half-
chewed in her lap.

The modern dilemma faced by every demented person living
alone, and by those most responsible for her – was dissected. Loss
of freedom versus loss of dignity. One daughter in America, another
in Cambridge, England. The series of little crises in K's life being
then enacted are being repeated in street after street, city after city,
all over the world, as highly profitable pharmaceuticals boost the
share prices, and thence the pensions, of a population which hence
outlives its mental capacity.

Despite the live-in carer, K took to wandering at night. Control
of bodily functions was uncertain, making taxi rides or visits to
restaurants and cinemas anti-social. Eventually the inevitable
decision was reached. The care home.

Yet by the time K was carted off to this inexorable fate, something
beautiful had happened between us. All the feelings of rage (on
my side), which could still, unpredicted, flare up, clashing with
genuine fondness, had evaporated. This was not by any effort of
will. What we went through in the last eighteen months of her life
at home had been a tragedy in the purely Aristotelian sense; fear
and pity had been purgative, cleansing.

The whole of life is repetition – so said Kierkegaard. The pattern of my difficult relationship with my first wife mirrored certain aspects of life with my difficult mother. No, not difficult; make that impossible. True, there was little or no marriage of minds between me and Jean Dorothy. There was, however, a comparable pattern. Extreme impatience and irritation (on both sides) in early decades, always repressed (with wife as with mother), gave way to a final period of friendship, tenderness, mutual respect. With Jean Dorothy this only became possible when the curtain had come down on her forty-year psychodrama of marriage into which she poured every ounce of her intense, furious and extraordinary mental energy. With K the friendship only developed when our children had fully grown up. I think that for much of the time – long before all memory faded – we forgot that we had ever shared a domestic set-up, let alone a bed.

2. Remind Me

'May I ask?' ventures the young man through his Perspex mask. 'I mean, may I ask?'

Visored, it recalls one of the faces looming up to the camera in underwater nature films on childhood television, Hans and Lotte Hass, or Jacques Cousteau, their snorkelled visage distorted by close proximity to the submarine lens, flippering their seaweedy path towards some dead-boring coral reef.

'Yes.'

'I mean, may I ask, what is your relation to …'

'We were …'

The word refuses to be spoken, not least because, all these years later, it seems so improbable. I can't say, 'We were man and wife.' On the other hand, nor can I say we are friends.

Jacques Cousteau leads the way into a small tent which has been erected in the garden. It is too cold for sitting out, but we are in the high days of the Coronavirus. Better to die of pneumonia than be one of the government statistics of deaths by Covid-19.

While I am not saying the improbable word 'married', Professor Katherine Duncan-Jones is being trundled through a French window into the freezing tent. I have had my temperature taken (sub-zero, I'd guess) and I've been arrayed in a plastic apron and a Cousteau visor, so it is no surprise that she spends a moment wondering who I am. She has been dressed in a straw hat covered with flowers. Inevitably, one thinks she is 'Crown'd with rank femiter and furrow-weeds / With hardocks, hemlock, nettles, cuckoo-flowers'.

Another quotation that inevitably comes to mind: those lines from *In Memoriam* which she liked to intone as we limped along through Port Meadow. The quoting habit had been annoying to anyone else who happened to be with us – but here, who cares? We are on our own, apart from Jacques C., and suddenly, what is more, the lines seem apt in this clinical Golgotha: 'They called me in the public squares / The fool that wears a crown of thorns.'

Tennyson! I lost my virginity, and our first child was conceived, at the White Hart Hotel in Lincoln. K had taken me to a meeting of the Tennyson Society, held in that Tennysonian city, in February 1971. We had heard Sir Charles Tennyson giving his wonderful roadshow, recalling his grandfather, the huge brown hands clutching the bannister at Aldworth, the wideawake hat full of edible fungi, which the aged Poet Laureate had gathered on his dawn walk, the Lincolnshire voice, with its short 'a's – 'GASTLY through the drizzling rain ...'

The trembling excitement of that hotel hour when we had retired to bed, the beauty of the woman beside me, with her long, thick, golden hair, the ecstatic joy of it. Were those two naked bodies, entwined in one another's love half a century ago in a Lincoln hotel, truly the same as the two bodies sitting opposite one another in this grotesque plastic garden tabernacle? Her hair, poking from beneath the straw hat, is wiry and grey. The hat lacks any dignity. On my side of the screen, plastic aprons hide the three-piece A. N. Wilson outfit. It was she who urged me always to wear a suit, all those years ago, citing Bowra, his eye darting up and down the grey flannels and sports coat of a Wadham Fellow, barking, 'Why are you dressed as an undergraduate?'

The old lady in the flowery hat peers blankly at the visored old codger.

'And you live? Where? Remind me.'

'London.'

'Of course.'

A few days ago she had been awake all night, texting the daughters. They had interpreted these frantic, incoherent messages to mean that K feared I was dead. That was the reason for my visit today, to reassure her. Yet, when I read the messages, it was clear to me that they did not concern my death. *Andrew Wilson gone – afraid gone.* And later – *Better for him, better off now. He NEVER wanted to be here* … She even managed – *He is in London.*

In the solitude of her locked room she was reliving the misery of abandonment thirty-something years ago, abandonment by one who had promised to be with her, for richer, for poorer, in sickness and in health … Had he kept the promise, she would not now be in a care home. She would be simply at home.

Through the Perspex mask I repeat what I had been told by the care home people, that K had been reading Betjeman's poems aloud to the other inmates. Her face looks puzzled by the information.

'You live where? Remind me.'

'London.'

'Of COURSE.'

I recite one of our favourites, 'Myfanwy at Oxford', and her lips seem to be moving, as I say the familiar words: 'Tubular bells of tall St Barnabas, / Single clatter above St Paul.'

The artificial flowers on the straw hat wobble in what might be recognition.

'Did you write it?'

'No. You remember old Betjeman? We spent an evening with him once.'

'You live where, exactly?'

'London.'

'Of COURSE!'

This conversation happened the best part of a year ago. Now, when I sit beside her, she stares blankly. She would not have a clue where London was, or what a poem is, or who I am.

Although Cambridge is in the east, it is another Betjeman poem that sings cruelly in my head, as, an hour later, I sit in the clattering train: 'The old Great Western Railway shakes, / The old Great Western Railway spins.'

Clearly, K – 'my' K – is no longer really 'all there'. Maybe my earlier self, or selves, have likewise evaporated. The masks or personae of an earlier self seem, as the years progress, scarcely recognizable as having any connection with the inner self, known to oneself alone – or, one hopes, to that self known to close friends or family. The self on the page is another thing. In my case he even has a name, the initials suggestive of anonymity or non-self. A. N. Other. That name sewn on to Cash's tapes and stitched on to grey socks, shirts, shorts, pyjamas for use at boarding schools: A. N. WILSON.

The old Great Western Railway makes
Me very sorry for my sins.

The mind drifts miserably back to memories when young A. N. was so thrustingly ambitious, so full of himself, so unfaithful, not only to his wife but to his own better nature.

Me outside my office at the Spectator *– 56, Doughty Street.*

3. Sorrowful Lay

That spring, forty years ago, I awoke in the dark with a stranger. The stranger was me. There was the old confusion, never solved – what makes us suppose that our waking hours are any more real than those spent asleep? What if both halves of life, waking and dreaming, are equally real? Questions which neuroscientists and philosophers would answer in their way, and writers – novelists, biographers, journalists – perhaps differently. So much of the truly significant experience in my life to date had happened when asleep, or when reading, or writing, a book.

For the last year or so I had been working in London, sleeping three or four nights in the house of a friend, and returning to Oxford at weekends. One of the young women who worked at the *Spectator*, where I looked after the books pages, had asked another, 'Do you fancy Andrew?'

After some humming and ha-ing, she had replied, 'I can imagine tearing off his three-piece suit only to find another three-piece suit underneath.'

This was when I was just about thirty. Nevertheless, the other stranger in bed with me that spring morning had discovered that there was no three-piece suit underneath. Her generosity – first welcoming me as a lodger, then as a lover – had made me very happy. Desperately happy, because the clichéd epithet was true, there was indeed something desperate, frenzied, in both our happiness, hers and mine. There had been nothing like this in my life before, and, in my clumsy, selfish way

I was happy, as only very selfish young men can be happy, desperate as only young people can be desperate. I had not dared ask myself the question – because I knew the answer – whether she wanted what I had – children. I took at face value her claim that we were only friends, even though, by then, we were so much more.

Waking in bed with her yet again, lying in the dark with my arms wrapped around her, I watched the daylight paint its bright edges round the curtains. Swallows were larking about in the rainy London air. Beneath the eaves of that little house they cooed their melancholy air, and involuntarily I thought of 'The swallow Proigne, with a sorrowful lay, / When morgen cam, gan make her waymentynge'.

Involuntarily, since, until so recently, my day job had been teaching medieval literature at Oxford. Then had come the offer via a friend, Peter Ackroyd (a poet at that stage, not yet a novelist), who worked at the *Spectator* and suggested my name to the boss. Why not come and be Literary Editor?

There had followed the most ridiculously enjoyable year, where almost every other day ended in some crowded publishing office, holding a glass of warm white, while we launched someone or other's book. That was how I met my landlady, who, though she was a publisher, looked like a young farmer's daughter who had just come in from gathering cloudberries a hundred miles north of Trondheim. I loved the fact that everything was treated by her as if it were a joke. I loved the fact – we all smoked like chimneys – that she seemed to kiss her cigarettes as she held them between her lips, and then, as she let out another lungful of smoke, burst into yet more laughter.

After a childhood spattered with unhappiness of various kinds, and about ten years of marriage, which had been the opposite of plain sailing, the happiness was something that was difficult to get used to. I suddenly appeared to have been given it all – professional success, amusing friendships, an emotional life which, though it filled me with guilt, was also extremely exciting.

I thought she was still asleep, but she said, 'You've forgotten, haven't you? It's just like you to forget a thing like that. I know you.'

But if she had known me, she would have realized that, far from forgetting, I'd been thinking about little else for the last two months.

4. Living up to the Blue China

Oscar Wilde was denounced by the puritanical dons, when still an undergraduate, for the supposed decadence of his confession that 'I find it harder and harder every day to live up to my blue china.'

A. N. Other, or whoever it was lying there in the Fulham dawn, had never found the observation in the least decadent. Now that I have reached the age of seventy, and I look back to my childhood in the Potteries, and to the ceramic genius of my father, I can say that Wilde's regretful words are my credo, and my story. I have spent my grown-up life failing to live up to my father's blue china.

Norman Wilson, my father, was managing director of Wedgwood until twenty years before that morning of guilty joy in Fulham. He was also a designer of distinctive brilliance. Those bowls and vases! I look at some of them now as I write. The messages they send are so pure. Staring at an exquisite Korean bowl in the British Museum one day when I was a boy, Norman murmured, 'They had abstract art two thousand years before we did.' Korea was really the inspiration, as it had been for his father and for Bernard Moore, the innovative ceramic artist. Norman longed to visit Korea, and it is on my conscience that I never made time to spend a month going there with him.

Lying there in Fulham, listening to the swallows lament the treachery of false lovers, I was conscious of a whole avalanche of guilt, mingling with the glow of self-congratulation and physical ecstasy. I was not merely behaving selfishly to my lover and, of course, to my wife and children, but I was also, by the way I was now beginning to live, betraying the essentially innocent and decent world of provincial Staffordshire in which I had grown up. My life was failing to live up to the blue china.

One simple test proved this. The quality of my writing had coarsened. The first few novels won prizes. The very first review I ever received was by Ferdinand Mount, whom I did not at the time know, but who was now the political columnist on the *Spectator*. It saluted the arrival of a new star in the literary sky, and the other reviewers followed him in their accolades and encomiums. They had seen something which, had it been worked on, might have allowed me to develop into something ... oh, I don't know, something better than I was.

Then I'd published *Scandal*, a vulgar easy romp about a politician involved with a prostitute. It was instantly bought for television and made into a mini-series starring Timothy West, an actor I admire. I was aglow, feeling that my 'career' had taken off. That is, until a wise old friend, Terence de Vere White, quietly remarked, entirely without malice, 'I hope you won't mind my saying, it's a terrible falling off from your earlier books.' I hope I took his words to heart. I hope I have since tried harder, and written better books. The words stung, though, because they were true, and he had noted a Fall.

Art is a calling, whether we hear its call or not. Writing bad novels, and thinking they might pass as good novels because they have been made into TV shows; going to early evening drinks parties; sleeping with people not one's wife; gossiping and chattering ... it was all too enjoyable, and it numbed the capacity, not merely to create, but to hear the messages sent to us by great art.

My friend Naomi Lewis, a poet of talent and a critic of genius, compiled a book called *Messages*. It was partly poems written by the famous, such as Milton, and partly poems written by her students at City Lit, where she conducted a legendary seminar on poetic composition. To none of the poems in her anthology was a name attached. Her editor at Faber, Craig Raine, told her, 'We'd sell more copies if we could re-name it *Massages*.'

'I know you,' came the voice from the other side of the bed. 'You've forgotten – you are meant to be having your photograph taken by Lord Snowdon.'

5. Best of Young British

Laurence Sterne, when he finished the first volumes of *The Life and Opinions of Tristram Shandy*, told his publisher, who, naturally had his eye on the money, that he did not want to be fed, he wanted to be famous. For most novelists, success does not depend on creating a perfect work of art, a haiku or a miniature. The novel is a messy form. But to be famous, now you're talking. That's why 'The Best of Young British' at this date, by a mile, was Martin Amis. Even if you'd never read him, you could recite the names of his girlfriends, and the foul things he'd said about them in interviews. In fact, reading such interviews only made more and more women join the queue, like groupies screaming outside the van of a lead guitarist on tour.

In the fame stakes, Amis was destined to be outpaced, easily, by Salman Rushdie, when he was condemned to death by Ayatollah Khomeini for writing *The Satanic Verses*. Whether you were gleefully watching this novel burn in the streets of Islamabad or defending the right to free expression, Rushdie's was a name, in every television studio in the world, that everyone, but everyone, in the whole world knew – because he had included a paragraph in his novel that he had been warned would be offensive to Muslim opinion. Clearly, poor chap, the affair blew up in his face, and he could never have guessed the trail of terror and murder that would ensue: his translator assassinated, he himself driven into hiding for years. But since the literary shape, and success, of *The Satanic Verses*

Me and Martin Amis drinking warm white wine.

would have been unaffected by the removal of the paragraph, you assume he left it in because he thought it would make a splash.

Young Rushdie at Rugby School was three years older than I was, and in a different house, so I never knew him in those days, although I vividly recall his appearance, his melancholy, sardonic expression and the glide in one of his eyes as one passed him on Barby Road. He told me when we came to know one another that he had been ruthlessly bullied by racist oafs, something I readily believe.

In the commercial world of 'The Best of Young British', writers were supposed to be performers, celebrities. While they may have hoped they would be famous for their work, the publicists were looking for something else entirely: the capacity to appeal to gossip columnists, suitability for television chat shows, hunger to cut a dash.

Self-projection is an ingredient in art, even when that self is unnamed: by which is meant, the pouring of oneself, all one's best skills and imaginative powers, into the work. Self-promotion was a very different thing. In my own small way I had been caught up into the mood of the age, only too happy, when the chance came along, to appear on television or to lay aside work on a book for the quick thrill of writing print journalism.

The difference between, on the one hand, the inner self, the good self I aspired to become, and, on the other, A. N. and his antics, was never put into more embarrassing perspective for me than when the family – Katherine Duncan-Jones, our two daughters (by then eleven and thirteen) and I took a holiday cruise in the Mediterranean. It happened a year or two after I'd left the *Spectator*, but this seems the moment to mention it

6. Masks

Charles Moore, a friend of mine, had by this stage taken over the editorship of the *Spectator*, to which I was still a fairly frequent contributor. He asked me if I'd like to go on a Swan Hellenic cruise, all expenses paid. It was too good a chance to miss, so, accepting the freebie for myself, I paid for K and the girls to accompany me.

My frivolous brief from Charles, on what promised to be a fascinating tour of classical and early Christian sites dotted around the Mediterranean, was to lampoon one of the guest lecturers, the Bishop of Durham, the Right Reverend David Jenkins.

This, alas, was an all-too-easy assignment, although at the time it was far from obvious why his faults were, to my eyes, so glaring, namely, that they were defects I shared: an addiction to cheap publicity, and, where theological questions arose, a laughable confusion of mind.

In newspapers, as in folk tales, there are, or there were when print journalism played a more exclusive role in forming the public's picture of the world, recurrent figures and tropes, characters whose outlines bore only a notional resemblance to actual human beings. (Hence, in newspapers, the cartoons invariably give a truer illustration of the texts than the photographs.) Among these stereotypes were to be found self-advertising aristocrats, emphasizing their difference from the norm by wild political views, or unusual dress, sports personalities whose booze-fuelled antics in foreign hotels made better copy than their skills on the tennis court or football pitch, fashion models whose inability to manage anger guaranteed satisfactory tantrums on transatlantic flights and adulterous politicians whose bedroom irregularities were of more interest than the clichés they uttered at the despatch box.

Like the damned in some medieval *danse macabre*, their antics turned effortlessly into spectacle. Almost all such figures are addicted to public exposure. Even their complaints about 'intrusion' into their private lives are themselves bids for yet more publicity. Even while making their complaints the addicts demonstrate their gibbering craving for notice, recalling the pale, sweaty face of junkies pressed against the locked glass door of a late-night pharmacy.

When, in my forties and fifties I worked for a daily newspaper (the *Evening Standard* in London), my early bids for publicity seemed mild beside those of the serious users: the occasional social use of weed, compared with habitual intake of heroin or crack cocaine.

Both the poet Stephen Spender and the philanthropist Lord Longford had become friends of mine over the years. Both, on different occasions, acknowledged to me that it was a sad day if they scoured a newspaper, preferably one of the red-tops or a tabloid, and found no reference to themselves. The image of these distinguished figures in their local newsagents, flicking through copies of the *Sun* or the *Daily Mail*, recalled the sadness of lonely mackintoshed men reaching greedily for magazines on the top shelf, in the days before internet porn.

To this list of stereotypes – sour media dons trading insults about their colleagues in the reviews, minor royals credulous enough to believe their charity work interests us more than their family squabbles – we must add, even in these secular times, the troublesome cleric, the pestilent priest.

Naturally, for the red-tops, the chief interest is to find some act of sexual hypocrisy: the cardinal who has denounced homosexuality propositioning handsome young seminarians; the dean molesting the choirboy. The trouble with the sexual offenders is that, once they are exposed, you have killed the story, shot the fox. A far longer shelf life was to be found in the clergy who think they are controlling their own publicity. In the 1980s there was still mileage in the clergyman who did not believe in Christianity. In those days there were still enough newspaper readers to be shocked when they learned that some cleric, often a senior bishop, believed less of the Creed than your average secularist. Whereas doubts about the Resurrection, or even the existence of God, hold back the scrupulous majority from participation in Church membership, the 'trendy vicars', as they were termed in the 1960s, actually made a career in the Church, advancing themselves through unbelief. Maybe they are thinner on the ground these days. As Church membership has shrunk, those who have remained appear to be the believers, while the 'trendy' parson seems as dated as the flared trousers he probably wore under his cassock.

Malcolm Muggeridge liked recalling the Bishop of Birmingham in the 1930s, who wrote an article for one of the papers to which he had given the title 'Reflections of a Troubled Theist'. A sub-editor, mischievously or with unconscious truthfulness, had set this as 'A Troubled Atheist'. Later in the twentieth century, a Bishop of Woolwich got a quick fix by telling the jury in the obscenity trial of *Lady Chatterley's Lover* that it would make a good handbook for Christian marriage, and thereafter soared to best-sellerdom with a paperback with the misleading title *Honest to God*.

The Bishop of Durham was gallantly trying to keep this slightly flyblown old tradition alive in the 1980s. His career got off to a wonderful start. Even before he was consecrated, he alerted the press to the fact that he could not be described as an orthodox believer. For the ceremony in which he was actually made into a bishop, at York Minster, he chose as a preacher a self-confessed atheist called Professor Dennis Nineham. Shortly after this event, the Minster was struck by lightning, an event which meant that God had clearly been reading the *Daily Mail*, and that the Bishop could be guaranteed headlines whenever he craved them.

So hungry was the Bishop for a fix that he seldom allowed any major festival of the Church to appear on the horizon without priming the gossip columns with his intention to deliver some myth-debunking sermon. Easter was dismissed as 'a conjuring trick with bones', for example.

As guest lecturer, for which people had saved up their money to be given actual facts, the Bishop was rather less good value. Many of those who went on Swan Hellenic cruises were not super-rich but were schoolteachers who had been saving up for twenty years while cramming the diminishing band of children who still learned Latin, or clergy widows whose knowledge of koine Greek was as good as their husbands', or singletons for whom a cruise with like-minded people offered harmless companionship. With all these 'little' people the Bishop was notably tetchy, preferring to fraternize with the richer passengers who had booked first-class cabins.

There was an obvious reason for this. The richer ones tended to be less well-educated, and more prepared to swallow the Bishop's ill-prepared talks. One day we all went to the Kariye Mosque in Istanbul, a former Byzantine church with magnificent frescoes and mosaics. One of the first-classers quizzed the Bishop about how the mosque got its name. Jenkins hastily looked in his Blue Guide and saw that it had been called the Chora, when it was a Greek church. It was a choral place, he said; it must have been noted for its choir.

The rich inquirer was entirely satisfied, until an old lady in ankle socks and sandals who was travelling steerage, a retired teacher of the classics, politely remarked that the word *chora* in Greek meant 'field', and this was a church which had been a little out of town, like St Martin-in-the-Fields in London. No wonder the Bishop felt safer in the company of the stockbrokers and the Harley Street dentists.

Had he been our only speaker, it would have been a poor lookout, but we were lucky enough to have three other excellent classicists on board. The star turn was Henry Chadwick, Dean of Christ Church, and a distinguished scholar of Late Antiquity. His disquisitions – at Cumae, beside the cave where Aeneas began his descent into the underworld, at Gallipoli, recalling the fallen of the First World War, at Delphi, shrine of Apollo (one of the places in the world where I have been most keenly and palpably visited by a sense of the numinous), at Nicaea, scene of the great fourth-century Council where the Creed was formalized – were unforgettable. Henry, his wife, Peggy, and their three beautiful daughters were all excellent company. They introduced us to June and Roger Lancelyn Green.

Lest the reader should think I've abandoned my confessional intention in favour of holiday reminiscence, I am about to disclose an incident which, although trivial in itself, still fills me with self-disgust.

I want to say, as I wanted to say then, surely this wasn't me? Not the me who responds to Bach and Rilke, who loves his children and has friends? Surely I, the inner me, is a decent, kind person?

On any Swan Hellenic cruise in the Mediterranean, in the height of the summer in those days, Roger Lancelyn Green was the Father of the Marshalsea. He and his wife would book for the statutory fortnight and then, when the sunburnt Latin teachers and dentists clambered ashore at Piraeus, bound for flights back to England, the Lancelyn Greens would stay on board and do the trip all over again. By now Roger was frail and felt each summer was likely to be his last.

His name will be familiar to anyone who, as a child, read his adaptations of myths and legends in Puffin books – *King Arthur and His Knights of the Round Table*, *The Tale of Troy*, *Myths of the Norsemen* and many others. Roger had been taught by C. S. Lewis at Oxford and maintained a friendship with him. Indeed, when, late in his life, Lewis married an American, Joy Davidman, who was dying of cancer, Roger and June took the pair on just such a Mediterranean holiday as we were enjoying – a 'Wings' tour.

Lewis, sixty-one years old, had never set foot in an aeroplane, and since 1917, when he was wounded at the Battle of Arras and brought home, he had never been out of Britain. The holiday with the Lancelyn Greens was joyous. June was a jolly, intelligent woman. She and Roger shared Lewis's faith. There were timeless moments, as when, after his wife had died, Lewis recalled, 'Joy knew she was dying, and she knew I knew she was dying – but when we heard the shepherds playing their flutes in the hills, it seemed to make no difference.'

Between us and the Lancelyn Greens there was much reminiscence about Lewis. K, as a member of the Oxford English Faculty, was friends with those older dons, such as Hugo Dyson, who had known him. I myself had been taught by Lewis's younger friend and protégé Christopher Tolkien, son of the author of *The Lord of the Rings*. Our talk with the Lancelyn Greens ranged from medieval literature – they lived at Poulton Hall in the Wirral, which they liked to believe was Bercilak's castle in *Sir Gawain and the Green Knight* – to Sherlock Holmes, on which Roger was an authority, and for which K and I shared an enthusiasm, often reading the stories aloud to one another.

As well as enjoying the sunshine and the swimming and the visits to sites familiar to all readers of *The Tale of Troy*, we'd made new friends, and that is always a happy feeling. Our two daughters seemed content, especially the elder – at home an often sad-seeming child but whose bright eyes were now taking in scenes from *The Odyssey*, a work that she would one day translate into matchless pentameters, to enormous international acclaim.

Then we reached Thessalonica, a tiny group of whose citizens had once received that strange letter from St Paul which is generally believed to be the earliest Christian document. We saw the stupendous archaeological museum, containing the Aravissos Hoard, with its gold artefacts dating to 4000 BC. We saw the gold hoard of Philip of Macedon and the extraordinary vessel known as the Derveni Krater. The experience of seeing these wonderful objects has never left me. Wandering back to the boat, down the steep, steep streets with June and the girls, K murmured, as she often did,

Once out of Nature, I shall never take
My bodily form from any natural thing,
But such a form as Grecian goldsmiths make,
Of hammered gold and gold enamelling ...

Yeats, with his preoccupation with masks, his pronounced sense of the difference between the inner self and the self displayed to others, was an appropriate spirit to have invoked.

June approached a flyblown, scorched news-stand near the wharf and came back triumphantly with a days' old, yellow, crinkled copy of the *Sunday Times*.

It had entirely left my consciousness that, some weeks previous, a journalist from that paper, Susan Barnes, had come to our small house in Oxford with a photographer to interview me. In so far as the hour or so in her company had left any trace at all, it was recalled as simply bland. It had turned out that she had once been married to a friend of ours, Patrick Skene Catling, a notably handsome Irish novelist who was what used to be called a 'ladies' man'. Susan had then married a politician called Anthony Crosland, famous, in so far as he ever was, for saying he wanted to abolish 'every fucking grammar school' in England. By the time of the interview she had begun a romance with another friend of ours, Auberon Waugh. I mention these things simply to explain why, although interviews normally make me nervous, this one had felt more like a cup of tea with a friend. After an hour or so this cooing, smiling bottle-blonde American left no impression on either of us. It was only when we returned to the ship that June, rootling through, exclaimed, 'Oh look! An article about you!'

She asked if we'd like to read it before she did, but, knowing that Roger, too frail for shore excursions, had been waiting for her, we urged her to keep the paper. We'd meet later – it had become a pleasant habit – for a glass of ouzo before dinner. Plenty of time before then to plunge in the pool on deck.

It was a shock, therefore, a couple of hours later, bathed, dressed, combed, glowing with sunshine and goodwill, to arrive at the bar and find a stone-faced June Lancelyn Green. I've emphasized her bonhomie, which was spontaneous, catching. The facial expression was all the more disconcerting, and my immediate thought was that Roger, in the course of an exceptionally hot afternoon, had succumbed to heatstroke.

She was standing stock-still and did not acknowledge whatever foolish pleasantry escaped my lips.

'We read the article.' She seemed coldly furious. 'We clearly did not realize what kind of a person you are. Roger has asked that you do not approach us for the rest of the cruise.'

June had handed back the paper, of course, and we both read it. My first reaction was to rage against Susan Barnes's pointless spite about K, whom she described as 'homely'. The photo, chosen with blatant malice, depicted a woman looking much older than her mid-forties, standing behind a chair on which sat a man who seemed much younger than his mid-thirties. The article was crammed with tittle-tattle, and it depicted a worldling, thrusting, ambitious, notoriously adulterous. This latter aspect was grossly exaggerated. Far from being a 'ladies' man' in the sense normally understood, I am much more inclined to hopeless romantic yearnings than to actual unfaithfulness. No doubt such yearnings are silly, when they become apparent, but they have always been part of my inner life. I have had very few adulterous affairs.

What made the *Sunday Times* article such a stinker was that it was based not on the interview, just on gossip picked up from others. What K felt on reading it, and whether she read it *through* – that question still gnaws. Of course, she did what she did, throughout her life, with all painful topics: she buried it in silence, behaved as if no such article had ever appeared, as if the Lancelyn Greens had never cropped up in our lives.

Only – the incident *had* happened. The Lancelyn Greens felt tricked. They had supposed themselves to have befriended a Fellow of Somerville who had known some of Roger's oldest friends. All that bit was true, and it had been fun to recall Oxford's golden twentieth-century decades when Tolkien and Lewis had been extant. The Lancelyn Greens also supposed themselves to have befriended a young man who had tried to follow in that golden path, teaching the very literature that Roger, and Lewis and Tolkien, had loved – *Beowulf* and Chaucer and *Sir Gawain*. Together, the four of us had attended the Communion service celebrated on Sunday morning by Henry Chadwick. And now they felt tricked. The Andrew Wilson they thought they had known had been a fraudulent mask, worn by that cad they'd read about in the paper.

7. Norman Wilson's Son

'The Best of Young British Novelists', of whom I was one, were to be immortalized in a group photograph, taken in Chelsea Harbour. Today was the day. It was bucketing down, and, try as she might to get me to the studio on time, my friend's car was stuck in the usual immovable, matutinal jam of the King's Road. At a certain point we both agreed it would be quicker for me to get out of the car and, umbrella-less and mac-less, leg it through the monsoon. It was a drowned rat who arrived to be pictured with his co-scribes.

Snowdon was an energetic, simian figure, notably short, professional, brisk.

'You're Norman Wilson's son,' he said, with a smile which revealed bright yellow teeth. (Later in journalistic life, when I occasionally had lunch with him, Nigel Dempster and Peter McKay, the teeth had been cleaned, presumably at the insistence of the current wife or girlfriend.)

He spoke about working with Norman at the Design Centre, and recalled his visit, with Princess Margaret, to the Wedgwood Factory in Barlaston, Staffordshire. Like all royal, or, in his case, royal-by-marriage, personages who know their job, he was good at working the room, with a breezy word for each of us. It was soon time to assemble the Twenty, being photographed in a group inevitably recalling school. You wondered who, in this assembly, would be made to sit cross-legged on the ground in front of the others, a football between the knees. At school, it would have been the smallest person there, but since, in present company, this was, by several inches, Martin Amis, such a positioning

An anxious Norman Wilson showing Lord Snowdon and Princess Margaret the works. Sir John Wedgwood is on the right of the picture.

would not have reflected the undoubted fact that he was the star. At the time it was really nineteen wannabes and Little Mart, this picture.

Looking at the photograph forty years later, one sees a gang of Salieris with not a Mozart among them. The best known to me personally was Shiva Naipaul, though I had known Julian Barnes vaguely for years and had been at school with Rushdie – for some reason absent from the photo shoot. Shiva's novel *Fireflies* is probably as good as any published by that stage, by that pack. Shiva knew, which I did not, that the heart condition which killed his father in young middle age could at any moment take him. Jenny, his wife, who was my colleague on the *Spectator*, shared this knowledge. It must have added to the intensity and devotion that he brought to his writing tasks, as well as tempting him, when not working, to numb anxiety by excessive drinking. So many of us then, at the *Spectator*, drank on a positively Slavic scale, for one reason or another. Shiva suffered, more than most writers I have known, from anxiety about his work. He was a perfectionist, and obsessive. He cared about every word of every sentence. His consciousness that the fiction and the journalism were both very good could not obliterate the paranoid feeling that the world was comparing him, to his own disadvantage, with his elder brother Vidia, with whom, it is no secret, he had a difficult relationship. At this stage of things Shiva, Peter Ackroyd and I would drink ourselves silly in a nearby Italian restaurant, or in the Duke of York in Doughty Mews, two or three times a week, often to be joined by cartoonist Michael Heath, Bron Waugh, Richard West and others.

The old man – that is me – looking at that group photograph now feels a wistful sympathy for them all. They had possessed the hubris to set up as rivals to the giants, to Joyce, to Nabokov, to Balzac, and the great Hegelian tide of history was against them. There have been some brilliant crime writers in our lifetime, but no 'literary' novelist to match the giants.

The figure in the group who I am compelled to acknowledge is – or was – 'me' is not really recognizable. Someone at the time, seeing it in the paper, said I looked out of place, as though, among the Young Novelists, Snowdon had cleverly pasted in a youth who had joined the Jesuit novitiate with Gerard Manley Hopkins. There was more truth in that than the joker realized. In the midst of the carnally obsessed love affair to which allusion has been made, many hours were also being spent sitting or kneeling at the back of churches, painfully aware that in this vale of soul-making, the addiction to writing more and more journalism, the marital failure and infidelities, the booze was destroying, not making, a soul.

Snowdon, like the expensive delicate ship in Auden's poem, had somewhere to get to, so the shoot did not last long. We all poured out on to the steaming pavement, the rain having at last ceased. Martin Amis approached and extended a hand.

On the few occasions we've met, this being the first, he has always been charming, a little flirtatious, a little chary, puzzled by my fogey suits and so forth. Once, attending some reunion dinner at my old college in Oxford with Craig Raine, then a Fellow, Martin looked down at the row upon row of bespectacled men in tuxedos, and said, 'One hundred and fifty A. N. Wilsons'. (As it happens, I hate dinner jackets and black tie, but one sees the point of the joke.) He knew, as he shook hands with me on the pavement, that I was a friend of his father, mother and stepmother, as well as knowing others in his world, so he did not approach, exactly, as a stranger. Yet there was a definite sense that he did so as *capo di tutti capi* and that McEwan, Barnes and Swift, huddling behind him like schoolboys, were a gang that I was not going to be asked to join. There was a sense of the Boss seeing off, not an Enemy exactly, but an alien to their approach. 'Martin can't understand,' said his father, Kingsley, to me once, 'that you do not at least *pretend* to be left-wing. All writers your age are supposed to be lefties.'

Fair enough. But then, I was also embarrassed by Kingsley's assumption that if I was not a leftie, I must therefore be 'right-wing', or anyway right-wing in his particular way.

The short exchange with Martin had a 'disconnect' feeling to it, comparable to the nightmare moment, some years later, with the Lancelyn Greens. There was the person he thought he was seeing or meeting, and there was the inner me, and they were very obviously different. Obviously to me, that is.

Shiva, who was a buddy of Amis – Martin was to speak movingly at Shiva's memorial meeting at the Art Workers' Guild, all too soon after this photo shoot – suggested he and I share a cab back to Bloomsbury. My resolve to do an hour's work in the office before lunch was undone, as we swung into John Street, by Shiva's suggestion that we repair at once to the Duke of York. Alexander Chancellor, the editor, Ferdie Mount, the scarlet-complexioned political columnist, Michael Heath and Peter Ackroyd would indubitably already be at the bar, buying drinks at the expense of our indulgent proprietor, J. G. ('Algy') Cluff – a figure who bankrolled the entire enterprise but was never once invited to join us.

'You're Norman Wilson's son.'

Seventy years and more before Snowdon made the remark, and took my photo, my nine-year-old father was larking about with his brother on a haystack at their farm in Rough Close, a few miles from Stoke-on-Trent, Staffordshire.

In the eighteenth century the Wilsons had been running a small pottery in Barnstaple, north Devon. When a fire destroyed their works, they moved to Staffordshire, and for a while enjoyed some commercial success, having gone into partnership with a London merchant called James Neale – who was also, for a while, a business partner of Josiah Wedgwood. Sometimes, rummaging in a junk shop, I have found a painted figure or plate and found the mark 'Wilson and Neale'.

Several generations on, in the mid- to late nineteenth century, my great-grandfather, James Wilson, established his Etruscan Works in High Street, Longton, advertising 'STATUARY, PEARL AND ALL KINDS OF CHEAP PARIAN' – busts of Petrarch's Laura or of Mr Gladstone, designed to adorn the cluttered chimneypieces of lower-middle-class Victorian parlours, the ceramic equivalents of copper-potted aspidistras and antimacassars.

James's son Tom (Stephen Thomas Wilson) – my grandfather – went in a different direction. Since 1898 the works, Wilson and Sons, had relocated to the unglamorous setting of Fenton. Arnold Bennett, four years after this, wrote his first Potteries novel, *Anna of the Five Towns*. He thereby sealed poor old Fenton's fate by airbrushing it out of the atlas. Even in fiction it had ceased to exist. The five towns that constitute the rest of the Stoke-on-Trent phenomenon are Stoke itself, Hanley, Burslem, Longton and Tunstall, all given fictitious names by Bennett. He said he thought Five Towns sounded 'more euphonious' than six. No doubt, had Livy or some other chronicler deemed that 'Six Hills' sounded 'more euphonious' than seven, we should disregard the Caelian or Esquiline Hill, and when we opened the Book of Revelation, we should find the Whore of Babylon perched on six mountains rather than seven.

Norman, who was quite prickly about class, and believed he had successfully passed himself off as a gentleman – 'The Colonel', as he was always known in our Welsh village during my embarrassed childhood – never displayed the smallest consciousness that Fenton was infra dig. Though painfully chippy about those who were richer than us (this wasn't difficult), and cringing, for example, when I went as a child to Christmas parties given by our cousins the Greens, because they were so obviously grander than we were (they had a butler), he was also, in other moods and modes, brimming with a confidence that his own character and circumstances were unimprovable. Pride is an insufferable quality. Vanity by contrast, I find endearing, particularly when it descends into clownish manifestations of bumptiousness. Norman's elder sisters, who mothered and 'spoiled' him – his actual mother having died shortly after his birth – continued to express, throughout life, exasperation at his need to 'show off', his jokes, his comic turns, his sudden bursting into music-hall songs or recitations of the *Rubáiyát of Omar Khayyám*, his pomaded dressiness, his personal vanity. How often, as a child, I watched him smoothing the crow's feet around his eyes in front of a glass, in the hope that age would go into reverse, or adjusting shirt collars to cover the telltale antiquity of his throat, or practising smiles.

There is a photograph of the four- or five-year-old Norman standing proudly outside the works at Fenton. Clad in a sailor's suit, he is also wearing an expression of irrepressible superiority to the rest of the humanity. To my eyes, this photographic demonstration that the child is father to the man makes the image unmistakable. It could be no other child.

These were the days, 1906 or 1907, before motor transport was common in the pottery towns. Dray horses, pulling the carts of finished wares, would dump on the straw-strewn cobbles. One of Norman's earliest memories would be of old women advancing hastily with trowels on the steaming horse shit, and hurrying back to fertilize the geraniums or spuds in their tiny back gardens. On one occasion, however, Fenton street Arabs got to the steaming load before the horticulturalists. These Fentonians were certainly not, as Norman was, in possession of a beautifully pressed sailor's suit; nor would they ever be. They advanced on the privileged little brat and lifted him into the air before giving him the pummelling for which his conceited expression appeared to be asking. For good measure, they then rubbed him in the horse manure, no doubt deriving great satisfaction, before they skedaddled up the street, from the front door of the 'big house' opening, and the nursery maid and the two elder sisters running in panic-stricken response to little Norman's anguished hollering.

Perhaps it was this incident, perhaps a more generalized need for fresh air and an escape from the smoky, clay-dusty air of the pottery towns, which led Tom Wilson to buy the farm at Rough Close. His

Norman and Stephen at Rough Close, a little while before Stephen's death.

own father, Stephen James, purveyor of 'ALL KINDS OF CHEAP PARIAN', had gasped to death of tuberculosis aged only forty. This disgraceful fact (disgraceful in Norman's eye) was still only whispered about, half a century later. If Aunt Elizabeth said, 'Grandpa Wilson died of TB,' Norman would attempt to silence her with the 'Tch, tch, tch, tch' noise with which he censored any subject too painful to be mentioned. He was evidently unfamiliar with Thomas Mann's *The Magic Mountain*, and considered tuberculosis an indicator of social inferiority, something only common people got.

In the presence of Norman's children there would be many unmentionables. When he was in his fifties, managing director of the most prestigious of all the potteries, Wedgwood, and by way of being a grandee – at any rate as far as the Five or Six Towns were concerned, – he would wander, as he loved to do, in Longton market on a Saturday afternoon, with his two elder children. Having surveyed the junk stalls, he would buy Staffordshire oatcakes and bring them home. We would all eat them, dripping with butter and Lyle's Golden Syrup. On one such afternoon he was approached by a friendly pair speaking with the strong Stokey voice. He apparently froze – my sister tells me of the scene, I was at home, as usual, with Blakie – while they chattered harmlessly. As they went on their way – 'Tarr-ah, our Norman! Don't leave it so long next time!' – my brother and sister asked who on earth they were. '*Very* distant cousins,' was the curt reply.

Tom Wilson – Grandpa Wilson to us – had troubles, however, that were of a more serious order than having relatives who spoke with North Staffordshire voices. (And maybe they were cousins, however distant, not of Grandpa's but of our grandmother.) Tom's loss of a forty-year-old father left him in charge of the business when he was very young. His business skills were non-existent.

Moreover, whereas 'ALL KINDS OF CHEAP PARIAN' made a modest income, Tom Wilson was not interested in money, and wanted to make something beautiful.

In *A Potter's Book*, Bernard Leach described Tom as the last great master potter. Tom's own personal hero was Bernard Moore (1850–1935), whose flambéed glazes and lustre pigments were some of the most beautiful productions of the aesthetic movement, easily worthy to be placed alongside the more celebrated William de Morgan. The deep red flambé glaze which was Moore's signature colour, so redolent of the 1890s, was one that my grandfather imitated, and Grandpa's skills at developing glazes and perfecting firing techniques was something he passed on to my father, who took it into more modernist directions, but, like his father, Moore and de Morgan, always with an eye to the east, especially to Korea.

Clearly, Tom would have been happier producing only 'art' ceramics rather than the cups and saucers that provided his children with their daily bread.

His melancholy temperament, flaring into uncontrolled rages, became a byword among both the workforce and his family. My Aunt Elizabeth, his firstborn, remembered as a child her Pa standing beside the exit from the kiln as the trolleys of finished ware were trundled out into the yard to be packed in straw. It was the impassivity of the men's faces that struck the clever girl, as they continued to wheel their barrows even as Mr Tom, with his walking cane, swept tray after tray of teacups to the cobbles, a look of abject misery on his moustachioed face.

'It could be,' she would say, 'that I am remembering the very day that Ma d—'

But, before the word 'died' had escaped my aunt's lips, Norman would cut short the recollection with his 'Tch, tch, tch, tch, tch', a noise that recalled a very small boy pretending to be a steam train.

Tragedies aplenty befell my grandfather, with the relentlessness of some doom-laden novel penned by his namesake Thomas Hardy. Having had four children, he became a widower. Like many Potteries people, he liked the Isle of Man. At one point he ventured into sheep-farming there and had the experience of Gabriel Oak, in *Far from the Madding Crowd*, losing his entire flock during a storm when the animals were blown off a cliff into the Irish Sea.

Very early in Norman's childhood, his father took off to the Isle of Man and married a Manxwoman whose name was Kate Kreer. The ceremony was solemnized in Douglas, the island's capital, and it was only after they had crossed to Liverpool by steamer and boarded the train to Stoke that her husband informed her that she had four stepchildren. Elizabeth, to whom her father's unannounced marriage was a great shock, ran immediately to live with her grandmother and her great-aunt Edith – Tom's aunt – who painted Scottish moorlands, and usually got a picture into the Royal Academy summer show. Later, Elizabeth went to live with two of her aunts, Hypatia and Horatia, staying with them until the outbreak of war in 1914.

Possibly it was his new marriage that prompted Tom to move to Rough Close. It was there, when my father was nine and his brother Stephen eleven, that we found them earlier in this chapter, larking about on the haystack in the yard.

Stephen fell.

At one moment, two brothers were in the midst of harmless fun, ignoring the cries of their sisters to be careful. A second later, Norman watched his elder brother lying in the farmyard mud. The child was carried into the house, but the dirt had infected his wounds and within a few days father and stepmother were watching tetanus, aptly called lockjaw, torture the child's last gasping hours of life.

Apart from being catastrophically sad, this pivotal event in Norman's life doomed him to become a figure whose presence to any child would be domestically, at best, semi-tolerable. He would marry late, when he was nearly forty, and with a longing for a huge dynasty. He told my mother he wanted eight children. Alas, when the children – there were to be three of us – actually appeared, the spectre of the farmyard at Rough Close could not leave him. The most harmless scene – a child toddling over clear soft sand on a beach, for example, or running through grass – could throw him into a panic. What if, beneath the sand, there was a jagged tin can? What if there was a broken lemonade bottle in the grass? 'You will be cut!' he would call. 'CUT! CUT! CUT!'

The list of possible calamities was endless. His clever brain invented them at every turn – two children on a see-saw would make him think of one at least, perhaps both, being hurled into the air and dashing their brains out. When my mother bought a little cottage in Wales overlooking miles of sand, and a glistening Towy estuary, Norman, who loved the place and would retire there for the last two decades of his life, saw nightmare visions that were totally beyond his control. The children saw golden sand. He saw a minefield in which careless picnickers had planted tetanus-enriched sardine tins. The children saw a muddy creek where they could moor a boat. He saw, long before they entered the boat and were swept to their inevitable death by drowning, the mud as a laboratory seed-tray of poliomyelitis. (My childhood coincided with the polio epidemic.) Only when he was absent was it possible for any of his children to climb a tree, ride a bike, plunge unescorted into the sea, without poor Norman seeing a repetition of the unmentionable – Tch, tch, tch, tch – tragedy.

He never spoke about it. One heard of it from Aunt Elizabeth. At Stephen's funeral, they sang 'Abide with me'. *Shine through the gloom and point me to the skies!* When this was sung at the football Cup Final on television, I would watch his forget-me-not blue eyes fill up. His loathing of religion, and of what he deemed its preposterous promise of a future life in exchange for earthly heartbreak – was bitter, unconquerable. Hatred of the God in whom he did not believe was part of the atmosphere in which I grew up.

His stepmother had adhered to the Edwardian High-Churchery which may be seen as the incense-drowned counterpart to her husband's love of red flambé glazes, a whiff of the 1890s surviving into the twentieth century. When Norman was twelve, in the opening months of the First World War, he was sent to Ellesmere College in Shropshire.

The school had been founded forty years or so earlier by Canon Nathaniel Woodard, a pillar of High-Churchery. Built with a quadrangle and a large Gothic chapel, it was a parody of the older public schools. Woodard had a twofold aim in founding his schools: the promotion of Anglo-Catholicism and the consolidation of class hierarchy.

Of the sixteen Woodard schools, the first rank was occupied by Lancing College, Evelyn Waugh's alma mater. It was clear to Woodard, however, that the words 'middle class' could now be applied to 'gentlemen with small incomes, solicitors, surgeons with limited practice, unbeneficed clergymen, naval and military officers' and also to 'respectable tradesfolk'.

Flushed with his success at catering to these lowlier categories of human being, the canon adventurously established a third category of school, such as Ardingly College (Sussex) and Ellesmere, initially intending them for the sons of 'second-rate retail shops, publicans, gin-palace keepers, etc.'. Such was the popularity of the schools, however, and such the fervour of the lower-middle-class hope that their children could pass themselves off as gentlefolk, that the margins between the second and third categories quickly became blurred. Ardingly and Ellesmere were initially intended to stop educating boys at the age of fourteen, and watch them return, admittedly with a smattering of Latin and the knowledge of the rules of Fives, to running their second-rate retail shops. By the beginning of the twentieth century, Ardinglyites and Ellesmerians were staying on until eighteen, just like the Lancing boys, preparing for the varsity.

Norman enjoyed the school, and he enjoyed telling people that he was a public-school man. Until he was in his forties, he played scrum half in the Staffordshire Public Schoolboys side most Saturdays. He had loved all the sporting activities at school, and it was a sad disappointment for him that neither of his sons showed much interest in games. He enjoyed bellowing the words of 'Gaudeamus Igitur', which, with its rousing Brahms melody, had been adopted as their school song.

In other respects, however, schooldays during those times were sombre, with the regular recitation of names of recent old boys dying on the battlefields in Flanders and northern France. His sisters, Dorothy and Elizabeth, had both volunteered and throughout the war nursed the wounded in field hospitals.

For Norman, the most nauseating school memory was of 'parsons' – always his word for the clergy – who had avoided call-up while their coevals crawled through mud, grazed with barbed wire and wounded with shrapnel. These impostors, these fake Catholics in their birettas and soutanes, confirmed his certainty that Christianity was something to be utterly derided and hated. He recalled the pleasure with which these perverts administered the cane. He claimed that the last time one of them had asked him to bend over he had grabbed the 'parson's' cane and threatened to chastise the little bugger himself.

Had Norman been only a year older, he would himself have been called up for military service. He was just sixteen when the war ended. After school, he studied at the Tech in Stoke before joining the family firm. It was, after all, Wilson AND SONS, even though there was now only one son to interest himself in the business.

He had inherited his father's combination of technical brilliance and aesthetic awareness. Working together, however, was not easy, and Wilson and Sons was slithering into ruin. Tch, tch, tch, tch – this was never mentioned, never. The firm went bust in 1926, but Norman always spoke of his departure, in that year, for Canada, as an entirely independent decision. He had always loved horses, and he set off to Calgary to break in polo ponies. He loved playing polo. In the day or two before the ship sailed from Liverpool Dock, the popular song on everyone's lips was

> Pack up all my care and woe
> Here I go, singing low,
> Bye, bye, blackbird!

Such was Norman's shame about the failure of the business that it was only after he died, and my brother was going through his affairs, that we discovered that Grandpa Wilson had died an undischarged bankrupt.

8. Leaving Germany

While the band played 'Bye, Bye, Blackbird', and the liner, Canada-bound, bore Norman from the Liverpool dockside, a skinny fourteen-year-old girl had been left alone in her boarding house at Cheltenham Ladies' College. It was Ascension Day 1926 and, because it was a holiday, most of the other girls had been taken on outings with parents or family. An older girl, Betty Mosley, taking pity on this little waif, whose name was Jean Dorothy Crowder, invited her for a tramp on Leckhampton Hill and a picnic with her mother and her father, who was the Bishop of Stepney.

'She was so alone-seeming,' Betty told me when, in extreme old age, Jean had staggered out of the room to make tea. 'She always seemed so sad.'

Whereas Norman's policy with regard to his past was scorched earth, obliterating as he went, keeping few family connections and no friendships outside the Wedgwood circle, Jean grappled her English friends to her heart with hoops of steel. Betty Mosley, later Dame Betty Ridley and a formidable presence on the General Synod of the Church of England, remained Jean's friend for life, together with a handful of Cheltenham girls and some of the girls with whom she'd shared lodgings when she worked at Wedgwood.

Jean's parents were estranged, her home life troubled. Selena Christian, her mother, was a spirited person with literary aspirations, who wrote occasional articles for the *Manchester Guardian*. She had a passion for the novels of Thomas Hardy, and, together with a Scottish

schoolma'am cousin, Agnes Peterson – 'Cousin Nan', always spoken
of by Jean in tones that would have been hyperbolic had a combo
of George Eliot and St Teresa of Ávila been embodied and under
discussion – would explore Hardy's Wessex. Selena believed herself,
on what authority her grandchildren never troubled to ascertain, to
be of the same family as Fletcher Christian, the mutineer on HMS
Bounty. It was averred that Fletcher and his brother John Christian
had been at school in Cockermouth with William Wordsworth, and
even that, later in life, long after the mutiny, Fletcher had escaped the
Pitcairn Islands and turned up incognito to visit Wordsworth and
Coleridge in the Quantocks, providing inspiration for *The Rime of
the Ancient Mariner*. True or cock-and-bull, these claims established
that Selena and her people were a cut above the Crowders.

Her husband was a child of presumably very innocent parents
who, unaware of the sniggers his initials would provoke when
engraved on suitcases, had named him Walter Clarence Crowder.
The initials must have rankled since it was he who pointed out to
a married pair as heedless as his own mother and father that, if
Jean and Norman named their second child Jean Elizabeth Wilson,
her initials would be painted on her school trunk. Such thoughts
were not based on anti-Semitic feeling, merely a knowledge of how
cruel children like to be. My sister's names were rearranged, by the
time her birth was registered, and her school luggage was always
initialled EJW.

Clarrie, whom I never knew, was what used to be described as a
self-made man, a businessman in the cotton line. He was proficient
in French, German and Spanish and spent much of his professional
life on the European mainland, away from his wife.

If this book were a biography of my mother, the author would
be obliged to research the probably irrecoverable truth of what
had gone wrong in Selena and Clarrie's marriage. Since it is an
autobiography, and both my maternal grandparents were dead
before I could speak, all that matters is the subjective truth, fed to
me by Jean Dorothy via her memories. Girlhood had been a dark
memory until boarding school rescued her from a mother who
hated her, locked her in wardrobes and smacked her.

In the Jean version Selena was a termagant, incomprehensibly punishing a saint. She liked to apply the lines in 'Tintern Abbey' to her father: 'His little, nameless, unremembered, acts / Of kindness and of love'. She remembered him cleaning her shoes before he left their suburban house to catch the train to Manchester. Never, in these recitations of Clarrie's kindness, did Jean ask why Selena was so perpetually foul to him, refusing to eat meals in his presence and insisting that he ate in the kitchen while she and Jean's much-petted elder brother, Felix, ate in the dining room.

The wretched existence was played out in a new-built villa in Bramhall, near Altrincham. (A politician once told me it is the most Conservative constituency in England.) Felix attended a local grammar school. A comparable place for girls might have been found, but by then the marriage had already started to unravel, to the point where a boarding school was advisable. Quite apart from wishing to remove from the scene a child witness to marital misery, another motive edged Selena towards the need for Jean to be sent away. A disturbing rumour was brought to their household by a neighbour, Mrs Berry, whose daughter Enid (a lifelong friend) was Jean's exact contemporary. The local girls' school was said to have a high academic reputation, but there was a rumour.

Mrs Berry had heard that some of the girls there spoke ... When Jean, who had, buried beneath her many impossible character traits, a marked sense of humour, recalled all this, she would imitate the way in which Mrs Berry was so appalled by the rumour that she could not say it aloud. She mouthed it silently. Some of the girls at the grammar school spoke with ... 'a northern accent'. The two mothers could not have been more shocked if told that some of the girls suffered from venereal disease.

Felix, who went to Cambridge and became a lawyer, spoke with a completely southern voice, in the rather prissy tones of a stage vicar. Presumably, Mrs Berry and Selena Christian spoke in what is now called Received Standard, though one would guess that Shaw's Professor Higgins would deduce from their voices that they came from Cheshire. It is all but impossible nowadays, when BBC announcers speak with the whole variety of British English voices, and where there is, really, no Received way of speaking the language any longer, to reconstruct a time when an accent mattered so much. Those at the top of the pile could afford to speak as they chose. Upper-class cockney still survived in the speech patterns of King George V, while his Foreign Secretary, former Viceroy of India Lord Curzon, spoke with short northern 'a' sounds. But for the middling sort, desperate to retain their middle-class status, and with the knowledge that recent family generations had been lower down the pecking order, elocution was taken with desperate seriousness.

Cousin Nan, the saint and fount of all wisdom, recommended, from her Scottish perspective, St Leonards School in St Andrews. Mrs Berry's researches, however, discovered that the school was liberal in its use of the tawse on the unfortunate gels. Selena liked the sound of Cheltenham Ladies' College, and it was to this celebrated establishment that Enid and Jean, aged eleven, were dispatched.

Jean's rewrites of personal history were frequent during her widowhood. Just as with statements emanating from the old Politburo, the version of history that had been peddled for as long as anyone could remember could change overnight. For the first thirty years I knew her the Cheltenham years were the happiest of her life. Betty, Enid and Dorothy Wallace (the half-Burmese daughter of the crime writer Edgar) were lifelong chums, and the arrival of the old girls' newsletter was a red-letter day. But in her widowhood, when the Party Line changed, it seemed that the schoolgirl bliss had been scorched through with moments of humiliation.

On her very first night in the dorm, one of the girls asked around among the other new bugs how they addressed the butler at home. Did they call him 'Mr So-and-so', or simply by his surname, or even by his Christian name? When Jean's turn came, she owned up that the modest suburban villa in Bramhall did not run to a butler, only maids. Contemptuous giggles greeted this information. Only when she was in her seventies did it dawn on Jean (who shared with her husband an extraordinary innocence) that many of the girls, perhaps most of them, had been lying about the extent of their family's equipage, and that the question posed to these children of dons, lawyers and doctors had, in the 1920s, been a spiteful tease.

Two passions, however, were nurtured by the school: sport and languages. Jean never got into the first XI, but she played cricket in the second XI. Tennis, hockey, lacrosse and swimming were all ardently loved. And she shared her father's fondness for languages (while speaking them with a completely English voice). When Jean was sixteen, Mother, who was severely asthmatic, was advised by the doctor to spend the winter in Antibes. Jean took a term out of Cheltenham to be the companion to her detested parent. According to the Lycée in Antibes, her French advanced to the point where a place at university could be considered. Felix had gone to Cambridge, but for Jean Dorothy it would be Manchester.

In preparation for this next stage she was to spend a term, after Cheltenham, at the Hilda-Schule at Koblenz, where the Moselle meets the Rhine.

Even as I wrote the last two paragraphs, the juxtaposition of French and German place names in the same sentence as the words 'Jean Dorothy' seems almost impossible. The Jean Dorothy I knew was what I suppose one would call agoraphobic. She was thrown into a panic by the idea of going anywhere. She had not left England since the 1930s, and if she was driven more than a few miles in a car, she suffered not merely from motion sickness but from near-hysteria. The lack of connect between the teenage Jean Dorothy and the woman I knew as my mother is total. What had happened to her?

I suppose the simple answer is 'marriage'. Seventy years on this planet have taught me, by observation and experience, that this cherished institution, while nourishing those rare beings for whom it 'works', is, for a significant number of those who risk it – I'd say most – an arrangement of life that is utterly destructive of the human soul. But then, the years have also taught me that simple explanations for things are not always the right ones, and my mother remains to me utterly incomprehensible.

Here she is, though, seventeen years old, twenty or more years before the tadpole that would one day be me appeared in her womb, and she is arriving at the Hilda-Schule in Koblenz. One thing is certain: it was a time of intense personal happiness. She lived *en famille* with the headmaster and his family, who were of an age with her. When, as occasionally happened, she recollected them, a change came over her face. The brooding, taut, so often furious features softened and became gentle. Photographs show a face I would not see until she reached old age – Jean Dorothy smiling, Jean laughing uproariously. This was a Jean who had found a family who accepted her, and loved her. How Clarrie became such friends with them – that is anyone's guess. It was he who had found the school, and arranged for her to go there.

While she was there, she received the news from England that her parents had separated. Clarrie was to live with a sister – I never met either of them. During his vacations from Cambridge, Selena was to continue to live with Felix, Jean's brother. Clarrie's career was in ruins. It was 1929/30. England was in the grip of a slump, and the idea that Jean could afford to go to university was shelved.

Going to university would have been the making of her. However 'difficult' and miserable she might still have been, there would surely have been consolation in filling her unhappy head with French and German literature. Becoming a graduate might at least have fought against that passive-aggressive inferiority complex which made her close down any conversation that was moving in the direction of being interesting. Mention of a book, or a work of art, other than a novel borrowed from the public library, would nearly always make her sulk, and if you tried to talk to her about the current library book, she peered at you suspiciously as if you were showing off, or trying to catch her out.

There were, however, moments when sunlight broke through the clouds. When she was old, and near death, having been twenty years a widow, she told me how surprising she found it that, having a reading knowledge of French, Russian and Italian, I'd never learned German. It was such a wonderful language. Imagine being able to read Goethe, Schiller and the other poets, admired by her friends in Koblenz!

She had never made such a remark to me before. She told me to open her cupboard and take out her German schoolbooks, her dictionary, Clarrie's dictionary and grammar. So began, for a grown man with other tasks on hand, the difficult task of learning German – but one that made it possible to write the biographies of Prince Albert and Queen Victoria, and to study in the archives at

Coburg, Gotha and Berlin! Now, a decade later, my German is good enough to read *Faust* and *Maria Stuart* and the *Duino Elegies* and Sebald's *The Rings of Saturn* in the original. And I feel I am enjoying them on her behalf, as if someone dying of an incurable anorexia had given me a meal ticket for all the best restaurants in Paris.

Her father's ruin, and the dismantling of her family, removed the incentive to return to Mother, Felix or the constraints of Bramhall. Germany – I can see it now, having started to write about it – was so much her kind of place, with its wholesomeness, its orderliness, its cleanliness. The headmaster she idolized. 'A real old Prussian.' Her face glowed as she said it. A stickler for discipline, upright, Lutheran, pure. When the subject of contemporary politics arose, he would say fiercely, at the supper table, 'If I found one of you reading That Book, I'd not only throw the Book out of the house, I would throw YOU out of the house!' So, of course, the boys became avid readers of That Book. The consequences were among the factors, I believe, which broke Jean's heart. Something had broken her, and it was not just Mother, or the collapse of her health through obstetric complications, or the challenges of being married to Norman. It was the Twentieth-Century Tragedy which all that generation carried inside them, and which she could not bear.

Once or twice I asked her if she had ever read That Book, the forbidden one, but she would merely shudder, and the curtain would descend beneath her stubborn, short-sighted eyes.

After a semester at the Hilda-Schule as a regular pupil, she remained with the family for over a year, earning her keep by teaching English conversation to the junior classes. By the time she had to return to England, she knew that she would have to earn her living.

It was Mother, the detested but feared Selena, who sent her a cutting from the Situations Vacant column from some newspaper, presumably the *Manchester Guardian*. The venerable old family pottery, Josiah Wedgwood and Sons, still housed in the Etruria Works at Burslem, as it had been since the eighteenth century, needed someone to translate and reply to letters in the European tongues. Jean Dorothy applied for, and got, the job. She left Germany and set herself up in shared 'digs' in Newcastle-under-Lyme, with two other young women.

9. The Works

After a year breaking in polo ponies on a remote Canadian ranch – nearest town Calgary – Norman Wilson received an invitation to return to England, as Works Manager at the old Etruria works, built by Josiah I in the eighteenth century. The summons came from the present boss of the firm, Frank Wedgwood.

My father was twenty-five years old. The world of the Potteries was small. Everyone knew everyone else, and the families who ran the, for the most part tiny, firms were interrelated and intermarried many times over. Frank Wedgwood had seen the collapse of Wilson and Sons, and perceived that Norman Wilson, by becoming a Canadian equestrian, would be a loss to ceramics. Like his father and Bernard Moore, Norman was a skilled master of the science of glazes. He had a good eye. He was a scientist, an aesthete and a technician, the three qualities needed to be a successful industrial potter. He came from a family of at least seven generations of potters, and he knew his craft by instinct. He was, moreover, a good manager of people, as would be demonstrated in the army. He had the soldierly combination of bossiness, charm, impatience, efficiency and good humour (much of the time), with occasional outbursts of rage. These skills brought out the best in others. You see why Frank Wedgwood headhunted him.

The Norman I knew was a man in his sixties and seventies. By then he had retired to Wales with his wife and his elder sister. My brother and sister had left home. Norman was lonely, and friendless,

and locked in a difficult marriage (difficult for them both!). As a
growing child and adolescent, I'd hear the Wedgwood anecdotes
over and over again, and, as he grew older, his need to repeat them
was compulsive. Waiting in shops, standing on railway platforms
or at the bar of an hotel, he would light upon total strangers and,
Ancient Mariner-like, catch their eye. Sometimes, when we had
been on a shopping expedition to Carmarthen, Norman would tell
me to meet him in one of the old inns where farmers congregated
on market days. As I advanced to the door of the saloon, I'd hear
his voice announcing, 'Frank Wedgwood – always known as Major
Frank, of course – was the nicest man I ever knew.' Not deflated
by the visible lack of interest in his hearers' faces, and brooking no
polite interjections such as, 'Well, now, is that so?' or 'Who is Major
Frank?' he would press on, the Last Minstrel strumming his Lay.

'We always followed the Beagles.'

'Oh, now beagling, it's interesting you should ...'

A look of impatience would cross Norman's face. The red-faced
farmer was about to make the mistake of treating this as a dialogue,
in which the other party had some role to play, whereas surely he
could see that he was simply there in order to listen?

'... many of the workforce at Etruria followed the Beagles,'
Norman would insist.

Etruria, anyone? This in a saloon bar full of hill farmers and
drovers, trying to discuss the price of sheep.

'... I was a young man in those days; Major Frank would have
been sixty or so. Huh! We thought that was ancient! You may or
may not know it, but many men and women in Stoke-on-Trent in
those days spoke the dialect. I'm not talking about an accent, but
the real Stokey dialect.'

He raced on, guessing that mention of people who spoke a
different language might easily deflect the audience into making
their own contribution: for example, by speaking of the question
of whether sheep auctions should be conducted in English or in
Welsh. No time for that sort of talk.

'Anyway, the Beagles. We ran at a fair pace, I can tell you. Old
Frank was older than most of 'em, and on one famous occasion' – all

occasions involving members of the Wedgwood clan were famous –
'he fell. Remember, or you won't get the point of the story – the
men spoke the dialect. Never occurred to them that old Frank
could do so as well! So, down he fell, and one man called out, "'e's
dine!" Frank, energetic as a boy, hopped up immediately and called
back, "'e isna!"'

I felt by now protective of Norman. I wanted these stories to
be greeted with the amusement and interest which at that date I
still believed them to deserve. Come on, someone. Give it a polite
laugh.

He would murmur, as he took a sip from his large schooner of
Amontillado, and sadly watched the baffled boredom on the faces
of his audience. 'Typical Wedgwood story, that.' How could his
hearers have known that 'dine' meant 'down'?

The more polite of the drovers and hill farmers would say, 'Well,
is that so?'

'Yup. Nicest man I ever knew, Frank. Always known in the
works as Major Frank. He was in the Boer War. Now, his brother,
Cecil …'

For all his niceness, and his surprising grasp of the dialect, Major
Frank had not been the best man to be running a business during
the 'Slump' that followed the Wall Street Crash. One day in 1930,
on his way to a business meeting in Brussels, he got off the train
at Euston Station and fell dead on the platform, at the age of
sixty-three.

His mantle as managing director fell on his thirty-one-year-old
nephew, Josiah V, known in his immediate family as Siah, at the
works as Mr Jos and by us Wilson children as Uncle Jos. Almost
certainly, had it not been for Josiah, the firm would have gone
bust. He was a person of singular gifts: the intensely musical cousin
of Ralph Vaughan Williams; a brilliant economist who was the
youngest director of the Bank of England in its history. He was
nervous, jumpy, moody, at times melancholy-mad. He quickly
became the most important person in my father's life, and he
would always remain so, especially after their tragic estrangement
in 1962/3.

When the pair come into my mind now, as they so often do, Uncle Jos in his well-cut double-breasted charcoal grey suits, Norman in his racier Prince of Wales checks, their costume does not fix them in the twentieth century. Jos of the Woeful Countenance is Don Quixote in a double-breasted suit. Norman is the faithful Sancho Panza. It is one of those duos, such as Mr Pickwick and Sam Weller, or Sherlock Holmes and Dr Watson, which was passing the love of women. Fine, if both parties are bachelors; less fun for the women. And that, as they say, is the story of all my early life.

10. Frail Travelling

The girls in the typing pool – we're in the mid- to late 1930s now – would snigger, 'No, but 'e's ever so handsome.'

'Dapper.'

'Them lovely suits, 'n all. They'd set 'im back a bit.'

'And them Bentley cars. And an Alvis.'

'Well, a bachelor 'as only hisself to please.'

'Shame, you'd think 'e'd be married be now. Them lovely blue eyes.'

'I think Dawn fancies 'im 'ersel'.'

'Geroff, Hilda Worrall!'

When the laughter died – 'Only one thing…'

'You wo'?'

'Ever remind you of Someone?'

The whispers would be followed by shrieks of laughter.

'And 'e's got the moustache 'n all.'

Overhearing these observations, the bespectacled young woman in the corner of the typing pool, concentrating on a letter from a department store in Hamburg or Berlin, glowed with the excited knowledge that the object of the discussion had recently asked her out on a date. And yes, it did amuse her. There was a resemblance, certainly – the moustache, the blue eyes.

By arrangement, top secret, not to be disclosed to a soul, he picked her up from her digs in Newcastle. This was yet a third car, a Lagonda. They roared off, down innocent, pre-war roads from Newcastle-under-Lyme to Whitchurch, from Whitchurch to Oswestry and over the border into Wales, little guessing that, in the unimaginable future, this was where they would spend decades together: early acrimony and squabbles becoming an ingrained habit, but the perpetual bickering, which made their joint company unendurable to one another, accompanied by mutual dependency. At last, when the bickering stopped, he would lie in a Welsh churchyard, and she would wait twenty lonely years before being placed in the same grave.

The swerving bends pursued by the swooping Lagonda made her feel a bit sick, and when, on their way back to Staffordshire, they stopped in a pub, she had not wanted alcohol. When did she ever? Her three children persuaded her on her widowed eightieth birthday to sip a glass of champagne, an experiment that she characteristically predicted would make her 'bilious'. He, by contrast, had needed a drink. Fidgety, nervous, his displays of fear shocked her. At the works he seemed so breezy, so self-confident. She had expected him to kiss her, but when a terrified lurch towards such a gesture began, she deflected it. She had only been kissed by one man before: Eric Woods, a Bramhall neighbour and coeval, now a clergyman academic at Cambridge who published under the name G. F. Woods. (The F was for Frederic – for which Eric was short.) Neither had said anything, but since her teens she had half assumed that Eric would be 'the one'.

Norman was ten years older than she was but, as she told me in our long talks, when I came to know her in her widowhood, she was convinced he was as virginal as she. He had once been engaged to a girl called Dorothy. What a lot of Dorothys there were in the story: there was his sister Dorothy, now married to a surgeon, Gordon Lewis, at the City General Hospital in Newcastle; there was Jos's (estranged) wife, Dorothy. Norman's girlfriend had been Dorothy Yates (Dot). He had fallen for her at a tennis party at Farley Hall, the 'stately', or semi-stately home, where he had lived as a lodger a decade before buying a small house of his own. Iris Wedgwood – wife of Ralph the railway millionaire, mother of the historian C. V. (Veronica) Wedgwood and of John Hamilton

Norman and Jean in the Welsh hills.

Wedgwood – had commended Dot for her 'child-bearing hips'. Norman used to say he had broken his heart over Dot, and that it was only his anti-religious principles that had put the kibosh on the relationship.

Like so many people in North Staffordshire, Dot was a Roman Catholic. In those days canon law was fiercely followed. When a Catholic made a match outside the Church, the non-Catholic partner was asked to undergo instruction in the Faith, and it was a requirement that the children would be brought up as Catholics.

Norman's hatred of religion, beginning with his brother Stephen's cruel death, compounded by the sadism of the biretta'd inverts of Ellesmere College, had matured into an intellectual certainty since his absorption into the Wedgwood entourage. Of course, he conformed to their world view. Had not the patriarch of the dynasty, Josiah I, known as Owd Wooden Leg – because he indeed had a wooden leg after the amputation of his lower right leg, following a riding accident – been the grandfather to Charles Darwin? And had not Darwin seen off the Almighty seventy years since? Colonel Jos (our Jos's father), Liberal, then Labour, MP for Newcastle-under-Lyme, had denounced the Prayer Book Revisions of 1927/8 in the House of Commons, not because this divorced father of seven children was especially religious but because he shared the anti-Romish prejudice entertained by the majority of decent English people. The new Prayer Book had a whiff of Popery about it, with its inclusion of 'Blessed is He who Comes in the name of the Lord' into the Communion, implying that Christ was about to descend into the bread on the Holy Table.

Years and years later, in 1982, when Veronica's brother John Hamilton Wedgwood was about to marry *en secondes noces* an Anglo-Catholic lady called Pamela Tudor-Craig, the wedding invitation bid us all attend 'nuptial mass'. Veronica said to Norman, 'You don't expect to see the words "mass" and "Wedgwood" on the same card.' Paris might have been worth a mass, but Newcastle-under-Lyme, where the Unitarian Meeting House attended by Owd Wooden Leg still stands, most decidedly was not. The prospect of Norman marrying Dot Yates was over before it began.

In old age Norman would speak airily of Veronica as a woman he 'might have married' or, in other versions, as himself having been 'earmarked' by Iris as a suitable partner for the famous historian. In these slowly enunciated reflections he never expressed even a glimmering of consciousness that C. V. Wedgwood, who had spent seventy years of her life living devotedly with Jacqueline Hope-Wallace, was highly unlikely to have opted to share her life with a chap.

In grown-up life, after I became Literary Editor at the *Spectator*, I came to know Veronica independently, and she even, before the cruel march of dementia, did some reviewing for the pages I edited. She and Victoria Glendinning, both friends of mine, were judges of the W. H. Smith Literary Award and gave it to one of my novels, *Wise Virgin*. At the lavish prize-giving luncheon I sat some way away from them, but I could see them casting their eyes in my direction, often bursting into laughter. Afterwards, as we were milling about, I asked Veronica what she and Victoria had been discussing. 'Your father,' was the reply. I felt, on Norman's behalf, a little stung. He was still alive, and he was so pleased that evening when I rang up, and lied, and told him Veronica had sent her love.

She probably wasn't being malicious in her chat with Victoria, whose father, Freddie Seebohm, funnily enough, was also known to Norman – they were in the Royal Horse Artillery together during the Second World War – but his innocence, or narrow emotional range, was marked. The thought that two women, let alone the fact that one of them was a Wedgwood, might live together as married people live … Had you put this to Norman, such a notion would have been laughed aside.

So, had Jean Dorothy, on her carsick journey back from Wales, begun to wonder about Norman as a life partner, she needed fear no female rivals. This was not, however, to say that no rival existed. The all-consuming friendship with Jos sealed off any possibility of Norman being interested in anyone or anything else for long.

11. Andrew Woods

Moreover, the difficulties and crises of steering Josiah Wedgwood and Sons through the 1930s were entirely preoccupying. Saving the old firm, and looking after the workforce, was Jos and Norman's prime concern.

The Wall Street Crash of October 1929 had a devastating effect on the Potteries, as on industry in general. In 1929 Wedgwood made a profit of £7,697. The auditors reported a loss of £6,829 in the first quarter *alone* of 1932. By then, in the Potteries, 36 per cent of the workforce was on the dole. In order to minimize the redundancies, the Wedgwoods asked the workforce to take cuts in wages of up to 20 per cent when trade dipped to its lowest point. The young idealists running the firm, my father included, were determined to save it. A stroke of luck came when Cadbury's, the Birmingham chocolate manufacturer, had a 'promotion' whereby customers collected labels from Bournville Cocoa tins and, in exchange, would receive a simple beaker and saucer made by Wedgwood. This wheeze saved Wedgwood from bankruptcy.

It was not enough, however, to go on making pastiche eighteenth-century blue and white jasperware. Most of the output of the factory since early days had been undistinguished, or downright ugly. Whereas Jos was guided by his business nous, financial know-how and, in those days, socialist zeal for the welfare of his employees, he knew that he also needed the artistic flare and design sense that were Norman's forte. In 1934 Norman persuaded Jos to take on

Victor Skellern as Art Director. Skellern had begun his career in the decorating department at the Etruria Works. Then he won a scholarship to the Royal College of Art in Kensington, of which Jos was a governor. Skellern returned to Etruria with the informed enthusiasm of the modern designer. At the Royal College he had made vital contacts which enabled the trio – Jos, Skellern and Norman – to transform Wedgwood. Chief among the new 'finds' was the young New Zealand architect/designer Keith Murray, but there were many others. A routine developed. Artists would be asked to come for a week or so to North Staffordshire to absorb the 'feel' of the old works, and to experiment with designs, paint some plates and try out some decorations and glazes.

Not all were successful. Visitors to the shrine of the Bloomsberries, Charleston Farmhouse in Firle, Sussex, are now reverently shown the blue and white plates depicting Great Women of History painted by Vanessa Bell. Although Norman liked Bell, and Duncan Grant, who accompanied her on that visit, the plates were unskilfully painted, and obviously unsaleable. Artists who did make it into the shops, however, began to give an entirely new 'look' to Wedgwood: Laura Knight, Eric Ravilious, Arnold Machin, John Skeaping, as well as Norman and Victor Skellern themselves.

In 1936 there was an exhibition of the new Wedgwood designs at the Grafton Gallery in Mayfair, containing work by all these names. It made a huge impression on the public, who now realized that the Wedgwood stamp on the bottom of a plate meant more than simply pastiche jasper ashtrays decorated with eighteenth-century goddesses. Between the death of the first Josiah and the arrival of my father the firm had not pioneered any original designers. Victorian Coalport, Royal Doulton or Worcester is likely to be much more beautiful than Victorian Wedgwood, though Mr Gladstone had been right, in his speech to open the Wedgwood Institute in Burslem, to say that you could always tell a pile of Wedgwood plates because they did not wobble, each was truly identical and fitted in a pile with the neatness of paper.

Now, in the mid-1930s, people could see that Wedgwood was once again, as it had been in the 1780s, a name to associate with the highest, most innovative aesthetic standards. Aided by the steady popularity of the beakers for Cadbury's, business began to boom, even while other potteries struggled. By 1934 there was a profit of £9,428; by 1938 it was an impressive £13, 651.

The money was sorely needed, since Owd Wooden Leg's Etruria Works was in a poor way. He built it, all unknowing, on the site of old mineshafts, and by the time they were celebrating the bicentenary of his birth in 1930, Etruria was sinking into the adjacent canal. When he had established the works there in 1769, the 380-acre estate was in the country, a safe distance from the growing towns of Hanley and Newcastle. George Stubbs's portrait shows Wedgwood sitting with the family in a rural paradise, with a tiny puff of chimney smoke glimpsed in the background, a mere allusion to his manufactory and the source of his prodigious fortune.

By the 1930s, the green fields captured by Stubbs had become a filthy industrial inferno. The average age of a potter's death in those days was in the early thirties. Silicosis clogged the lungs of young men with coal dust and clay dust. All the picturesque little bottle ovens were coal-fuelled, and the air over the Pottery towns was a thick smog. Even on a clear day you could not see across the valley in which Etruria snuggled.

Etruria, the birthplace and childhood home of Charles Darwin's mother, had long since been abandoned by the Wedgwoods. The family had decamped to Maer Hall, a few miles to the west of Newcastle-under-Lyme. Josiah I's widow had moved to the village of Tittensor, and nearby Barlaston was soon colonized by other members of the family. Major Frank, the nicest man, etc., lived at Upper House in that village. Norman himself eventually abandoned Farley Hall and bought a little house in the village. Iris lived at the Old Dairy. Some of Jos's childhood was spent in the village when Colonel Jos, his MP father, took a lease on the handsome old Barlaston Hall.

Etruria and the district of Shelton, where the majority of the workforce, by force of circumstance, had to live, was a death-hole of filth. The railway chugging through it coughed out smoke and smuts towards the works. If it snowed in Etruria, the snow was black by dawn. The nearby Shelton Bar steelworks belched fumes that contained metallic particles. Between seven and fifteen hundredweight of dirt was deposited monthly on Etruria by that steelworks, mainly iron or iron oxide. As the pots were trolleyed into eighteenth-century kilns, iron filings clung to their damp surface. Half the potential profit of the firm, about £2,000 worth of damaged wear, was lost every year.

The case for closing the works and moving to a cleaner site was overwhelming. By 1936 a number of sites had been surveyed. Norman asked two of his workers, Claude Walker and Bill Clenton, to collect soil samples from Barlaston. The estate surrounding Barlaston Hall was the perfect site for a new factory. The Trent and Mersey Canal, still used in those days for freight transport, ran through the village. There was good access to the railway, so Manchester, Liverpool and London were all within easy reach. It was highly unlikely that any other industry could encroach on the new factory, which was planned as an electrically powered, clean plant. In the unpolluted air, a model village could be constructed for the workforce, with sports facilities and schools. (No pub, however – some of the older members of the family were still Puritans, who felt that the public house was the ruin of the working classes.)

In May 1936 Jos summoned the entire workforce into the canteen. Flanked by Norman, John Hamilton and Tom Wedgwood, Jos broke the news. It came as a bolt from the blue, even though some of them later claimed they'd known something was 'up'. The general reaction was puzzlement. They had been used to 'popping home for dinner' during the weekdays, and back to work – how would this be possible in the new village, which they regarded as 'a picnic kind of place, a Sunday school kind of a place'?

The responsibility for constructing the new factory fell upon Norman Wilson. He and Keith Murray toured the United States for months, inspecting factories. Their aim, which was realized, was to construct the first electrically powered industrial pottery in Europe, free of pollution. Details of their researches and journeys are to be found in the vast record now deposited in the Wedgwood Museum in Barlaston.

The foundation stone was laid on the eve of the Munich Crisis, 10 September 1938. Around 1,600 Wedgwood employees and their families arrived either at Trentham or Barlaston, and tramped across the empty fields to the site. Who would lay the stone, and begin the symbolic burial of plates and pots, enacting the ceremony performed by Old Jos at Etruria in 1769? Each pot contained a plate inscribed: 'Within this cavity, are buried pots to commemorate the founding of this factory in a garden village by the sixth generation of the descendants of Josiah Wedgwood who founded his factory at Etruria, Staffordshire, 170 years ago. By Their Works Ye Shall Know Them.'

Rumours had flown around about which dignitary would be chosen to grace the ceremony. The front-runner was Queen Mary herself, a devoted Wedgwood collector who had visited the works more than once. (She created a whole Wedgwood Room at Windsor Castle.) After her last visit the lavatory seat on which the royal bum had been lowered was auctioned, and it now hung in one of the 'shops', as the workrooms were called, framing her photograph.

In the event, with impeccable instinct, Josiah decreed that the foundation should be laid by eight veteran potters, who had devoted their lives to the company, their combined age 411 years, whose names were chosen by ballot among their fellow workers. In his speech one of them said: 'We know, had you so desired, you could have had any high person in the land to have declared the founding of the new pottery and village of Barlaston. But as you and your forebears have often said, you preferred to honour some of the craftsmen who have helped to make the name of Wedgwood world-famous.'

The casket containing the foundation pots was sealed by the youngest member of the family, Alan Wedgwood, with my father holding his hand and guiding the trowel, which his three-year-old fingers could scarcely hold. It is Alan's pram, with its jasperware pale blue medallions, which is one of the more amusing exhibits at the Wedgwood Museum.

Then Norman made a speech:

May the occupants of this factory be happy and without fear of
the future. May they be smilingly efficient and never imagine
a grim countenance is the hallmark of a hard worker. May the
wisdom and experience of the older men be used and added to by
the younger ones, and may the management, when young, learn
tolerance quickly. Let us hope that silicosis and other industrial
diseases be conspicuous by their absence.

Then they sang Parry's setting of Blake's 'Jerusalem'. Many were
weeping. William Blake had designed and engraved the first sales
catalogue for old Josiah I, and he had painted a ceiling at Etruria
which, sadly, faded in the course of the next century.

The next day Mr Chamberlain flew back from Munich waving
his piece of paper promising Peace for Our Time, signed by the
man who was deemed, by the girls in the typing pool at Etruria, to
be a dead ringer for my father.

Norman, in addition to his energetic work for Wedgwood,
had been, ever since his return from Canada, a volunteer in the
Territorials. He chose to join the Royal Horse Artillery precisely
because it was a regiment of horse. By now he was a captain. As the
factory at Barlaston began to arise, he continued to go on training
camps. When he could not be with Wedgwoods, he was happiest
with horses.

In 1939 his platoon presented Captain Wilson with a silver
cigarette box on the occasion of his engagement, and by August
of that year they were giving Major Wilson another silver cigarette
box to celebrate his marriage.

The skills displayed in factory management – efficiency, ability to
command, brisk insistence on cheerful diligence – were welcome in
the military. He also had a passion for artillery. Unlike the Modern
Major General, he did understand the mysteries of field weapons
and, all too necessary in the coming war, of anti-aircraft artillery.

The skills required of a good husband had been left out of his
store of gifts. The capacity to make a woman feel loved; a fondness

for, even minimal respect for, the opposite sex; the capacity to curb impatience and smother irritability – he never showed any awareness that these were desirable qualities. Like his bride, he came from a broken home. His had been broken by the God in whom he did not believe killing first his mother and then his brother. The bride's home was simply broken, now no longer existent, with father and mother in separate dwellings. When Norman proposed, Jean had readily acceded to his one condition: that her mother should never be allowed to cross their threshold.

The tiny wedding ceremony took place at Macclesfield parish church – Macclesfield, in Cheshire, being the place where Selena now lived. Clarrie, Jean's father, sat in a front pew with his sister. The bride was led up the aisle by her diminutive, wheezing mother. It was a gloomy occasion, soured by the inability of Clarrie and Selena to be on speaking terms. Norman's sister Elizabeth came. It was the first time Jean had met her. Elizabeth's opening salvo was a question – 'Can you cook?'

Perhaps a clumsy remark, but it was smoulderingly resented by Jean for the next half-century. A truthful answer to the question would have been in the negative – though she could bake, and her Scotch pancakes were good. Ditto the 'date bar', the recipe for which she got from her Newcastle rooming mate, Winnie Young.

The bridal pair drove away in the Lagonda. It was a long wedding journey. They were heading for Constantine Bay in north Cornwall, where a week in an hotel had been booked. Within days of their arrival there, the wireless had told them that the German army had crossed the Polish border and Norman had received a telephone call at the hotel reception desk, summoning him to report back to the barracks in Staffordshire.

In the hot, bright weather they drove back. She felt hurt by his excitement. The prospect of war, which horrified her, thrilled him. She felt that the precious few days in her company had bored him. He showed no consciousness that she was in turmoil about the outbreak of war. The only completely happy years of her life had been spent in Germany. She had made visits back throughout the 1930s. Her surrogate family, and all its ethos, had changed horribly.

The boys who had been brothers to her, for whom reading That Book had seemed like a piece of adolescent naughtiness, now took the book deadly seriously. She was furious with them, not merely for believing what it contained but for destroying her happiness. In a chaste teenaged way she had loved the boys. The joy on her face in the photographs is something I never saw – not happiness of that abandoned kind.

On one of those later visits she had asked after the doctor who had been especially kind to her while she was operated on for appendicitis. Her host, the headmaster, who had been the old Prussian head of his household, Lutheran, stern but upright and good, now cowered before the sons. He seemed frightened when the name of the doctor was mentioned.

'But he is a friend of yours,' Jean said. 'He used to come to dinner here.'

'We do not know him,' said one of the boys haughtily.

The sister said quietly, 'The doctor and his family have gone to live in America.'

'It is better that way,' said the eldest boy. 'Germany will prosper without ...'

During the phoney war, when Norman fairly frequently got leave to return to Barlaston, he taught Jean the use of a pistol, and they did target practice in the garden.

When she first told me about this, I exclaimed, 'But what about your friends in Koblenz? Suppose there had been an invasion, and one of the young men in that family had come marching up the garden path?'

A truly terrible look came across my mother's face. It was not blood lust, not at all. I felt, though, that I knew how, in the Greek tragedies, men and women, wrenched between the rival loyalties of family versus state, or between wounded love and the need for revenge, can decide for reasons of honour or affronted rage to kill those they most love.

'I'd have shot him in the head,' she said quietly.

Shortly after the outbreak of war, my mother returned to the church in Macclesfield where she had been married. Mother, small, overweight, a chain-smoking asthmatic, had succumbed to her last choking fit. Over the funeral baked meats, Jean looked about at the faces from her Bramhall childhood: Felix, fussily handing round sandwiches; Clarrie, shy, furtive; the Berrys – and there was Eric Woods. He offered her his felicitations and, as he held her hand, he murmured the inevitable words.

'But you never asked me,' she protested, feeling furious with him.

As she said this, she discovered in her heart that, had he asked, had Eric Woods only asked, she would not be in what she knew to be a marriage that could not make her happy.

'And,' she added, as she told me this, 'you would have been Andrew Woods instead of Andrew Wilson.'

'Only I wouldn't have existed, would I? I'd have been a different person altogether. If I'd existed. If you'd had children.'

This thought was left in the air.

'How d'you mean?' she asked.

12. Contrasts

The contrast between G. F. Woods – mild, gently ironic, unflappable, palpably at ease in his own skin – and Norman Wilson – tense, vulgar, volatile, by turns testy and hilarious – could not have been more marked. When I was a young child, Jean was quite open with me in her expressions of regret that she had not married Eric. Some of my most confused hours as a child – miserable, but also shot through with a guilty kind of thrill – were those in which my mother would come upstairs to my bedroom to calm me from a hollering fit before I went to sleep. In the darkness, as she smoothed my brow, she would speak of our running away together to the remoter regions of Scotland, escaping the marital rows, and the cigarette smoke. She taught me to fear my father in those early days, just as, later, he taught me to sympathize, deeply, with his being married to a neurotic killjoy.

I suppose a Freudian analyst would say that it was obvious why – though in every way unsuited to the role – I should have considered, in my late adolescence, being ordained as a clergyman. I wanted to be the man my mother wished she'd married? Neat, eh?

I remember sitting, as an eight- or nine-year-old, with my mother and Eric in the tearoom at Marshall & Snelgrove in Manchester. Quite close to our table, on the fourth floor of that department store, was a large plate glass window against which a complicated, Heath Robinson assemblage of ladders and winches had been placed. As we ate our buttered teacakes, a cloth cap appeared on the ladder, then the man's head, his shoulders; then his arm and his hand, holding bucket and mop.

'Do you think,' Eric Woods asked me in his gentle northern voice, 'he didn't realize there were lifts in the shop?'

A moment of double-take in my childish head, before the satisfying 'click' of a joke. The man outside the window, rather than being a Mancunian window cleaner, had momentarily become a Harold Lloyd-like figure, confusedly trying to make an entry by preposterous means. There were many funny moments at home with Daddy, but for him humour consisted in funny turns, rehearsed stories, usually about the Wedgwoods ('Well done, thou good and faithful servant', the epitaph chosen for a gamekeeper at Maer Hall who had accidentally shot a member of the hated Johnson family) or jokes that might have been told on stage by a stand-up comedian. His talk did not catch, as Eric's did – and as Jean's did, when I got to know her in her seventies – 'Life's Little Ironies'. It was an educative moment – putting it another way, a corrupting moment – Eric's joke about the window cleaner, in which I learned a comic potential in language and observation of which Norman would never have been capable.

In the early years of the war Jean Dorothy found married life difficult, to the point where she could not decide which was worse – the long periods when Norman was away, when she was having to negotiate her position with Mrs Hassall the housekeeper, or those periods of leave when her man returned. There was the nicotine addiction. Those silver cigarette boxes, filled each morning with fifty untipped Senior Service, would be empty by the evening. He smoked incessantly. The fingers of his right hand were sticky and orange. Clothes and moustache reeked. And smoking continued in the bedroom. The first thing he did, upon waking, was to light up. Then, when he'd stubbed the first fag, put his teeth in.

For, yes, this man who was not quite forty was toothless. Mr Skae, the dentist in Longton, had recommended the removal of all Norman's teeth when he was thirty. This was completely normal practice in the past: one of the many indications that the past is a foreign country. My friend Beryl Bainbridge (born 1932), who grew up in Formby, outside Liverpool, was kindly offered by her parents the chance to have all her gnashers removed as a twenty-first-birthday present. (She declined the offer.)

Apart from the toothlessness and the smoking, Jean found the swearing intolerable. On her way to the works at Etruria, in the bus from Newcastle-under-Lyme, she had seen a word beginning with F daubed on the purplish brick of a factory wall. She had never heard it spoken until after she was married. Before the wedding Norman had been courtly, almost everlastingly smiling; but then, she realized in retrospect, she had seen him almost exclusively in the two places that made him happy: at work, and behind the wheel of a swanky car. She had never seen him at home, never sampled domestic life, still less slept with him. His tendency to fly off the handle and to swear was something to which she could never be reconciled. She herself was a smouldering crater of bad temper, but with her it was expressed by little outbursts of breath; profanities and obscenities would never have crossed her lips.

At the works, where he could command, and expect, absolute obedience, and where his cleverness had translated, by the end of the 1930s, into a huge, modern, electrified factory, and workshops where row upon row of decorators, modellers, saggar-makers, porters, foremen, were all doing what they were told, Jean Dorothy had had no opportunity to sample his impatience with the simple intransigence of matter itself. He could give commands, and create a modern 'works'. He was scientifically and technologically aware, he could calculate the necessary temperature of a kiln to the nearest half a degree to produce a particular glaze. This did not, however, make him a practical person. At home, if something broke, and he attempted to mend it – a new wheel for a barrow, a fuse in an electric plug, a washer for the tap – he was clumsy, and when the device did not respond to his botched attempts at repair, there would be outbursts. She found them frightening, but she was also appalled by the coarseness.

This translated into his particular way of being an atheist. Among his repertoire of comic songs from the music halls or the rugby club, to which, since school, he had so happily belonged, there were also songs that ridiculed the Bible. One of them perkily suggested the same subversive message as Gershwin's 'It Ain't Necessarily So':

There was a man named Abraham
He had a son called Ike.
He took him up a mountainside
Upon his motorbike.
But when he reached the top, he said,
'Oh, Ikey, you must die.'
But Ikey said, 'Oh, no, Papa.
'An angel will rescue I.'

And so on.

Jean, a quietly observant member of the Church of England, neither high nor low, who on most Sundays of her life attended what she called The Early Service, found flippancy about the Bible horrific. It was not because she was a fundamentalist or a bigot. When I got to know her, she told me she had always been agnostic about the Divinity of Christ, for example. But the Sunday-school-mocking song, like the swearing and the heavy smoking, was coarse. The humour was so un-nuanced. Eric Woods, who became a Professor of Theology, was what would be called a Modernist, which was all of a piece with his ironies and understatements.

As if the smoking, the uncertain temper and the atheism were not enough of a shock, Jean had to come to terms with Mrs Hassall. Norman had a very small house in Barlaston. Next door, in a similar dwelling, he had established Mr and Mrs Hassall, he to do gardening and odd jobs, she to keep house. The brusque question posed at his wedding by Norman's sister – 'Can you cook?' – was an irrelevance at the time, since the cooking was done by Mrs Hassall. Presumably, in those days, Jean sometimes ate a 'normal' meal? Or perhaps Mrs Hassall contributed to her anorexic, picky ways with food?

Jean's arrival undoubtedly put Mrs Hassall's nose out of joint. She was a frightening bully, a suburban Mrs Danvers, with a bony, hard face and little ratty dark eyes. She resembled Mrs

Samuel Whiskers. One of the first things Jean noticed about Mrs Hassall was that she was a thief. Mr Hassall was to be seen in the village sporting Norman's expensive handmade shirts and, on one occasion, a pair of his trousers which had been elegantly tailored by 'old Holmsey'. When Jean told her husband that he should confront the Hassalls, the response was the 'Tch, tch, tch, tch' with which any unmentionable subject was closed down.

Perhaps he did not wish to admit to himself that he was the Hassalls' dupe. Perhaps he felt that, despite their unpleasantness, the Hassalls were of use. Either way, he preferred to keep on the right side of the pair, rather than confronting them, which was Jean's instinct. Jean won. She did confront Mrs Hassall and there were the predictable protestations of innocence.

In later years Norman made the Hassalls into one of the few non-Wedgwoods in the anecdotal word-hoard. In these versions Jean, the young bride, said that she could not but notice her husband's beautiful shirts flapping on Mrs Hassall's washing line, and then appearing on Mr Hassall.

'Yes,' Mrs Hassall would say, in the Norman version, if he was able to stifle his guffaws, 'isn't it a Co-Inside-unce, my 'Assall and Mr Wilson 'avin shirts so, lahk, simla.'

As the laughter died, this would usually be followed, in his recollection, by Jean having complained that the electric flickered on and off in those war years. 'Yes,' the housekeeper would explain, 'my 'Assall says, the trouble with this wartime electricity, it's got no BODY to it.'

It must not be supposed that all the suffering, in those early years of the marriage, was felt by the woman. Norman was not a huge culture-vulture, but as a bachelor, music and art had played a part in his inner life. He found he had married a philistine. Although Cheltenham Ladies' College had Delius on the teaching staff when she was a girl, and although Sir Adrian Boult came to conduct the school orchestra and choir (as she would recall if he ever appeared on telly), she was cloth-eared, and liked to claim that the only music she enjoyed was colliery brass bands from the north. As a bachelor, Norman, sometimes alone, sometimes with

Uncle Jos, would go to concerts. He had driven down to Oxford, and stayed the night at the Mitre, in order to hear Rachmaninov play in his Third Piano Concerto at the Town Hall. Afterwards, Jos had taken Norman backstage to meet the composer. On another occasion – 'famous occasion', rather – Norman had watched Sir Hamilton Harty conduct César Franck's *Symphonic Variations*. So impassioned was the maestro that the baton had flown from Sir Hamilton's hand into the orchestra stalls. Norman had caught it and took it up to the stage when the tumultuously emotional piece was played out. This memory was recited every time Norman played Franck to us on the wind-up 'gram'. He loved his small collection of 78s – Borodin's *Prince Igor*, Beethoven's Fifth, Franck – and their repeated, half-wheezy playing would bring back the stories – some culled, presumably, via Uncle Jos – from Vaughan Williams, such as the fact that Franck had hands so enormous that they could span twelve white notes on the piano keyboard.

Such observations and memories were interpreted by Jean as 'showing off', and would make her chunter with discontent, or simply sulk in silence. When she smouldered, he reached for the gin bottle.

'Your Uncle Jos says I am his second-best friend,' he would say, 'but this' – tapping the green bottle of Gordon's – 'is the best friend a man could ever have.'

'And Jos hasn't got to live with you when you're …' – she seemed to search for a sufficiently belittling epithet – '*tiddly*.'

Choosing not to notice, he would repeat, 'Best friend a man could ever have.'

As well as Jean Dorothy's cloth ear, there was the absence of any aesthetic sense. This jarred more painfully than her unwillingness to attend concerts. When he had bought the little house in Barlaston, his excitement was quickened by the pleasure of designing his own furniture – glass tables, glass shelves displaying his own burgeoning body of work, bowls and vases of wondrous glaze and clean, spare lines.

It was a great shock to my father, when the glad news of his mother-in-law's early demise was followed, all too soon, by the arrival of a furniture van from Macclesfield containing her criminally lumpen Edwardian mahogany wardrobe, a pseudo-Jacobethan 'grandmother clock' (a miniature long-case affair) that had tolled out the miserable hours of that suburban house in Bramhall and other monstrosities. The dynamic of marital power is one of the most fascinating of all subjects. You would think that Norman would have been able to dispose of these hideous objects of furniture with ease, but he lived with them to his dying day, regardless of how small the (many) houses to which they decamped were. His art deco bachelor paradise became merely a thing of anecdote and memory.

Quite how the aesthetic horrors struck two stalwart survivors of the Arts and Crafts Movement may be readily imagined. Jean's loneliness in the war, and the fact that the housekeeper had so little to do, suggested the obvious solution of her having lodgers. Alfred and Louise Powell had been coming to Etruria since 1906 to teach painting in the 'shops', i.e. workrooms. Alfred had trained as an architect under John Dando Sedding (of Holy Trinity, Sloane Street, the 'Cathedral of Arts and Crafts'). Louise, born Lessore, daughter of an artist, was a superb painter, embroiderer and textile designer. It was agreed that when in Staffordshire – two or three nights a week – and longer, during the London Blitz – this octogenarian pair should lodge with Jean Dorothy.

It was always impossible to predict which way my mother would leap in her assessments of others. You could imagine the Powells, with their devotion to art, their personal memories of the Burne-Joneses and the de Morgans, might have awoken Jean's chippiness, her passive-aggressive (and not always so passive) insistence she was only a very 'ordinary' person who 'knew nothing about art'. On the other hand, there was her capacity for reverence, especially towards the old. Alfred Powell's long white beard, and the perfect manners of the pair, made them instantly beloved by my mother. They also provided a welcome buffer between herself and Mrs Hassall, who drew in her breath at their vegetarianism ("Assall said they'll eat us out of eggs') but had no scruples about spending their meat ration coupons on herself and her greedy life companion.

The Powells were kindly companions while Norman was away at the war. 1940 was a year of constant travel for him, since he was involved in setting up coastal defences. It was during this year that he first visited, and fell in love with, South Wales, where he would spend the last quarter of his existence.

Even the defence of the realm, however, was not to be compared, in the scale of importance, with the mutual dependency of Don Quixote and Sancho Panza. The prospect of running the new factory without Norman plunged Josiah into one of his periodic fits of melancholy-madness. Brilliant as he was in so many areas, Jos was plagued by demons. He pestered and pestered until, some time after the Battle of Britain, Norman was allowed six months' leave from the army to solve the teething problems of the new works, to encourage the depleted workforce in their new factory, to help Jos reverse the potentially catastrophic loss of trade caused by the outbreak of war. He therefore abandoned the army life he was so enjoying, with its camaraderie and its challenging series of short-term soluble problems – deciding the best place for gun emplacements in Pembroke Dock, in Milford Haven – and returned to the two emotional tyrannies between which he would be torn for the next two decades – the impossible Jos and the impossible Jean. From the pounding of ack-ack guns, set up in Hyde Park Lane and directed at enemy bombers, even as, on the other side of Park Lane, diners continued to sit forking in their unrationed dinners at the Dorchester,[1] from the coastal defences of Hull, catastrophically incapable of preventing the near wipe-out of that proud old port, he returned to the safe little village, to the Wedgwoods, to Mrs Hassall pinching his shirts and socks, and cooking their meagre rations, the fag dancing on her mean lips as she overboiled the vegetables.

[1] Food served in restaurants was not subject to rationing regulations.

13. Warfare Accomplished

Some Victorian wag said, 'How kind of God to make Carlyle marry Mrs Carlyle, thereby making two people unhappy instead of four.' I used to think this joke applied well to my parents; but I've revised my view as, in time, one revises almost all views. While irritating the hell out of one another, they were always, in a maddening sort of way, in love. Just as some very smelly people presumably do nothing about it because they do not know they are smelly, so Mummy and Daddy were unaware that their everlasting bickering made their company all but unendurable. Yet, as Jean would recall in her widowhood, there was a deep physical bond. Though (the smoking!) she insisted on separate bedrooms from an early stage, he would continue, until weeks before he died, to ask her to slip into his bed. 'Stay with me,' he said to her, just before going to hospital for the last time. 'Even if it is only to warm me.'

Anyone leaving it until he was forty before marrying takes an enormous risk, and given the extraordinary (to our generation) fact that it was perfectly normal in those days for couples to wait until the marriage ceremony before discovering whether their companion made a desirable domestic, or sexual, partner, they now seem to me to have made a pretty creditable fist of the whole adventure, even if their dogged, and for the most part bad-tempered, absorption in the marital enterprise rather shut out anyone else.

Village life, moreover, when they started on the journey, had its quiet amusements. Jean resolutely continued to go to church, despite what bees might have flown in the bonnets of the great Victorian agnostics. Charles Darwin could think what he liked about the origins of earthly existence. Jean persisted in going to hear the Revd Albert Freeman, the incumbent of St John's Church, Barlaston, recite the words of the Communion from the Book of Common Prayer.

This harmless innocent loudly informed the queue in the village shop one day, 'My wife is expecting a child.'

While congratulations were offered from both sides of the counter, he continued, 'We waited and waited before being so blessed. I mean, we did *everything*. We prayed. No child. We went to the doctor, and nothing appeared to be amiss. Still, no child. Then, my dear wife went back to the doctor on her own. He explained it to her! But how on earth were we supposed to know how a baby is conceived? No one had told us, and it was not a thing you could possibly imagine wanting to do unless someone explained it to you.'

Norman and Jean had been almost as innocent before marriage. Marie Stopes's *Married Love* was one of the volumes, along with Herbert Spencer's *First Principles* and *The Saturday Book*, that were to be seen in the beautiful art deco bookcase. There was a directness about Jean from which Norman, with his need to protect himself from shocks and fears, would always shy away. When my first marriage failed, my father was already dead, and my friendship with my mother had begun. 'Don't make the mistake of thinking you can live without sex,' she said firmly. 'That's one of the worst mistakes a person can make.'

Other people's sexual lives will always be mysterious, which must explain why we love to discuss them or, if they are famous, speculate about them in print. By contemporary standards, it is probably incomprehensible that two people in the early to mid-twentieth century could wait until one was thirty-seven, the other twenty-seven, before undoing 'one of the worst mistakes a person can make'.

Their first child, my brother Stephen, was born in May 1941. Since the beginning of the nineteenth century, the firstborn of our family had always been called Stephen – alternately, Stephen James, Stephen Thomas, Stephen James.

'But surely, not just Stephen?' Jean asked. 'Your father is Stephen Thomas …'

But the last Stephen James had choked to death aged eleven, while a heartless God, who did not even have the charity to exist, did nothing. Norman dismissed the subject with a 'Tch, tch, tch, tch'.

The firstborn was registered simply as Stephen. Later, Norman's sister Elizabeth told Jean, 'You were right. Norman's barmy. Pa would have been so pleased if you had called the baby Stephen James.'

Fifteen months later, in August 1942, Elizabeth Jean, always known as Jeannie, was born.

In defiance of the bewhiskered sages of yesteryear, and in the absence of their father, who had returned to the Royal Horse Artillery, the two babies were baptized by Mr Freeman on the afternoon of 21 October 1942. In the parish mag he wrote of my brother and sister, 'Of course, we welcome you! And hope Father will soon be home for "always".'

It would need a real student of parish mags, such as Barbara Pym or Ysenda Maxtone Graham, to explain the inverted commas in the vicar's usage.

Inevitably, the homecoming happened. My father had both loved and hated the war. Loved the feeling of being useful, loved the bossing, loved the all-male environment. Hated the bone-headed philistinism and the snobbery of the officers' mess, and of the officer class generally in the regular army. Once, when Norman had invited Geoffrey Gilbert, probably the most distinguished flautist of his day, to an evening concert to entertain the troops, his commanding officer had insisted they go through the tedium of a formal mess dinner, with dress uniform, the port circulating, before the great musician could play a note (Mozart, Debussy's *Prélude à l'après-midi d'un faune*).

By then, of course, the men had long since had their teas and there would be a bored, restless audience. When the absurdity of dinner was at last over, the Colonel looked down the table contemptuously at Gilbert, who was himself a serving officer in the Coldstream Guards.

'Right!' snapped the Colonel. 'Now I suppose we must let the bugger play his penny whistle.'

In 1945, as the war was coming to an end, my father was transferred, as an acting brigadier, to the Oxford and Bucks Light Infantry, and put in charge of the Slade Camp, just outside Oxford. His job was to expedite the demobilization of hundreds of soldiers, many of whom had fought in the toughest campaigns of the war, in North Africa and in Italy. While they were killing time at the Slade, a huge training camp that stretched from where the Oxford ring road now whizzes between Headington and the Cowley works to the Shotover estate on the London road, these men were preparing for civilian life. Each was to be found a job in civvy street – where possible, the same job they'd done before call-up. Each was to be given a demob suit and hat. Much more significant, they were to be offered personal advice about return to the non-militarized world.

There was no 'counselling' as there would be now, no warning that their return to domestic life would be potentially fraught, with their children finding the presence in their house of a man threatening, and the women who had coped without their partner for five years and often done 'men's jobs' receiving the return of The Master and the loss of their job with a mixture of feelings. The men did, however, receive more than career advice. Norman organized concerts, shows, plays, films. They were kept abreast of what was happening in the great world, with a vast news cinema, which filled one of the hangars on the camp site. It was here that they all watched the footage of the concentration camps being liberated in Central and Eastern Europe. It was here, before they walked back in stunned silence to their Nissen huts, that these men confronted the full enormity of what, in the crazed death cult of Nazism, they had been fighting.

There was also a General Election to organize, the Khaki election, so called because so high a proportion of the electorate were still in

uniform. As well as historical talks by A. J. P. Taylor, who held his
huge audiences in thrall, there were political speeches by all three
major parties. Regular officers, with whom Norman ate his dinner
every night, felt complete confidence that a grateful nation would
return good old Winston to Downing Street, and that Britain
would return to its Tory norm.

Some of the Tory officers had been fighting in the Western
Desert, dodging bullets on the beach at Anzio, slogging up
Monte Cassino in the cold, driving February rain as enemy pilots
peppered them with gunfire. They could be forgiven for not having
had the leisure to read the Beveridge Report. Nevertheless, their
complete ignorance of the way that their men were thinking never
left Norman; and because I spent so much of my time, from the
age of twelve, sitting alone with him and hearing his endlessly
repeated memories, it has never left me, this sense of the complete
failure of the governing class to relate to the thought processes of
'ordinary people'. In 1945 this class was that of the officers and was
'Tory'; more recently it has been the university-educated 'liberal'
or 'metropolitan elite'. Such a failure to connect, which would be
fatal to anyone trying to run a business, is endemic to the way the
British choose to do things. The officers with whom Norman had
dinner every night regarded as nightmarish what Nye Bevan and
Clem Attlee were offering Britain – a welfare service that protected
the most vulnerable, nationalized industries, decent housing and
education, and free healthcare. When Norman expressed the view
that Labour was bound to win the election, they looked at him
as if he had uttered treason – which, in their scale of value, he
had: sort of. That election swept away forever the pre-war Britain,
with its class certainties and its acceptance that those who had
ruled the roost since the Glorious Revolution of 1688, by virtue of
being richer or owning more land than anyone else, were therefore
entitled to do so in perpetuity.

14. Miscarriages

So, like the hundreds of men he had dispatched in their large-lapelled demob suits and trilby hats, Norman came home to Staffordshire. The little house in Barlaston, conceived as a bachelor pad, elegantly deco but now darkened by the ugly brown furniture bequeathed by 'Mother', was plainly unsuitable. Instead of being a small house where two newly-weds with mixed feelings about one another tried to live as a pair, it was an overcrowded family house with two children, who stared at the arrival of the father as at a stranger.

They moved house, to a hamlet called Burston. It was a substantial Georgian house nestling on the edge of the Sandon estate, which was subsequently sliced by the main road roaring and honking between Lichfield and Manchester. Sandon Park is the seat of the earls of Harrowby, their other place being Burnt Norton, Gloucestershire, made famous when visited, in the late 1930s, by T. S. Eliot and Emily Hale. It was there that they saw 'the door we never opened into the rose garden'.

Hobnobbing with aristocrats was not an activity to which my mother or father ever aspired. They would speak of the Ryders (the family name of the earls) with that nervous jocularity with which middle-class people, in those days, regarded those who were landed. Jean, who went to tea with Lady Harrowby, was surprised that such a person should offer Lyle's Golden Syrup direct from its beautiful tin, as an accompaniment to white bread and butter.

(Did she imagine that an aristocrat would, or should, decant the sticky goo?) Norman, for his part, was invited by Lady Harrowby's son Sandon (Lord Sandon, the son and heir, was ten years older than himself) to shoot, but spoke with some satire of this bookish, Wodehousian figure's inability to shoot a pheasant even if it flew directly at him. (When he subsequently inherited the earldom, Harrowby's only speech in the House of Lords was to launch a campaign for 'a lavatory in every lay-by' on public highways.)

Because they were intimidated by the class divide, and in awe of their neighbours' titles, my parents liked, when discussing the Harrowbys, to remind us, and themselves, that They were no better than Us. Indeed, was not Lady Harrowby the granddaughter of W. H. Smith, a mere shopkeeper? The very fact that the middle classes adopted this jokey tone was, of course, self-contradictory confirmation of the fact that, in those days, the class system still existed, although Norman and Jean affected to have no interest in it. Like the majority of the middle class, they were anxious about their own place in the hierarchy of things.

During my teenage years with them in Wales, long after my brother and sister had left home, Jean befriended a local farmer (female) who lived not far from us. By then, my father had not a friend in the world – not one – so there was a strong element of envy as he observed his wife's very cautious ability to step outside the domestic stockade. 'Why can't you have friends of your own class?' he snarlingly inquired.

This was because she enjoyed drinking tea in a Welsh farmhouse with Nin, a pretty woman whose lover was the cowherd. By that stage Jean was angered by most of what Norman said, and she professed herself appalled by the petty snobbery of the question. As it happened, Nin's maternal family, the Morrises, had owned land and farms in that part of Wales since records began, certainly since the Middle Ages, but that was not a point Jean would ever have wanted to make. The bitterness of the exchange sprang from her knowledge – which Norman was too innocent to possess – that he was not in a position to ask such questions. What class, after all, was he?

Known in the village as 'the Colonel', Norman believed himself to be a gent, which he most certainly wasn't. (After 1945, those civilian soldiers who returned to their pre-war avocations were told they were entitled to refer to themselves with a military rank, the convention being that you took a rank lower than that which you'd possessed while in the service. Retiring as a colonel, Norman was therefore 'entitled' to be called Lieutenant-Colonel Wilson, but was breezily unaware that there was something cringe-making about all this pretension.) He thought that wearing 'natty suitings', driving stylish old cars and calling himself Colonel Wilson made him grand, whereas those who were regular army officers or actual gents saw through the play-acting at once. It was a stinging moment when Katherine Duncan-Jones first juddered up the steep drive of Hill House, Llansteffan, and was greeted by the Colonel in one of his bright check suitings. She told me, a few hours later, when we were walking on the beach to let off steam, that as he approached her, she felt she had never met anyone in her life who was grander, and, half an hour later, never anyone who was commoner. Like many of the things she said in those early days, this would have been better left unsaid, not least because I had begun to be corrupted enough to learn what she meant.

Both my parents, who idolized Sir John Wedgwood, baronet brother of Veronica, who resided in some style at the house once occupied by his cousin Ralph Vaughan Williams – Leith Hill, Surrey – would have been utterly mortified had they heard his verdict on them – 'the sort of people who eat High Tea' (quoted to me decades later by another member of the Wedgwood family). The fact that this was not in fact the case – Jean, indeed, did not eat anything in my recollection except the occasional Jacob's Cream Cracker – does not alter how others perceived them. Jean, with her much subtler social antennae, could see that the Colonel's persona was always on the verge of seeming ridiculous. Though she disliked having done so, she had learned lessons in the dorm at Cheltenham Ladies' College.

She kept becoming pregnant. Feeding Jeannie, the second baby, brought on excruciating mastitis. She never wanted to go through that again. Norman, however, had patriarchal ambitions, and wanted a huge tribe.

The family physician, Dr Inman, was totally bald. Alopecia had removed every follicle from his pinkish skull. There were no whiskers, no eyelashes, no eyebrows, just a gleaming pink egg surmounted by steel-framed spectacles. His happiest hours were spent on the golf course, and he saw in my father a health-obsessed *malade imaginaire* who vied with his hero Jos Wedgwood in his preparedness to summon expensive medical aid at the slightest sign of bodily malfunction.

On one occasion, Inman returned to the house three times to syringe ears. 'Honest-LEE!' my father exclaimed when the bill was sent in. It was £40, the equivalent in today's money of nearly £1,000. A part of Norman's nature was proud of the bill. Inman had recognized him as a man of substance, someone worth swindling. By any standards, Inman was an abysmally incompetent doctor. My mother's whole life would have been in every way happier had she had a female doctor during her many pregnancies. Because she so dreaded becoming pregnant over and over again, Inman recommended cigarette-smoking as an excellent way to calm the nerves. Virginia tobacco, which Norman smoked during every waking hour, made her throw up, so Clarrie, her father, kept her supplied with Turkish cigarettes.

There was a small dame school at Burston, but the time came when Stephen, approaching seven, and Jeannie, six, needed to be educated. Norman, the ardent materialist-atheist, and Jean Dorothy, the observant Prayer Book Anglican, were persuaded by the *on dit* that by far the best school in the vicinity was at the Dominican convent in Stone, their nearest small town. Jean drove the children to the convent each day in the Riley while Norman swanked off to the works in Barlaston at the wheel of the Bentley. Then came the winter of 1947, and for weeks Burston was marooned in deepest snow. Norman could not get the Bentley out of the drive, and trudged in boots to Sandon Halt to catch the train to Barlaston on the newly nationalized, but still steam-powered, train.

That winter drained them. There was another miscarriage. Although the children loved Burston, with its space and its freedom, their parents' mental health suffered, cut off by winter weather, from any company but their own. Stone beckoned, and by the time Jean was found to be pregnant yet again, moving house felt like a necessity.

Some human beings who will agonize over the choice of a new shirt or a different car make life's larger decisions – the choice of a life partner, or of somewhere to live – on impulse. When my father saw Stonefield Cottage, Newcastle Road, Stone, his eye took in a pretty little Georgian box with an enclosed garden backing onto the canal whose waters mirrored the overhanging alders, hazel bushes and hawthorn. The garden was made all the prettier by a summer house, built with its back to the canal, pressed on the one side by abundant hazels and on the other by an orchard of Bramleys and Coxes. Between two wooden-floored rooms, there was an open verandah looking back to the house. When, in grown-up life, I eventually visited Tolstoy's country house, at Yasnaya Polyana, and stood on the fretwork-framed wooden-floored terrace, it felt like a much grander version of 'the verandah' at Stone. We always called the whole structure 'the verandah', and some of my happiest hours were spent there, in that condition of perpetual make-believe in which children live. Slopping about with a bowlful of water and silver sand, I was a great potter forming vases and bowls; draping myself in the sample banners for the Coronation which had been given to us by Clarrie – printed velour or satin sheets depicting the young Elizabeth II in her crown – I was myself a monarch or, just as often, a priest approaching the altar of God.

Norman, presumably, was enraptured by the prettiness of house, garden, verandah. What he failed to notice was that, half a century after the house had been built, some stinker had come along and built the railway alongside the north flank of the garden. A huge railway bridge lowered over the little cottage as it peeped over the privet hedge to Newcastle Road. Smuts and smoke and clouds of steam, in those closing days of the Victorian railway world, billowed across the orchard and the lawn, blackening roses, hollyhocks and delphiniums. An apparently incurable insomniac (I never once heard either of my parents admit to having enjoyed a good night's sleep), Norman would come down in the morning, his third or fourth cig of the day smouldering between orange fingers, to assert that the house agent who had failed to point out the proximity of the railway line to any potential purchaser deserved shooting.

Jean, sick, furious at being pregnant yet again, saw the house in Newcastle Road differently. Although she had a greater capacity than anyone I ever met to squeeze discontent from the happiest of circumstances, and to find in neutral or sunny prospects the occasion of complaint, she had immediately loved that house. She liked its scale, and she loved its position, with all that implied. It meant an end to the school run in the Riley. It was just over the road from the tennis club, and in those days she still loved that game. The public library and the pretty little Georgian town of Stone were all to be reached on foot. So was the Rector, Mr Herbert, whom she had known and liked when he took the services at Sandon. The Georgian Gothic parish church, though at the other end of the town and more easily reached in the Riley, provided what sustained her inner life, the weekly Communion at 8 a.m. She knew, from early acquaintanceship with neighbours in Newcastle Road, and at the tennis club, that she was going to have friends here. Inside her was a new life. Me. Whether this child would make it the full term, or whether, like the others, it miscarried, remained to be seen.

15. What is my Name?

Being born, in the cottage hospital at Stone, was the easy part. For me, at any rate. Staying alive presented a challenge. I had a condition known as pyloric stenosis, which is a narrowing of the opening from the stomach to the small intestine. Food, therefore, could not reach the small intestine, and the milk – after her trouble feeding my sister, Mummy put me on the bottle from the beginning – came shooting out as projectile vomit. The only remedy was to operate, a simple but dangerous surgical procedure involving the removal of some of the blocked intestine. Norman, programmed since childhood to see disaster in every circumstance, consulted his brother-in-law Gordon Lewis, the chief surgeon at the City and General Hospital in Newcastle-under-Lyme. Gordon said there was a strong danger of losing the baby, and it was therefore better that the operation should not happen on his watch, with all the subsequent difficult feelings this would involve. (They were very close to Gordon and his wife, Dorothy, my father's sister; Jeannie and Stephen played with their cousins Joan and Tony; Sunday lunches together were a regular, frequent occurrence: all this would have been clouded had Gordon been blamed for the loss of a baby.)

Intensely squeamish, convinced that even the healthiest child was in imminent danger of death, Norman went to pieces. Jean, accompanied by Dr Inman, took the puling, puking little boy to the North Staffs Infirmary in Stafford.

They'd somehow assumed that the baby was going to be a girl, and, having used up family names on Jeannie and Stephen, they were toying with the idea of calling me Susan. Since it looked as if the new baby was going to leave the planet within days of having arrived upon it, the question of what I should be named had been driven from their minds.

The ward sister at the North Staffs Infirmary took the matter out of my mother's hands. She told Jean to steel herself for the death of the baby and offered to baptize him. Since she was the sister of the future Cardinal Archbishop of Armagh, Sister Conway had a semi-professional interest in guaranteeing that I did not go unprepared into the Beyond. Jean readily agreed.

The operation was completely successful, and I was soon fit enough to return to Stonefield Cottage. Amid the jubilation that their baby was going to live, Jean felt it safe to let fall the detail that I had been admitted to the Church. An almighty row ensued, with Norman inveighing against the superstition of the Roman Catholic Church and the impertinence of some Irish nurse *daring* to name *his* child.

All baptism in the name of the Holy and Undivided Trinity is a Catholic baptism, as Jean endeavoured to point out. It would still have been a Catholic baptism, had it been carried out by Mr Herbert, or, come to that, by Norman himself. In Baptism, there is no division between the Churches. It is only in their ideas of who is or is not an apostolically ordained priest, and in their understanding of the Sacraments, that the divisions open up between the Churches. She did not expect Norman to grasp these ideas, which he would have seen as mumbo-jumbo, but ... Hold on, a moment, please.

Jean was recalling these events during her widowhood and old age, when I was a man in my thirties. She recalled her own sense of comfort and relief when I was baptized, and the conviction that it was worth doing, even if it would later provoke her husband's wrath. As she told me the story, there was one question that came naturally to mind.

'Did Sister Conway baptize me as Andrew, or with some other name?'

She smiled back at me. Her usual way of deflecting unwelcome questions was immediately brought into use.

'How do you mean?'

Had I been baptized 'Andrew', she would, of course, have replied, 'Yes – I told Sister Conway you were to be baptized Andrew, and that was the name she gave you.'

Quite clearly, by asking what I had meant, Jean was obfuscating. She clearly knew the name the nurse had given me. If I had to bet on it, my guess would be Patrick. Maybe Michael? Perhaps that was why my father had been so particularly angry.

It was he who settled matters by going to the registrar's office and recording the birth of Andrew Norman Wilson. Though the life of A. N. had begun, I suspect that this was not the name known to his Guardian Angel, or to Sister Conway. The mismatch was perhaps a foreshadowing of A. N.'s life as a confused, and very disobedient, Christian.

16. Convent Thoughts

Sometimes, if my mother required Blakie's presence in the house, or if Blakie was busy with her husband – Our Cyril – or child – Our Vron – I made the journey to school on my own. It was a journey of a few hundred yards, down the Newcastle Road, over the canal bridge, to the small Gothic-pointed door in the redbrick wall of the convent. Naturally, I felt much safer when Blakie accompanied me. I loved holding her rough red hands. I loved her smell, and her comforting, fleshy body behind her pinny. I loved her very thick black hair and her shiny face. I loved stroking her cheeks.

My father said she was a gypsy. He told me this after the disappearance of Blakie from my life. By then, they deemed me old enough to be told that her mother lived in a caravan somewhere out of town near the Downs Banks, and that this mother had had at least ten children by a variety of fathers.

'She's not a very nice person,' Jean shuddered. 'She organized cockfights and …'

I was about ten when they told me these supposedly shocking facts. I had no idea what a cockfight was, but, since they had unwittingly plunged me into a boarding-school world run by sexual perverts, I totally misunderstood their meaning, and imagined they were saying that Blakie's mother presided over orgies. I was surprised, indeed appalled, to hear my mother speaking so freely of cocks, since she normally veiled her references to bodily functions with euphemism.

'Don't let any of the other boys be silly,' had been her only warning against sexual predators, for example. But all this lay in the future. I am writing now of the idyllic time, the Stone childhood, the Garden of Eden before the gate was shut.

Beyond loving Blakie more than anyone in the world, and knowing myself loved in return with complete lack of reserve, my five-year-old self would not have been worried by considering her family connections, however (another Jean euphemism) 'unsuitable'. Indeed, in so far as I knew Blakie's family I liked them very much. True, Our Cyril was a little frightening, but this was partly because my mother said he had 'a nasty tongue'. Of course, to my mother, he was not Our Cyril. He was Mr Blakeman. His epic row with Jean over the lupins in her herbaceous border had become the stuff

Me and Blakie. My idea of heaven.

of legend. He had peremptorily removed these phallic-seeming, sun-loving blooms, claiming they'd never appealed to him, lahk. Jean had told him that if this was his attitude, he'd better leave. Blakie, in floods, had then said that she felt she should leave us, too, and Jean had asked, reasonably – what about little Andrew? If Blakie left him, it would break his heart. More tears, as I was enfolded in Blakie's warm arms and felt her wet cheeks against my own,

I don't suppose that Our Cyril's work as Jean's gardener was ever his chief employment. I'd guess he picked up jobs here and there casually. He was always very nice to me, a big, swarthy man with a tufty, hairy chest and a thick moustache. He smelt a bit sweaty, not a quality I minded in the least. Forty years after the time described, we were all made aware that Kuwait had been invaded by Iraq, and that the Iraqi dictator had set light to the American oil tankers in the Persian Gulf. Our Cyril's face appeared on every television screen – only it was Saddam Hussein.

Our Vron, their only child, was about my age, maybe a bit older, and for those periods, which retrospect suggests was most of the time, when my mother was too ill to be seen, I would be allowed to spend time in Blakie's house, on the edge of the canal, with its tangled garden filled in my memory with sweet peas, geraniums and rows of carrots, potatoes and cabbages.

Donald Winnicott, pioneer of developmental psychology, told an aspirant child-analyst that if the juvenile patient offered its hand to the therapist, it was essential to hold it. In those moments, the child's analyst represents the outside world, with which it learns to come to terms. The attractive, and safe, person can offer to the very young child a bridge out of the collective family thinking, and the chance to develop a primitive smokescreen between the family and the self. These first steps lay down imprints. The first expectations that the possibility of pleasure is to be found outside the family are an essential factor, determining whether or not a person can feel at home in the world. The first such hand that reached out towards my own was Blakie's, enabling me to feel at home on this strange planet. The closeness to Blakie, however, confirmed in me an awareness which I never saw better described than in Georges

Simenon's autobiographical novel *Pedigree*: '*sa vie est ailleurs, il ne sait pas où, il cherche dehors et continue à la chercher.*'

Of the rest of Blakie's extended family – the supposed many half-siblings – I knew only her much elder half-brother, Our Art, a notably handsome man with swept-back white hair and rather orange teeth who had the economical habit of smoking half a cigarette, stubbing it gently and preserving the other half behind his right ear. He worked at Joules's brewery, more or less opposite the convent, so if, on our way to the little Gothic door, we passed him, trundling beer barrels on a trolley, we'd stop and fraternize. The conversations would end with a friendly orange grin and, to Blakie, 'Bye, ducks' and to me, 'Bye, Our Andy', an inclusive vocative that made me very happy.

Our Vron was also educated by the nuns, but for reasons which I never questioned she went to St Joseph's, the school on the other side of Margaret Street. I no more found this puzzling than I

My adored headmistress Sister Mary Mark, OP. Bottom right is her brother Sebastian Bullough, OP.

thought it strange there should be lay sisters at the convent, such as Sister Bridget in the laundry, and some others who served our meals and cleaned the classrooms. They spoke with Irish voices, and they did not have Mary in their names. Just Sister Deirdre, Sister Maeve, rather than the choir sisters, who spoke with voices like my mother's and had Mary inserted into their (often male) names – Sister Mary Aquinas, Sister Mary Alban, Sister Mary Mark.

My brother and sister had attended the convent before me, but they were already away at boarding schools, so I was in effect an only child.

'Tarr-ah, pet.' Blakie would crouch down and my head, first buried in her breasts, would be raised to her lovely, smiling face.

'Tarr-ah.'

'Remember now, what Mummy said.'

'I won't go near Mr Murphy. He's silly.'

'Good boy.'

A final hug, and the little door opened.

An opera-minded reader accompanying me on this journey might have supposed, before our eyes adjusted to the steamy atmosphere in those cloisters, that the execution of an entire community of religious sisters had taken place, just such an atrocity as Poulenc chose for his immortal *Dialogues of the Carmelites*, only these were the habits of the Order of Preachers, the Dominicans. Everywhere you looked, in the steam, nuns appeared to be suspended. As the eye adjusted, you saw you were passing the laundry, presided over by Sister Bridget. The array of esoteric gear – long white habits, white woollen stockings, starched wimples, starched white sleeves – filled the corridor, together with the black items of regalia, the veils and scapulars. Since the Second Vatican Council, religious sisters, in so far as there are any, wear modernized uniforms, if, indeed, they choose to wear any distinctive clothing. In the mid-1950s, nuns were still dressed like characters in *The Canterbury Tales*.

In his diaries, Chips Channon, in April 1935, was staying in Asolo with his porter-millionaire in-laws the Guinnesses (Lord and Lady Iveagh). It was in that beautiful hill town that the legendary

Italian actress Eleonora Duse conducted her affair with Gabriele D'Annunzio. Channon was shown her house. 'It was inherited by her daughter, a selfish bigot … Priest-ridden, she had two children, a son and a daughter, and she bullied these unfortunate, highly strung young people to go both into a religious house, and one is now a nun and the other a Brother of sorts.'[2]

It is a good example of how unreliable gossip can be. The 'Brother of sorts' was Father Sebastian Bullough, OP, one of the most distinguished Cambridge theologians – a friend, as it happened, of my mother's friend Eric Woods. His sister was my headmistress, Sister Mary Mark, OP. It may be that Chips Channon's tittle-tattle was correct, and that these two were forced into the religious life. My recollection of Sister Mary Mark, whom I came to know quite well in later years, was of a well-grounded person of good humour and common sense. I would imagine it would have been impossible to force her into anything.

Informing and shaping the English Dominican life was, as I subsequently would learn, a world outlook that would be deeply sympathetic to me. The encyclicals of Pope Leo XIII in the nineteenth century, with their denunciations of capitalism, inspired such phenomena as the Ditchling Community of craftspeople in Sussex – Eric Gill and friends – as well as, in the United States rather later, the Catholic Worker Movement of Dorothy Day. The motto of Gill's community loses none of its validity, even if, when read beside Fiona McCarthy's lurid biography of the man, it might seem absurd: *Men rich in virtue, studying beautifulness, living in peace in their houses.*

William Morris – non-Christian – and Tolstoy and Gandhi would all have seen the point. In its Catholic context, the Dominican spirituality, linked with political and economic understanding, combines a troubled sense of the difficulty of leading The Good Life in a badly ordered world with an awareness that many of these questions are not new, and are rehearsed in the writings of the

[2] Chips Channon, *The Diaries*, vol. 1, p. 419.

medieval Dominican philosopher Thomas Aquinas, as they are in the Gospels themselves.

———

Across the little garth, with its row upon row of nuns' graves, little wooden crosses in the grass, round the corner of the vast convent building, in those days filled with sisters, and into the garden. There was Mr Murphy offering sweets to the little girls, and allowing the favoured ones to sit on his knee before he resumed his hoeing or trimming. And here is The Croft, the large Victorian house where the younger children were taught.

My first teacher was a laywoman, Miss Meehan, always referred to by Norman as Me 'n My Shadow. I did not know the song, so did not get the joke. Her mother was Sri Lankan, so we learned a lot about tea plantations. Sister Mary Edith was our form teacher. Often watching us file into class was the tall headmistress: the only visible part of her was her face, which was of quite breathtaking beauty, a face painted by Giotto.

Like Plato, some of the prophets in the Bible denounced the worship of idols. For another type of human being, an idol is a lens through which the great Unseen can be inferred or discerned. I am by nature an idolater. When, aged eighteen, I went up to New College, Oxford, and first entered the chapel, my eye rested on the huge stone reredos peopled by saints and biblical figures. It has often occurred to me since that just such a reredos exists in my skull, peopled by idols. The stern iconoclast would bid me, like the zealots of Reformation times, to hammer the statues to dust. Yet, I close my eyes, and see Blakie and Sister Mary Mark, OP very near to the centre of the great mental iconostasis of memory.

I kept up a correspondence with Sister Mary Mark until my mid-twenties, when it became clear that my departure from her ideals and beliefs made me ashamed to continue it. Every now and then, however, one of her treasured letters tumbles out of a book. It happened the other day when I looked at the old paperback written by her brother Sebastian. The Pelican edition of *Roman Catholicism* was a present from her, sent about six months before, in my late teens, I formalized my belief in that religion and was received into that Church.

I am struck in this and other letters from Sister Mary Mark by her solicitous inquiries after my mother, who was exactly her age. Some time in the early 1970s there was even talk, when Mark was in Wales, of her visiting Jean, but nothing came of this. Hindsight made me realize that Jean had indubitably confided her troubles in Sister Mary Mark. Although Jean told me that I broke her heart by formally becoming a Roman Catholic, she also, on another occasion, told me that, while we were still living in Stone, she had felt very tempted to do so.

When, much later in life, I saw photographs in books of Eleonora Duse, it was the face of her granddaughter, my teacher, staring at the lens. Great teachers continue to teach us, long after we have left their presence. Still, as a man in his seventies, I find she teaches me, not least about the true absurdity of almost all the ambitions which coursed through my younger self when I wanted to be a famous writer.

Leonora (Mark's baptismal name) and Hugh (later Sebastian) Bullough, pitied by Chips Channon for their bigoted upbringing, were the children of La Duse's daughter and the Professor of Italian at Cambridge. Blackfriars, the site of the Dominican house in that university, was their childhood home. Their neighbours were the Ramseys – their contemporaries Michael and Frank, destined to be famous as (respectively) archbishop and mathematical philosopher.

With her stunning looks, high intelligence, sharp wit, money and connections, Leonora Bullough could have had the kind of raffish life among famous bohemians that I, as a thirty-year-old, would have most ardently craved. Instead, for well over half a century, she based herself in the nondescript town of Stone, ending her days, after retirement as headmistress, helping out at a local charity shop, parish visiting and caring for the elderly in St Mary's Care Home. Through those years, she would look about in the choir stalls which had once contained dozens upon dozens of religious sisters chanting the Divine Office in Latin, and now see a diminished band of sisters singing the Gelineau psalms.

You never meet anyone who knew her whose face doesn't change at the mention of her name. All of us whose lives she touched saw that there is a higher way of living, that human nature is capable of transformation if one is humble enough, simple enough, to submit to the Gospel of Christ. (I've never quite done it, much as I have hoped or aspired, in pious moments to try.)

Although she was devastated by the death of her brother Sebastian at the altar of St Dominic's Priory, Stone, when he was in his fifties, I am quite sure she never wavered in her faith. She struck everyone who met her (*pace* Chips!) as an absolutely fulfilled human being. Of the two people I met most recently who had known her, one was a woman who'd worked with her helping out in the charity shop – 'She was the Queen of Stone'. It was said with the kind of laugh you would give if the actual Queen spent half her week sorting used clothes and Maeve Binchy paperbacks into saleable piles and placing the pastel-shaded acrylic knitwear – tea cosies and bedsocks – in the window.

Ah! Bedsocks. I remember my mother giving a pair to Mark. Also, there comes to mind her unworldliness. When Jean lent her and Sister Mary Alban a hot water bottle to keep them warm in the couchette when accompanying a school trip by train to Rome, it came back smelling of coffee. Mark had decided that if it retained the heat with water, it would surely do the same for caffè latte, bought at Milan station before she and Alban turned in for the night, and recited the night office as the train rattled through Switzerland.

Another verdict, from a distinguished journalist who, I discovered, had also been at the convent – years after me: 'We loved her, in so far as she let us near her. But she was bloody terrifying.'

She was certainly formidable. I've lost the letter in which she described to me the academic triumphs of one of my contemporaries at the convent, a notably clever young person, who, being female, was allowed to stay on until she was eighteen. (We boys had to leave at the age of seven.) Mark decided that Mary would benefit from going to Trinity College Dublin. She easily passed the exam, but this was still the late 1960s, when the application from a convent girl to the great Prot university was a matter of note.

In no time at all, a letter appeared on the desk of my old headmistress from the Archbishop of Dublin, John Charles McQuaid, described by his biographer as the last of the 'Renaissance-style prelates'. It informed Sister Mary Mark that not only would her student, if she committed the mortal sin of going to Trinity, be excommunicated. He would also excommunicate the entire conventful of Stone nuns.

With what quiet, ironic joy Sister Mary Mark composed her reply, written in small, elegant italic, pointing out to the archbishop that his jurisdiction did not stretch beyond the archdiocese of Dublin, let alone across the Irish Sea to Staffordshire. The student went to Trinity, where she was very successful.

No wonder the Greeks made Memory the Mother of the Muses, for Memory is a creative process. For me, the convent, and its school, are best described in the liturgical phrase applied to the blessed afterlife, a place of light, refreshment and peace. There were excellent teachers, lay and religious, and I liked my fellow pupils, though I found it hard at first to adapt to the company of other children. The nuns – especially Sisters Mary Alban and Mark – became family friends. My mother once observed to Sister Mary Alban, who often came for tea in our garden, and even once accompanied us on a holiday to Wales, that the Order of Preachers must be very liberal in their Rule.

'Oh, we are forbidden social visits,' Alban explained. 'But Reverend Mother has been given to understand that the Wilson family are under instruction. You are all on a journey of faith.'

I do not recall Norman ever being present when Sister Mary Alban came round. His scepticism was ingrained, as was my mother's devotion to the church of her baptism. Yet Jean was fascinated when the nuns gave her Thomas Merton's *Elected Silence*. It was an edition illustrated with photographs, and we often pored over them together. A neighbour of ours in Newcastle Road, Mark Lavalle, had lately become a Cistercian monk (Father

Marcellus) at Mount St Bernard Abbey in Leicestershire. Sister Mary Mark gave me Hugh Ross Williamson's *A Children's Book of Saints*, followed by the volume that was by far my favourite book as a child, *A Children's Book of French Saints*. Jean read to me the chapter about Joan of Arc again and again, and she remains my favourite saint.

It is probably a commonplace of materialist scepticism that Joan, the violent teenager-soldier who heard voices inside her head, was a classic case of paranoid schizophrenia. Equally, I have always liked the exchange in Shaw's *Saint Joan* when, at her trial, she is told that her voices are only her imagination, and she replies that of course this is the case, for how else, save through our imagination, could God speak to us? I know that Shaw was a sceptic, but the exchange can be interpreted to justify either opinion. Whatever we understand of the divine surely comes to us through this means. During the dark phases of life when I have told myself that I have lost my faith (and the central decade of my life, my forties, was one of almost total scepticism), what I have actually been suffering from is a failure of imagination.

It was Jean, and not the nuns, who first taught me to pray, coming to my room before I slept, and singing a verse or two of a hymn: sometimes Mrs Alexander's 'There is a Green Hill Far Away' or, my favourite, Jane Eliza Leeson's 'Loving Shepherd of Thy Sheep':

Keep Thy lambs in safety, keep!
Nothing can Thy power withstand,
None can pluck them from Thy hand.

It sometimes occurs to me to wonder whether my changeable attitude to spiritual questions stems from the three contradictory influences of early infancy: the quiet personal faith of my mother, reinforced by the Early Service and *The Book of Common Prayer*; Blakie and the nuns' devotion to the rosary and the mass; and Norman, with his fanatical zeal for Victorian agnosticism. If I attend the mass at St Dominic's, near where I live in London – once a week it is celebrated according to the old rite, with a voluntary choir of young

Eastern Europeans singing the *Missa de Angelis* – I am transported back to the convent gardens at Stone during the months of summer. The older girls are throwing rose petals in front of the monstrance as the priest carries the Blessed Sacrament through the grounds. Blakie and I are on our knees. We are not simply being well behaved, as I am when I accompany Jean to Mr Herbert's church, or quiet so as not to annoy Mr Herbert. We are awestruck because God Himself is passing by, as He did in the wilderness of Sinai. On the other hand, if I attend a well-rendered Anglican service, I feel not merely devotion; I feel mysteriously 'at home'. When I read the Victorian poets – Matthew Arnold on Dover Beach, or Tennyson 'with no language but a cry' – I empathize completely with their sense of the sheer futility of claiming knowledge of the Unknowable; and of the three contradictory mental conditions – Roman Catholicism, Anglicanism and agnosticism – I find as I grow older that agnosticism is for the most part predominant.

Norman knew two long poems by heart. One was Gray's *Elegy*, which, at the wheel of the Bentley, he could ponderously recite for the whole journey from Stone to the works. The other, which I much preferred, and always hear in his voice when I read it, was Edward Fitzgerald's translation of the *Rubáiyát of Omar Khayyám*:

> Myself when young did eagerly frequent
> Doctor and Saint, and heard great argument
> About it and about; but evermore
> Came out by the same door as in I went.

17. Newcastle Road

The illnesses of both my father and my mother were phenomena around which my mind, for many years, placed scornful inverted commas. Norman, despite heavy smoking and drinking, survived until he was eighty-two. Jean lived well into her nineties. It was difficult to sympathize with their obsessive consultation of doctors, just as it was difficult not to notice, even as a child, their indignation upon being told by expensive physicians that there was nothing seriously amiss. So ingrained was my impatience, during my teens, with their health obsession – they vied with one another as to which felt iller – that I suppressed in my sympathy the obvious fact that my poor mother's thirties (she was thirty-eight when I was born) must have been truly hellish, and her suffering, from successive miscarriages and clumsy surgery by male doctors, genuinely awful.

I could not write a continuous narrative framework of early childhood. It is, rather, a series of smudged, non-chronological impressions: of the grandfathers, for example, I remember nothing – only Jean, standing in the hall of Stonefield Cottage crying, as she received the news by telephone that her father was dead. My brother and sister flit in and out of memory like the sporadic passing of school holidays in which I saw them, during which they would play with me – for example, when they opened the dressing-up boxes in the verandah and emerged on to the lawn as cowboys. Here is Stephen helping Norman to inflate a rubber dinghy to launch on the canal, unable to suppress his laughter as the Colonel, bossing and cursing, repeatedly told us of the dangers of standing up when the dinghy was

Alastair Smith, Charles Jerratt, Timothy Fretwell,
Linda Weaver, Madeleine Jones, Mary Do, Teresa Beddington
Trudy Hall, Julie Munroe, Joy Holley, Rosemary Finney, Pamela Coops,
Andy Wilson (now A.N. Wilson, author!)

My class at St Dominic's, with Miss Meehan. Annotations to the snap are in the handwriting of Sister Mary Mark. The nuns called me 'Andy' as Blakie did.

afloat, disobeying his own advice and falling into the water. In those days, when he was a figure of some dread to me, I found the spectre of my father being humiliated both hilarious and disturbing.

Memory paints Blakie as the constant presence. Sometimes this was interrupted by Sam Harold, my father's batman, who, after the war, gained employment at the works. His hair was shaven almost to the crown of his head, and the rest of his Brylcreemed hair was a glossy, immovable splash across the top of his skull. Sam was responsible for my father being known in Llansteffan as the Colonel, since – when my mother bought her cottage in the village, and Sam was enlisted as an assistant in painting and rebuilding works – he would repair to the pub and regale the regulars with completely misleading accounts of Norman's wealth and grandeur. He never showed any sign of resentment at being patronized, when my father repeated Sam's version of Welsh place names – 'We nearly got lost in Lan-diddle-oh'. His perfect manners hid from all of us the smallest smidgeon of resentment. Perhaps he did not feel it. Perhaps he really did hero-worship Norman, as he appeared to do.

After the lupin controversy (as heated in its way, in our small world, as the Wars of the Roses had once been in a larger) and the departure of Mr Blakeman, Sam was the figure who did the rough work in the garden. This included pushing the lawnmower up and down in immaculately straight lines, making the grass seem as velvety neat as the front quad of an Oxford college. 'We're winnin'!' he would say, when reaching the end of a line, displaying no irritation about my tagging along at his side. 'Champion, Andrew! Champion!' he would say. 'Champion', as an adjective, like Blakie's 'Tarr-ah' was adopted into my own vocabulary.

If my early smudged album of memory contains more snapshots of Blakie and Sam than of Norman and Jean, this was because, during those years, Norman was often preoccupied by work and travel, and Jean was seriously ill.

To this fuzzy, unchronological phase of mixed memories belongs one of the most powerful – my mother taking my head and placing it against her belly as she told me I was going to have another brother or sister. Only years later did she tell me that there had been a very premature stillbirth and that, following a decade of obstetric catastrophes, the doctors recommended a hysterectomy.

In the 1950s this operation was nearly always performed by men. By necessity it was invasive; by custom it was brutal. Perhaps family teasing is a form of love, even though it is rough love, but I now flinch at the way we all laughed at Jean's anxious preoccupation with the lavatory. Apart from the psychological trauma of losing the womb, and the great pain following the clumsy 'op', there were many side-effects, including incontinence. I do not know how many months Jean was *hors de combat*, but this was when I was thrown back on the company of Blakie most fully. Nor, until I sat down to write these words, did I ever ask myself how irritating this must have been for Our Vron and Our Cyril. For the rest of my childhood Jean would be a semi-invalid. Some of the time she appeared to recover, and to play tennis and swim as she had done with such joy in the past. But I can never remember a time when one could take her health for granted.

Did she eat normally before the operation? I can't remember. I certainly have no memory of seeing her eat a meal – not a proper meal. She took the cooking upon herself. There was no Mrs Hassall any more. With what fuming bad temper and poor grace Jean would bring the food from the 'back kitchen' to the little dining room, too small for the repro-Georgian table and the sideboard which had accompanied them from Burston. Vastly over-roasted meats, vegetables boiled, seemingly, for bad-tempered hours. Her way with potatoes was to boil them until they all but dissolved in the grey water. They would then be half-drained in a colander, hit furiously with a fork, and slopped into a Pyrex dish. She treated the harmless spud as semi-toxic, often saying that none of us could guess how nauseating she found their smell. Why she thought we could not guess this was difficult to imagine, since, after slamming down the dish of mash on the sideboard, she would run from the room and put her head in the kitchen sink, with melodramatic groans.

Jean's unrivalled capacity to extract unhappiness from any situation, however neutral or cheerful, coloured all my early life. Such was the paradox of her nature, however, that she was also capable of surfacing with flashes of enjoyment or humour. She was a keen member of the tennis club, and would spend as much time there as she could. While memory paints her 'home cooking' as some of the most unpalatable ever forked into my mouth, the teas she helped prepare for the tennis club were among the most delicious. No one made better tomato sandwiches on thinly sliced white bread and butter.

At the tennis club, her face would be wreathed in smiles. Likewise at the convent gates, talking to the other mothers or to the nuns, I can recall her laughing, but never when her husband was present. On a family picnic or a seaside holiday, Jean was a nightmare companion, everlastingly afraid of travel sickness and in a seemingly perpetual bate with Norman, sucking in her breath rather than laughing at his jokes, wincing with fear as the Bentley swooped round bends in the road, groaning with theatrical boredom whenever the Wedgwoods were mentioned – and of course, when weren't they?

Norman's absences were therefore times of peace. Once a year, he and Uncle Jos would cross the Atlantic to visit the New York office. They would travel on one of the big liners, the *Queen Mary* or the *Queen Elizabeth*, and make a holiday of it. In New York they would take in a show on Broadway, one of the Rodgers and Hammerstein revivals or, the first one I can remember their enthusing about, *My Fair Lady* – 1956. Sometimes, Norman would stay on in America for a few weeks. He was tremendous buddies with Hensleigh Wedgwood, who ran the New York end of things. There was a memorable summer when Norman drove Hensleigh right across the US to Reno to obtain one of his many divorces. There is a photograph taken of Norman during this drive. He appears to be smiling beside a milestone, but in fact it is a commemorative monument announcing that, in a spot near by, Josiah Wedgwood I first bought white clay from the Cherokee nation. (This photograph, and my enthusiastic discovery, during my fifties, of Cherokee artefacts in the National Museum of the American Indian in New York, was the inspiration for what I think is my best novel, *The Potter's Hand*.)

We do not know whether, when he went to Reno with Hensleigh, Norman ever contemplated getting divorced himself. When Clarrie died, Jean had come into a tiny amount of money, and spoke openly of her desire to escape her husband. She'd found a house advertised in *The Lady*, in the remotest part of Wester Ross in the Scottish Highlands. She wrote off for the particulars, and when she came up to sing 'Loving Shepherd of Thy Sheep' at my bedside she would share her plans of running away with me. I half thrilled to the idea, and half dreaded the possibility of separation from Blakie, the convent, Candlemas processions and handwriting lessons with Sister Mary Mark.

Uncle Jos's own marriage had painfully unravelled and, in consequence, he was not on terms with his son – Doctor John, so called (of *course*) to distinguish him from Sir John, who was (do pay attention) always known as John Hamilton. Uncle Jos lived with an

Austrian housekeeper – Paula. Norman, in a poor imitation of her voice, would say, '*Mr Veelson, wiz you, he admit vat ve are togezzer, I eat viz you, ve go to Wien zusammen, but when Sir John come or Iris, he say, Paula, you housekeeper, back in ze keetchen. He hypocrite!*'

There must have been many relationships like this in the past, especially in small provincial towns like Stone, where openly living with a mistress would have occasioned comment. Nowadays, even the word 'mistress' would seem absurd, of course. As well as the annual trip to America, Norman went every year to Vienna with Paula and Jos, to visit her family. Sometimes this would be followed by business trips to Milan, well lubricated with many a Negroni in expensive hotels.

Uncle Jos, lonely, and dependent on his Sancho Panza, often dropped in to Stonefield Cottage at the end of the working day. The elegant little sitting room with its two half-D Georgian tables on either side of the chimneypiece, adorned with Chinese horses which had belonged to Grandpa Wilson, and its scenes of London by Thomas Shotter Boys on the walls, became thick with cigarette clouds as the two chums imbibed gin with Noilly Prat. Jean, too furious even to set eyes on Jos, let alone join the merriment, would send me in to hint it was time for him to leave, and then the pair would implore me to stay to hear the end of a narrative. Incomprehensible though they were at the time, these stories were evidently hilarious, since, when the punchline was reached, there were explosions of mirth, as when they recalled Jos, on some balcony overlooking Lake Como, imploring the waiter to bring still water – '*Acqua semplice, per favore, acqua non fizzimento!*'

By the time Jos was willing to drunk-drive the short distance to his house on the other side of Stone, Jean's mood was understandable. Not only was the small house choked with nicotine fumes but, as she would darkly remark, gin either made Norman 'ratty' or 'silly'. Decades later, when she was at least seventy, she consulted my brother's wife for suggestions about how she could dampen Norman's amorous propensities, perhaps believing that an American would be better informed about such matters. Clearly, through four decades of marriage, the relationship did not, from a physical standpoint, lose its intensity. The clash of their two egos, however, was an everlasting war. The atmosphere was bitter.

The friendship with Josiah caused Jean as much grief as adultery would have done. It was, moreover, the direct cause of a surely very legitimate resentment. Hanging out with Jos, who was a rich man, made Norman live beyond his means to a truly idiotic extent. Jean had heard about the request for *acqua non fizzimento* far too often for it to be amusing. She was not interested to know that the pair had sat together at the captain's table on the *Queen Mary* with the likes of Elizabeth Taylor and Michael Wilding ('extraORD-inarily nice man, and as for her – well, Elizabeth Taylor is a real BOBBY DAZZLER'). Nor did Jean want to hear the sordid details of Hensleigh's divorces. These reminders of a life more glamorous than her own were not merely inherently annoying, they explained the emptiness of the bank account.

Partly because they were high-minded friends of G. E. Moore and the Bloomsbury Set, partly because they were heedlessly rich, the Wedgwoods did not really need their directors' salaries. Norman might have been a director of the firm (the only non-Wedgwood to have such an honour), but his salary nowhere near covered the fare for travelling luxuriously on transatlantic liners, or spending weeks in hotels in Vienna and the Italian lakes. Only cads would have claimed such luxuries as 'expenses'. Jean and her children lived modestly, not because we were Puritans, especially, but because Norman had spent all his money on his friendship with Jos. There were marital rows when the bills for school fees came in.

If we can't afford to send the children to Rugby or Malvern Girls' College, she would argue, why not send them to the perfectly good local grammar schools? He would indicate that they now had a certain position to keep up. Then, with Micawberish lack of self-awareness, he would say she was the one with the money, so why didn't she pay the fees? In so far as this was possible, this was what she sometimes did. Somehow, she managed to conceal from Norman the existence of a number of the tiny trusts which she had from her father, but he was aware that there was money there somewhere. Clarrie must have sussed Norman's spendthrift ways, and he did not want Jean's money squandered on foreign hotels, cars and 'nice natty suitings'.

As the youngest child, at home throughout this period while the others were away at boarding school, marital warfare was the air I learned to breathe. Only after she was widowed, when Jean asked me to do her tax affairs, did she tell me about the trusts, and of her father's dread that Norman would spend what little was left of her money.

Yet such is the paradox and complexity of family life that, though I saw no evidence then for their love of one another, I never doubted their love for me. I was a brand snatched from the burning. I was their last shout. Had they not operated on me as a baby, I might so easily have been dead. My brother and sister were right to think I was a spoilt brat. Norman was far less strict with me than he had been with them on his immediate discharge from military service. He would chastise Stephen with his officer's swagger stick – the dreaded 'leather-covered stick'. Such horrors would have been unthinkable for me. From Norman, from Jean, from Blakie and from a loving elder sister I received indulgence of every whim.

There was an exclusive society called the ANWIL Club. I made cards, which were numbered and given out to the membership. Armed with these necessities, Jeannie, Blakie and my mother would be expected to sit through 'shows' in which I recited my own compositions, sang, strutted about or occasionally delivered short sermons on such subjects as the Joyful Mysteries of the Rosary. I assumed I was going to be liked. I probably had a lot in common with the bumptious five- or six-year-old Norman who, in his immaculate sailor's suit, was rubbed in horse manure by the juvenile class warriors of Fenton in 1909.

Being confident of my parents' love, however, was not the same thing as being happy in their company. Hardly a day of my childhood was spent without, by implication, my being asked to take sides with one or the other. When Norman made jokes, should I scream with laughter, as he was doing, even before reaching the punchline, or scowl, as Jean was doing? Involuntarily, I found him entertaining, but part of the entertainment was in being able to see how near the wind he was sailing. Was there a guilty pleasure in my noticing that his japes and jollities were going to infuriate Jean? Even when sober, he would veer from quiet gloom to high spirits. Then he would sing old music-hall songs, sometimes seizing the tea cosy which for some reason sat on the sideboard beside the Skeaping gazelle and the Napoleon-ivy-adorned Queen's ware lamps. With the cosy on his head, he could become Napoleon himself, or suddenly burst into 'Has anyone here seen Kelly? K-E-DOUBLE-ELL-Y.' If Noilly Prat and gin had been taken, he would often become Irish, and, with his arms tightly beside his side, he would imitate the jig of poor children begging on the quayside in Liverpool or New York docks. Tears would flow from the forget-me-not blue eyes as he tried to say, 'They were so poor, they could not even lift their arms.'

These histrionics would make Jean mutter, 'It's so undignified,' and when the tea-cosy routines were enacted, she would sometimes try to snatch the offending object from his skull. It seemed possible, at such moments, that she might actually strike him. Yet by then, awestruck by the plight of the poor Irish children, or laughing at the prospect of Norman as 'one of the ruins that Cromwell knocked about a bit', I'd see Jean as a mere spectre at the feast, a killjoy. Her snatching of the tea cosy would freeze the atmosphere, just as sudden headaches or 'bilious attacks' could ruin a picnic or a quiet drive in the countryside.

Yet I could be easily persuaded by her version of events. For example, until I was about ten, I was annually persuaded that Norman was 'trying to spoil Christmas' by inviting his elder sister, Aunt Elizabeth, to stay with us. Jean's antipathy to Elizabeth was never explained. It was a given. I was taught to view my aunt as a sort of witch. The fact that she brought with her mince pies made by herself (meltingly delicious pastry, wonderful filling), rather than being seen as the kindly act which was obviously intended, was viewed as the purest malice, designed to remind us of the cardboardy crunch of Jean's pastry and the boringness of her bought mincemeat. Far more confusing than the quality of the mince pies was the fact that the company of the wicked witch turned out to be invariably enjoyable. Like Norman, Elizabeth was good at recitations. In her well-modulated voice, we heard Cowper's 'Boadicea' – a particular favourite, and, hence, to this day, one of my favourite poems – or Cassius' speech from *Julius Caesar* – 'I know that virtue to be in you, Brutus, / As well as I do know your outward favour.'

Of course, the party line was that to enjoy declaiming poetry was simply 'showing off'. Boxing Day, when Elizabeth went to stay with her sister Dorothy at their house in the hospital grounds in Newcastle-under-Lyme, was always a relief. The terrible tensions were over for another year. Jean was never able to pretend, for so much as five minutes, to be pleasant to her sister-in-law.

18. When I Get There, I'll Be Glad

There had always been a succession of cats and dogs around the place, but the arrival of little Friskie, a King Charles spaniel of the white-and-tan colouring known as Blenheim, should have sounded a warning note. Friskie was a present to my sister Jeannie from Barbara; or, as Norman referred to her, Good Old Barbara.

She was a family friend, Good Old Barbara. She and her husband ran the boarding school in Malvern where my brother had been educated before he went to Rugby. Jeannie was just round the corner at Malvern Girls' College. But, what was that to me, in my convent-surrounded, Blakie-dominated Paradise?

Friskie was a nasty little dog, yappy, bitey, smelly and a bit lame, which is presumably why Barbara palmed her off on those hapless innocents the Wilsons. Friskie had been the runt of the litter. As I watched the ill-natured little bitch limping round the house, snarling at the good-natured Labrador Jim, snapping at Sam Harold's ankles as he pushed the lawnmower, yapping to be let in to the house, yapping to be let out, fawning on Norman when he came home from the works, growling at Blakie when she arrived to dress me in the mornings, I had no notion that I was soon to be placed under the absolute power of Friskie's donor, my torturer and tormentor for the next four and a half years.

For the time being, I was safe in Stone, safe in the Shire before the Black Riders had been glimpsed or heard of. I loved the little house, the garden, the canal-bank overhung with boughs. Nor were the bickering and rowing constant – there were moments of sunshine. Throughout seventy years of life I have had amazing good luck, and enjoyed many experiences of joy; but no period of life has been so happy as that last year in Stone before I was sent to a boarding school. My mother's health must have been improving. She took me, and little friends from the convent school, for picnics on the Downs Banks or for long sunshiny afternoons at the tennis club. Sister Mary Mark had begun to give us lessons. Blakie was always around.

Part of the fabric of life was to watch Norman drawing his designs. He did so in large scrapbooks bought at Woolworth's. First he drew the shape of the bowl, vase or jug or teapot in pencil. Then he would ink over his final designs. There would be many accompanying notes, relating, no doubt, to the technicalities of glazing and firing. The nicest of his commercial designs, from which I still eat most of my meals, had a glaze of his invention called 'Summer Sky'. It was his favourite colour, about two tones paler than his own, summery, forget-me-not blue eyes. Greater pride was felt in his 'unique' shapes – bowls and vases that I still buy on eBay if I can afford them. He derived inspiration from Korea, and used to say that the Koreans outsoared the achievements of China or Japan. Presumably, his mind sometimes strayed back to Fenton, and his father's work with Bernard Moore, but if so – Tch, tch, tch, tch … we would soon be in unmentionable territory.

His life as a director, eventually managing director, of Wedgwood was all-in-all to him. It was pure joy to climb into the passenger seat of the Bentley and to be driven to the works on a Saturday morning. (People worked until midday on Saturday then.) You would see the whole factory, a workforce of well over a thousand, lined in row upon row, turning, modelling, painting, affixing handles to cups, while from loudspeakers *Music While You Work* blared forth from the Light Programme. I remember once walking with my father and pausing next to a lady who was painting flowers on a teapot. She turned, when she had laid down her brush (like Lily Briscoe?), and with a broad grin she said, 'Aren't we lucky to work here?'

I am sure she was not saying it to impress the boss. In those days 75,000 men and women worked in the Potteries. True, for the more skilled workers there was the opportunity to serve apprenticeships, but in the great majority of cases this was scarcely necessary. Mothers would teach daughters how to paint flowers, or how to stick on a handle. Modellers would teach their sons before they had left school. Thanks largely to Jos and Norman, the electrification of the industry had cleaned up the polluted atmosphere of the six towns. Silicosis and other industrial diseases were on the wane. That factory in Barlaston, their brainchild, was in its day a glory.

When I made friends with my tutor at Oxford, Christopher Tolkien (of whom more, far more, later), he described going with a friend to the relatively new factory building at Barlaston. The rows and rows of workers, all producing pots to the accompaniment of popular music, struck him as sinister, nightmarish.

'I felt I'd looked into Mordor!' he said, with that contemptuous toss of his head.

He did not know, when he said it, that this Mordor had been created by my father. As a child, I certainly did not view the works in this light. Norman, in effect the boss of the whole set-up, was not merely a big cheese in the eyes of his children. He clearly was, objectively, a big cheese. He was always coming home with accounts of other Big Cheeses who had been to lunch in the boardroom – Chancellors of the Exchequer, well-known journalists and the like. Royal visits threw both my parents into a tizz. Jean, who was always well turned out, dressed, all the time I knew her, in an immaculately clean blouse (twinsets in winter) and a well-pressed skirt. More formal clothes made her feel uncomfortable. She allowed Norman to take her to some outfitters in London to find something deemed 'suitable' for her to be 'presented' in. This rig would be hoiked out of the gigantic Bramhall wardrobe, reeking of mothballs, whenever a royal visit was in prospect. It spoke eloquently about Norman's idea of ... of her? Of women? Of his fear that she would let the side down by throwing up? A broad-brimmed black hat and harshly cut charcoal-grey suit made her look as if she were attending a funeral, rather than being lined up for a ten-second encounter, poor thing, with the succession of royals who came to the works – the Queen, the Dukes of Kent, Edinburgh, Gloucester. After Jean and the other wives had bobbed to such personages, they could disappear and relax, while Norman, taut and terrified, would have to escort the royal party round the works. The only time this was a pleasure was when Lord Snowdon came with Princess Margaret. Norman and he 'clicked', which led to my father working with Snowdon at the Design Centre on a number of projects.

Unsurprisingly, Mr Jos, Mr Wilson, Sir John (please remember, not to be confused with Doctor John) and the other directors of the firm were treated with deference by the potters who worked at Barlaston. I cringed, at the Christmas party for children of the workers, where I was treated as a little prince, while the village policeman sang 'Rudolph the Red-Nosed Reindeer', and asked for me, as son of the boss, to stand at his side while this excruciating ditty was bawled, his large mouth far too near the mike. Whenever heard, the song brings back the embarrassment.

Since I was treated like a Crown Prince, you might think I might have expected that one day I should go into the industry. One of the music-hall songs Norman liked to sing, with or without the tea cosy on his head, was:

I don't know where I'm going,
But when I get there, I'll be glad.
I'm following in father's footsteps.
I'm following my dear old Dad.

Years later, after Norman had died, my brother Stephen told me he'd asked Norman whether he should consider going into the business and was given the firmest of negatives. The last thing the old man wanted, after generation upon generation of Wilsons doing nothing else, was for any of his children to pursue a career as a potter.

One of Uncle Jos's whims had been to commission a good eighteenth-century scholar to compile a selection of Josiah I's letters, and then to write his biography. On the advice of Jos's sister

Helen Pease, a Cambridge intellectual and fringe Bloomsberry, they alighted on a Fellow of Christ's College, Cambridge, called Jack Plumb. He'd eventually be the Master. It was accordingly to Christ's, after a period in Geneva, perfecting his already excellent French, that Stephen was dispatched, eventually to become an academic historian writing books on subjects as various as the *Action Française* movement, Corsican bandits, the cult of saints and popular magic.

Such a career path was clearly what Norman wanted for his sons. He seized on the funny little stories which, like so many children, I scribbled all the time, proclaiming that these outpourings prefigured my destiny.

'This boy's going to be another Arnold Bennett!' was the repeated refrain.

Me trying to follow in father's footsteps as a potter?

Strange as it may seem, it never occurred to me, whatever other ambitions I nursed from time to time, that I would *not* be a writer. The achievements of all but the very greatest writers (Goethe, Milton, Dante) seem much less than those of a soldier-industrialist like Norman. Here was someone who was largely responsible for building an enormous factory, for transforming an entire industry and, with it, improving the lives of thousands of human beings who might otherwise have choked to death aged thirty-five. He did this while designing and making objects of purity and elegance, whose beauty continues to adorn any room, any human life, in which they find themselves. Yet Norman believed that to be a writer was a higher calling than this. Having been a literary editor on two papers, and watched the mountains of literary productions overflowing from the postbags, almost every volume of which will be forgotten in a few weeks, I have come to question the reverence felt for the printed word, and for writers, that is often to be found among those of a practical turn.

Jean's chippiness in relation to my Aunt Elizabeth's literary references likewise derived not from a lack of interest in books – far from it – but from a sense that, had things turned out differently, she might have been a writer herself. If it had not been for Mother, or the Slump, or her failure to go to university, or the war, she too might have written as well as her heroines; perhaps she would have married G. F. Woods and, returning from a bike ride along the Backs in Cambridge, have penned novels such as those of Josephine Tey or Margery Allingham. Throughout her twenties she had compiled files of quotations from the poets. These collections, kept in small green ring-files, were not dictionaries of quotations, exactly, nor were they anthologies. Like many of the 'authors' of the Middle Ages, Jean regarded it as in order to read extracts and snippets rather than tackling the whole book. Of no book was this truer than of the Book of Books. She spoke in awestruck tones of 'Mother's cousin Nan' (Agnes Paterson), who was said 'to know the Bible very well'. The amazement of tone here would not have been out of place had Nan Paterson deciphered cuneiform inscriptions. Jean revered the Scriptures, but she only consulted the Bible to verify quotations. Her way of reading the New Testament, which she did all the time, was to re-read the passages set aside for the Epistle and Gospel during that week's Communion. In extreme old age, when she was suggesting readings for her funeral, she said, 'Let not your hearts be troubled.' She said we'd easily find it.

'In the Fourth Gospel?'

'How do you mean?'

'Well, it is in the Fourth Gospel, surely?'

'It's the Gospel for Whit Sunday.'

That's how she thought of it, just as she thought of the Beatitudes, which she knew by heart, as the Gospel for All Saints' Day.

So, with secular authors, she had divided them up into manageable 'extracts'. Wordsworth figured largely. Having tried, unsuccessfully, to get a publisher interested, she wrote to the poet and literary editor J. C. Squire, and, on his suggestion, rashly entrusted these precious files to the post. I am sure she knew nothing of his reputation as a roué. He posted them back, and a short correspondence ensued. Who are we to question a man's motives? He was probably just being kind, and would probably have offered advice had a middle-aged man requested it. He told her they were unpublishable.

Jean liked writing to the famous, and was surprised, for example, to receive a curt postcard from Somerset Maugham, suggesting that when she had written novels and short stories as successful as his own, then she might be entitled to criticize the psychological plausibility of one of his tales. She had expected him to find her observation helpful.

Anyway, suffice it to say that both Jean and Norman fantasized about writers and their lives, and bred me up to be a writer. As far as Norman was concerned, the Wedgwoods were to be revered not merely as potters but as the tribe who produced the author of *On the Origin of Species*, as of Veronica's histories of the seventeenth century – *The Thirty Years' War*, *The King's Peace*, *The King's War* and so forth. Had not Uncle Jos himself gone into print, as a young Marxist, with *The Economics of Inheritance*, a Pelican book advocating the state confiscation of all a person's property on death? Whenever I see this little blue-and-white paperback, usually for sale on the dusty bargain shelf of a second-hand shop, usually selling for a pound or less, I buy it, with wistful thoughts about the mutability of things, and of opinions, since – the cause of the painful severance between Don Quixote and Sancho Panza – the public flotation of the company left the heirs of Josiah and the other directors prodigiously rich.

Unlike the Brontë sisters, or C. S. Lewis, I did not keep my childhood stories, though, like them, I did illustrate them, since, as well as wanting to write books, I also thought of myself as an artist.

There were rows between Jean and Norman about where I should go to school after the convent, a school where boys could only stay to the age of seven. If Norman persisted in his belief that his children must be privately educated, what was wrong with Yarlet, a perfectly good small prep school only a few miles away from Stone, which I could have attended as a day boy? Sister Mary Mark suggested that I was too young and too 'sensitive' to be sent away.

Of course, I was privy to none of these discussions. Jean only told me about them in her widowhood. Suddenly, at the end of our summer holiday in Wales, I found they'd bought a large trunk on which my name had been painted. Blakie, her face blotchy with crying, was helping Jean fill it with items on a printed list – football boots. What on earth would I want with those? Grey socks, six pairs. Grey shorts. Grey shirts – rather nice, these, it must be said, soft Viyella. The most poignant item on the list was '*Teddy Bear – optional – First Term Only*'.

19. Put Your Cap On, I Should

Some days later, my father and I made the journey. Every step of the way is etched in excruciating memory. The walk past the convent, down the avenue of Station Road, which terminates in the charming Dutch-gabled, purplish-brick 1840s railway buildings. The platforms were wooden, as were the floors of the waiting room, where a few Welsh coals glowed in the grate, somehow cruel in their homeliness. Cruel, because by lighting a coal fire they seemed to imply we could stay there: but this was a place of departures, not of remaining.

We were ridiculously early for our train. Earliness is a family trait, but in Norman it ran to extremes. First he twiddled with the fittings of the gaslight, turning it up and down so that his face became now a palish green, now darkly shadowed, rather than its natural pink. Poor man, I had not yet started to weep, but he could tell I was on the verge, and I could tell he would do anything to avoid a scene. Yet the knowledge was, by this stage, my only weapon. Given the fact that he hated to see someone cry, would it not be possible, even at this late stage, to persuade him to let me stay at home?

He began to speak of my brother catching the train from this very station when he had first started at Hillstone. Eventually he became old enough to travel alone. Watching my lip tremble, Norman hastened on with his theme, becoming a routes bore. To reach Great Malvern, you needed to change stations at Birmingham, from

Snow Hill to New Street, whereas when he went to Rugby, Stephen would be able to go direct from Stone. My sister's railway journeys to Malvern were also recounted. She was now in Switzerland at a finishing school and good old Stebby was at Cambridge with Plumb. As we moved inexorably to the merits of Josiah I's letters, I blurted out:

'I don't want... I don't WANT to go away.'

My voice was cracking.

Norman said how little he had ever wanted to go away.

'Then why ... Why send me?'

'... but when you get used to it, school isn't so bad. Stephen enjoyed Hillstone.'

It wasn't a cruel place, not like Norman's school, Ellesmere. Stephen had loved all three places – Hillstone, Rugby, now Cambridge. Schools were nice places nowadays. Why, at Ellesmere, the parsons, in their soutanes and birettas, had whacked you for the merest thing, whereas ... He let out a mirthless harrumph. Rudolph! Norman doubted Rudolph knew what whacking was. They don't go in for that sort of thing nowadays. And there was good old Barbara.

'Barbara gave Friskie to Jish [my sister], remember. You'll like Old Barbara.'

The umpteenth nervous cigarette was ignited. I was shaking. Convulsed. Could only gasp, out, 'I don't ... I don't WANT ...'

Once the train came, and we were aboard, there was the further agony of having to look out of the window and to see Blakie and Jean, standing in our garden waving handkerchiefs as we passed.

As we rattled south towards Stafford, he fell back on Wedgwood lore, trying to ignore my sobs. There was a limitless range of characters to mention, of course. We had scarcely left Cecil Wedgwood on the battlefield of Passchendaele before we were once again with Uncle Jos at the petrol pumps during a motoring holiday. We could assess Veronica's status among the critics, some of whom could be a little bit snooty about her, but there was a place for books that were readable, as well as for those which were strictly academic. Hello, Wolverhampton already. Soon be in Brum.

'Do you know what people in Birmingham are called?'

By now I was incapable of speech. Disappointed that I'd forgotten this part of the catechism, for if a thing was worth saying, Norman always said it over and over again, he reminded me that the inhabitants of England's Second City were the 'Birmingham Tykes'. This was well known.

One of the things that caused puzzlement to come over the face of strangers was his assumption that doodles, wordplay and nicknames of his own invention had instantly passed into common currency. For example, he called those who had attended Rugby School Rag and Bone Men. When I eventually attended that school myself, I never met anyone who was familiar with the usage; it must have been Norman's invention. This would not stop him feeling hurt if any of the other fathers, sporting an old boy's tie, responded with incomprehension to his genial observation, 'I see you are a Rag and Bone Man.'

'Birmingham Tykes!' he repeated. 'Remember it.'

Another sad little harrumph. Surely the boy would laugh at this? Then he lost patience with my histrionics, just as he lost patience with Jean's self-pity.

'Oh, Andrew, honest-LEE!'

When we hit Tyke City, it was a walk of ten minutes or so between the two stations. I was silent when asked whether I'd like him to buy me a sandwich, whether I'd like him to carry my small leather suitcase which contained pyjamas, a wash-bag and Teddy (First Term Only) – but no book. It was strictly forbidden to bring your own books into the school.

At New Street it was all too easy to recognize the party returning to Hillstone since the gaggle of little boys on the platform were all wearing the uniform in which I was so ridiculously clad: polished black leather shoes, knee-length grey socks, grey shorts, the rather nice grey shirt, a black-and-yellow striped tie, a grey blazer with yellow, black and white piping, and on our heads, a vividly egg-yellow peaked cap, adorned at the brow with the letter H.

'Put your cap on, I should,' he said with some asperity.

I had assumed, until this point, that my father would be coming with me all the way to the school. There even lurked – or had done, until this moment – the cruel hope that when I met Good Old Barbara and that softy Rudolph – the one who'd never heard of whacking – that we could explain. A mistake had been made. In fact, I did not wish to come to their school, and I'd much prefer to stay at home with Blakie.

But, what was this? Norman was bending over to kiss my cheek.

'Better not to linger it out,' said the schoolmaster on the platform. 'It's very usual to be a bit upset in the first term, but, by the time we get to Malvern …'

'Oh!' Norman agreed readily. 'He'll soon be happy as a sandboy.'

And with that, he skedaddled. I watched the back of the large fedora and the overcoat, elegantly cut by 'old Holmsey', disappearing into the crowds. If I knew Norman, he'd be heading for the nearest bar for a very large one, poor fellow.

'You're Wilson,' said the teacher, who explained he was called Sir Conan Aske, a moustachioed, boozy military man, whose features come to mind when I read of Major Bagstock in *Dombey and Son*. His assurances to my father that I would settle down, as soon as the train set off for Malvern, were optimistic. I cried all the way, not caring that the other boys were staring and some of them giggling.

When we reached the other end, I was in no position to admire the Victorian allusion to a German spa, in the wooded mountain Gothic of that charming station. We were lined up in a crocodile and marched up the hill towards the school. I cried all the way. I cried over the baked beans on toast which were served in the large communal dining hall. I cried as we stripped down and brushed our teeth in the nude. Cried as I put on my pyjamas. Cried as the foul, delicately moustachioed Welsh matron, Miss Clark, reminded us that talking after lights out was punishable with a caning: 'and no exceptions, no excuses'. Cried as, clutching Teddy, first term only, I fell into a fevered, terrified sleep.

20. Notes for Boys

I first published an account of what it was like to be a pupil at Hillstone School, Great Malvern, Worcestershire, in a popular national newspaper (the *Daily Mail*). The article was a general reflection on the strange British custom, among the middle classes and above, of sending children to boarding schools. There was some allusion to sexual abuse in what I wrote. In so many walks of life, but especially in churches and schools, our generation has begun to confront the effects of sexually abusing children and, in the case of the bigwigs (bishops, bosses of the BBC, etc.), the effects of covering up such crimes. In my article I expressed relative gratitude for the fact that our headmaster, Rudolph Barbour-Simpson, though a sexual pervert, had never gone much beyond mild fiddling about.

I had never spoken to anyone about what happened at my school – not about what really happened. The article was a little gesture towards trying to come to terms with the memories. I concentrated on the headmaster, Rudolph, and in so doing entirely blinded myself to my relationship with Barbara, his wife. It is now clear to me that this was the really damaging thing in my experience at that school. But first – Rudolph.

He would prowl the dormitories at night, after lights out. He liked to attend bath-time, peering through the waters of the tub for signs of incipient pubic hair. He would stand watching as we had showers after games. The most obvious way he demonstrated his sexual feelings was in persistent caning, and it was only after I had been caned half a dozen times that I began to notice, peering through my legs as the cane came down on my arse, and the excruciating pain and humiliation of it was endured, that he would masturbate while he hit me, usually keeping his penis, his 'tube', as he liked to call it, inside his trousers, but not always.

In the first couple of school holidays, when I had returned home, bath-time had become something to dread. Most boys of seven or eight are beginning to feel shy of being seen by their mother, and so would get out of the tub showing only their back. In my case, I was so anxious to conceal my bottom and back, that I showed my front, hoping she could not see the welts, cuts and scars. I must have succeeded, since I am sure, had she seen these wounds, she would have insisted on my being removed from the school.

Corporal punishment is now more or less illegal in most European countries. In my article about Hillstone, I argued, caning was thought normal almost everywhere in the 1950s, and at least the sexual abuse was *relatively* minor.

The article had scarcely appeared before I was deluged with messages. My doorbell rang. A young woman whom I had never met before was standing there and asked to come in. Her father, she said, was a little older than I was. He was a normal – that is, slightly emotionally pinched – Englishman, unused to emotional display. He had never told her, or any member of his family, about his childhood. When he read my article, however, he had burst into tears and said that he had been anally raped by Rudolph Barbour-Simpson. The injuries were severe and identified by his family doctor.

Naturally, the family removed him at once from the school, and asked the doctor to be a witness in criminal proceedings. The doctor replied that he was willing to do this but that they must understand the consequences of such a course of action. Barbour-Simpson would almost certainly deny the charges. (He was a much-respected member of the educational establishment in Malvern, a Justice of the Peace, etc., etc.) There would be a trial. The child victim would be compelled to relive his ordeal in court. A senior barrister would be engaged by the defendant, and he (it would certainly be a man) would belittle the child in court. And pour doubt on his story. This mental torture in the witness box could last for days. Of course, the family brought no charges.

Several of the many letters I received from former pupils at the school spoke of anal rape. One such child had grown up into a severe depressive who took his own life in his early twenties. His family wanted me to know that Barbour-Simpson's activities had *not* been minor and there was much more to it than a little fumbling, as I had suggested.

By then I had heard from dozens of families and individuals, all telling similar stories of men unable to put the demons of Hillstone behind them. There were stories of depressions, suicides, drug dependency, alcoholism.

Some of those who have written to me, or met me since, have spoken of Barbara, and of her hateful daughter Jill, who, they said, made the suffering much worse. You could say that Rudolph was sick, out of control. Not so his poised, ladylike wife, with her raven hair, her fluffy, brightly coloured mohair cardi-coats, her upper-class tones, whose modulation was very faintly Welsh. (She said 'years' for 'ears'.)

Until all this happened, I had entirely obliterated from my memory the behaviour of Barbara at bath-time. Whereas Rudolph would merely come into the room and stare at us in our tubs, Barbara would kneel beside the bath of her little friends, of whom I was decidedly one, and stroke our genitals. I was not in love with her, but I was entranced. While also hating her.

They were a handsome pair, Barbara and Rudolph. She, daughter of a headmaster of Harrow, had a long, gypsyish face, and an ironical expression. She was a flirt. A number of the masters at the school clearly adored her, and even at the time I suspected that the French master was her lover. Two reasons for this suspicion. One, it was impossible to understand why this prodigiously clever man, fluent in French, German and Czech (and presumably with some Le Carré-ish involvement with military intelligence – Malvern was in those days the centre of a big radar station), could have ended up teaching in this grotesque dump of a place unless he was in Barbara's thrall. Both Barbara's children were described as 'adopted' – there was a weedy son called Michael – and one assumed that Rudolph had played no part in their arrival on the planet. It was very easy to imagine being in love with Barbara. Perhaps my father was, a little bit, hence the gifts of Wedgwood vases and bowls and the murmuring of her name – 'Good old Barbara'. He was far too innocent to guess what sort of person she was.

My second reason for suspecting she was the lover of the French master is more sinister. He was married to a mousey, put-upon woman and they had one son, who was a pupil at the school. Although the casual infliction of pain on any of the boys was an habitual game for Barbara, none of us ever saw anything to match her relentless persecution of the French master's son. She liked to find out food he especially disliked, and she would then force-feed him with it. Day after day she would drag him into the school kitchens. Jill, the odious daughter, would come along to watch the show. We would peer through the kitchen window, as Barbara sliced onions. When the child began to retch, she would spoon more and more of the nauseating things into his mouth, as he gagged and struggled and wept and Jill held his arms.

Beside the hutches for pet rabbits and guinea pigs was a larger cage, shown to gullible prospective parents as an aviary, should any pupil choose to bring a parrot to school. In fact, the cage was only ever used for boys who got on the wrong side of Barbara. The routine would be to lock the victim in for a few hours and then, by the time he was bound to be wetting himself, to collect an audience of the younger boys to watch.

For me, summer terms were the worst. The smell of chlorine – even occasionally, the sight of a bright blue swimming bath such as our local lido – is enough to recall appalling horror. I can remember Barbara's eyes lighting up when Norman, who, like my mother, was a keen swimmer, artlessly told her that I was being rather slow to learn how to swim, and that I showed a slight terror of the water.

'We don't understand it,' he said, standing beside the fireplace in her drawing room, with a cigarette between his fingers and a glass of gin in his hand. 'Jean and I both love swimming. And diving.'

'He'll get used to it if he isn't forced,' Jean murmured, but again, like her husband, not noticing the glint of excitement in Barbara's face.

For, yes, my mother and father were now friends of the bosom, and, even if they did not actually stay overnight with Barbara and Rudolph – usually putting up at a gloomy nearby hostelry called the Goldhill Hotel – they would always be invited in to the headmaster's house for drinks before taking me out for a Saturday or Sunday. By this time, I had come to an understanding of what Barbara was like, and wished they were not giving her so much information about my vulnerable points. There she sat, fondling one of her chihuahuas, or stroking one of Friskie's able-bodied spaniel siblings, who ran in and out of the room, snuffling, and yapping and farting.

The room was by now adorned with quite a collection of Norman Wilson ware, bowls and vases, whose clean lines and glazes, part art deco, part oriental, reminiscent of a night sky, or shimmering with lustre, were to be seen on chimneypieces, tables and shelves.

'Once when I was sailing to Madeira, I dived off the ship into the sea!' Norman boasted. 'Andrew seems more timid.'

Next day, when the parents had driven back to Staffordshire in the Bentley and normal Hillstone life resumed, Barbara would have me on the high diving board with an umbrella pointed at my arse, forcing me further and further along the board until – over and over again – THE BIGGER SPLASH. Over and over again.

'Again, Ma!' Jill would call from the side.

What abusers know, and what is so difficult for anyone to understand who has never been abused, is the shame felt by the victim. This is evidently multiplied a thousandfold in the case of rape victims, but even in the case of ordinary bullying, beating, wanking, routine torture, you cannot be easily persuaded to tell of it. You felt – in my case still feel – shame.

The names of those who were going to be swished were read out before breakfast. Their torment lay an hour in advance. Before it happened, they would have to eat their breakfast and attend chapel. In Rudolph's study the canes were kept, melodramatically, behind a curtain. Almost every child in the dining room knew what lay in store for the victims, but, such is the strange psychology of these things, one always slightly despised the victims, who, with difficulty, were to be seen eating their way through lumpy, viscous, grey porridge (salty, for Rudolph was a proud Scot, with his Edinburgh University BA), followed by some flaccid pieces of bacon, very undercooked, floating in rank, sour lard.

After the breakfast, and after playtime, we would be marched into the chapel, and Rudolph would appear in his BA gown, covering the very well-cut suits, pepper-and-salt grey tweed in coldest winter, or lovat green worsted, or delicate Prince of Wales checks. He had silvery hair, bushy dark eyebrows and a prissy, feminine-seeming pink face.

That handsome head was brimming with nonsense bordering on insanity. Upon arrival at the school, each child was given a small printed booklet entitled NOTES FOR BOYS. It contained such pieces of information as 'A gentleman is one who uses a butter-knife, even when alone'. A gentleman did and didn't do a wide range of things. For example, he never punctuated an envelope. Any cad putting a comma after '10 Downing Street' would be letting down the school. Clearly, there was no etiquette which prevented a gentleman from raping a nine-year-old child, but woe betide anyone who put commas on envelopes, or who addressed their mother as Mrs Jean Wilson rather than Mrs Norman Wilson.

The school library was filled with stories of male heroism: Captain Scott, Sir John Franklin et al. The only fiction was G. A. Henty or Captain W. E. Johns. We were only allowed to read books from the school library. When a Puffin of *Tom Sawyer* was discovered by an officious matron among my belongings, out came Rudolph's cane from behind the curtain in his study. And out came the tube.

The discovery of Dickens (I've written about this in my book about him) was a revelation. We could read him in English classes, selected chapters from *Oliver Twist* and *Nicholas Nickleby*, revealing to me not merely the saving power of literature but a lesson even more valuable. They brought the subversive knowledge that human grotesques such as Barbara and Rudolph, as well as being terrifying, were also ridiculous. They could cause suffering, but they could not compel you to take them seriously. Since Hillstone, I have never taken any authority figures seriously.

When someone causes another person deliberate pain, an undoubted bond is formed. There is no vestige in my nature of sado-masochism, and if there is violence in a television drama, I have to leave the room, particularly if a child is being beaten or caned. Between me and Barbara, however, there was a relationship which was almost a *tendresse*. She knew how homesick I was. On a Sunday evening, when I'd watched the tail-lights of the Bentley pull into the evening traffic, Barbara knew how close to tears I would be. My capacity for grief fascinated her. From my angle, her interest felt like a kind of sympathy. On such evenings, when my face was still blotched with tears, and we had taken part in Evensong with its inevitably moving hymn tunes, Barbara would ask me back to her drawing room for half an hour or so, to play records on her gramophone. She knew that Harry Belafonte's 'Island in the Sun' would set me off. Thus, when she had seated me directly opposite her and given me a mug of cocoa, she would put on this disc. Her right hand would hold her face; her large gypsy eyes would stare soulfully, and she would stare and stare as my tears flowed. On these occasions, I felt I was very special to her.

Sometimes, I ask myself this question. Suppose I was thirty years younger and all these things had taken place during the era when child abuse had been publicly recognized as evil? What if the Barbour-Simpsons had become the subject of police inquiries? What if I had been approached and asked to give evidence? Would I have said yes?

Partly because the abuses doled out to me by Rudolph were so minor, my answer to the last question is no. I only heard much, much later (as I have said) about his rapes. But it is not just because I was not seriously molested that I would not go into court to condemn the Barbour-Simpsons. It is because I can remember those evenings with the Harry Belafonte record. In spite of everything, Barbara was a sort of friend. More than this. Hindsight makes me think that her marriage must have been hell, and God knows what it must have been like to be the headmaster's daughter, if she had contemplated marrying Rudolph. Dickens has taught me that it is redemptive to view human beings as grotesques, as puppets in a theatre show.

Besides, as a child, you accept, very largely, the cards that have been dealt to you. It does not occur to you that you could change them; and that is for the very good reason that you COULD NOT CHANGE THEM. That's the chief difference between the suffering of children and that of grown-ups. It is the chief reason – again, Dickens reveals this so often – that children are better than adults at coping with suffering. Believing that they can cure or remove their unhappiness only adds to the misery for millions of grown-ups: this is one of the many reasons why therapists, in my observation, tend to increase, rather than diminish, the sum of human misery.

At the beginning of the holidays – eight weeks without canings, eight weeks without Hillstone, its smells, its pains, its atmosphere of oppression and evil – I had returned home with the happy thought that I would be reunited with Blakie. On all previous returns, there she had been, and I had rushed into her arms unaware of how either my father or my mother must have felt when they witnessed these outpourings of love. This time, there was no Blakie. I did not dare ask. When Norman returned from the works, he had asked Jean whether she had told me the News.

'I'm afraid Blakie ...' his voice trailed ... 'She's been rather naughty.'

'What?'

'She was found stealing,' Jean replied. 'In a shop. She'd been doing it regularly. They had no choice but to prosecute.'

'But she's not in ...'

'Once they rang the police, the shop had to prosecute.'

'But she's not ... she's not in prison?'

'Daddy had to go to speak to the magistrates in the court.'

'Of course,' Norman resumed, 'I told them how fond we were of her. There'd never been any pilfering from us.'

'Only,' Jean began.

They spoke of mysterious sums of money which had sometimes gone missing. Jeannie had once lost a ten shilling note from her bedroom.

Fury welled in me at these accusations.

'But, Blakie ...'

'She's not in prison,' said Norman.

'She was crying so much,' Jean said, 'when she told us about it. But we could not keep her on. Not after that.'

'You mean ... you mean that ...'

'Blakie won't be coming to us any more,' Norman said.

It is only as I write these words, sixty years later, that I realize I never knew Blakie's Christian name. I never asked my parents about her again. Sister Mary Mark told me many years later, in a letter, that Blakie had managed to get another job, in a supermarket; but that must have been some years later, after we had left Stone. There were no such things as supermarkets in the golden age of my childhood.

———

Retrospect makes it obvious to me that something at Hillstone would snap, though it did not do so until the following summer. Before this dramatic episode, a painful episode in the picturesque Cotswold village of Broadway. What hell those school outings must have been for my mother and father! She, who hated being away from home, suffered from motion sickness and anorexic panic in hotel dining rooms; he, who had no idea how to cope with 'scenes', and who knew that when the supposed treat was over and the little boy was driven back to school, there would be blubbing at the gate. We would all do our best, however, on these occasions, and there we were sitting at a table for three in the Lygon Arms, Broadway, eating (two of us) roast of the day, while Norman told a puzzled waiter that his wife would not, as such, be eating. The waiter had then tactlessly made it all worse by suggesting that maybe an omelette? A light salad, perhaps?

The high point of these hotel luncheons, in the days before the Food Revolution, was the arrival of the Sweet Trolley. The trifle was what one had one's eye on, lashings of Bird's custard and whipped cream atop a very sweet fruit jelly, the rubberier the better. Of course, one sat patiently while a waitress recited all the other options – leathery apple tart and so on – we were still in an era where there were not even profiteroles, nor, I think, Black Forest Gateau.

One felt a bit sick after so much trifle, but here we all were again, standing outside the hotel on the pavement. Norman was proposing a visit to Slimbridge Wildfowl Centre. An anecdote hung on this. Peter Scott, ornithologist founder of the sanctuary, was famed in that alternative universe populated by the majority of the human race as the son of Captain Scott of the Antarctic. In Norman's head, however, there was some 'famous occasion' in which Peter Scott had been at school with, or befriended, or annoyed some Wedgwood or another. On this occasion, rather than allowing the gleeman to continue his lay, I had interrupted to say I did not want to go to Slimbridge. I had not planned to say this; it just came bursting out of me.

A look of panic in the forget-me-not eyes.

'Honest-LEE ...'

'I don't want to go to Slimbridge, I don't want to go ANYWHERE.' A tantrum was brewing. I was too old for tantrums, but I was now drumming the bonnet of the Bentley with my fists and screaming that I hated Hillstone, did not want them to drive me back there, never wanted to see the place ever again.

'*Please ... please take me h-o-o-o-me!*'

I was by now completely out of control. I do remember my mother saying they should listen to what I was attempting to say, and Norman, poor man, paralysed with horror at this display, trying to explain that one could not just leave school, that we all had moments of discomfort. Why, there were days when he thought he would just 'pack it all in' and not drive to the works, if Jos was in one of his bad moods.

I do not remember how they persuaded me to get back into the car, though I do remember them quarrelling when they had done so. Jean said they should drive me back to Staffordshire and reconsider the matter, Norman arguing that I must return to the school and tough it out.

It was a summer evening. No longer weeping, but numbed, I attended Evensong. Rudolph, in the green academic hood trimmed

with fur, and the Edinburgh BA gown, had led in the tall figure of a
suffragan bishop who had a strong Scottish accent. I was fascinated
by the bishop's rig – what my friend John Lucas would call a House
of Lords outfit, a long white rochet with gathered, sixteenth-
century sleeves, and a black shiny chimere. They were clothes that
might have been seen at the court of Henry VIII.

'John the Baptist was borrrrn into the worrrrld for a purpose –
and sae are we all – all borrrn into this worrrrld for a purrrpose!'

For some time now I had realized it would be unendurable to
remain at Hillstone under the Barbour-Simpson regime. There had
been two recent breakouts. A boy of partly German, partly South
African, origin had been picked up trying to hitch a lift on the
main road to Worcester. But there had been another boy who had
somehow managed to get on a train to London and been allowed
by his family to leave.

I did not plan to get myself sacked, but there must have been
some logic working inside me by instinct. There was no point in
appealing to Norman – he would not let me leave. The only way
out was the sack.

What happened next would not have occurred if I had not spent
years in a state of inward rebellion.

The dining room was divided into tables, each one of them
representing a 'house'. These 'houses', like many things at Hillstone,
were figments of the headmaster's imagination. There were no
house buildings, or house tutors or housemaster, but we were each
assigned a house, named after a British naval hero – Anson, Blake,
Collingwood, Drake, Effingham, Frobisher, Grenville.

I was Anson, which meant I sat on Table One, presided over
by Barbara.

Breakfast was, even by Hillstone standards, especially disgusting that
day, the porridge lumpier, the slimy bacon even more undercooked
than usual. One little boy at our table was still struggling with the
porridge when the bacon was brought to the table.

Barbara, in one of her fluffy mohair numbers, a billowing
magenta-coloured housecoat, was in the custom of bringing her
post to the table, and having opened each envelope with a silver

paperknife she would survey their contents through a pair of reading glasses, which she kept suspended on a golden chain round her neck. But now, her attention had been diverted from her mail. She spied the little boy with his head still bowed over his bowl of unfinished slime.

She stood up and told him to bring the bowl to her end of the table, and to finish his porridge in front of her. Trembling, he brought the bowl, but with the first attempt to swallow a salty spoonful of this muck, he gagged, and spewed.

'Now, eat,' she said calmly.

Rashly, and praised be rashness for it, I found myself standing up and walking towards the pair, the shivering boy, vomit still on his lips, and the impressive Gypsy Queen with her large, seductively cruel eyes. No thought was required. I picked up the cereal bowl with its mixture of cold porridge and warm sick and hurled it at her. The bright magenta housecoat, the reading specs, the sallow cheeks, even wisps of her raven-dyed hair were spattered, and the bowl was in her lap.

In *Nicholas Nickleby* this would have been followed by a school rebellion, but I was frogmarched out of the hall by Barbara, across the tarmac to Rudolph's study, where, with her watching, the walloping of all wallopings was administered. Exhausted and tear-blotched, I was then incarcerated in 'the San'. The matron there was an Irishwoman, not entirely unamiable. Her words, 'You're for it, you know that?', were accompanied by a smile. Was there an element of conspiracy here?

Lying on the bed in the San, I was calculating the hours it would take. Barbara would have rung Daddy to explain I'd been sacked. Mummy or Daddy would then have to reach Malvern – that would take two or three hours, probably. By teatime, though, I'd be gone.

But the hours passed, and no one came.

It was decades later, indeed, only after Norman had died, that I heard what had happened. He had pleaded with Barbara on the telephone. Begged her not to sack me. In the late afternoon the school doctor, one of the weak, besotted men who were in Barbara's thrall, came and gave me a Valium.

21. Little Bryan

Every week of my life, when at boarding school, I wrote a letter home. For the first few years at Hillstone, these letters were dictated (by the master on duty) records of matters of the utmost indifference to myself, the performances of various school teams in matches against other private schools in Malvern. Every week, without fail, Jean would type me a letter on her Imperial portable, two sides of blue Basildon Bond paper. If Norman was at home, he would add a short note of his own to her envelope, penned in his spidery, beautiful italic. These were as sparsely worded as my mother's letters were chatty. They were impersonal, and made reference either to current affairs (in which I was as little interested as in rugger matches against the Downs or Wells House) or to the weather. 'Selwyn Lloyd's Budget looks promising.' When not at home, Norman would send me postcards from New York, Vienna or the Italian lakes. These would end, 'Your Uncle Jos sends his love, Yrs affctly, Daddy'.

Monday was the day when these letters would arrive, so it was a surprise, one December day later in the week, to receive an envelope typed by Jean with a Worcester postmark. The letter informed me that Mr Barbour-Simpson had given permission for me to leave early for the Christmas holidays. I should, however, be prepared for some changes. We no longer lived in Stone. We had moved to Worcester. Daddy had left Wedgwood.

You would expect, from what had been written in earlier chapters, that I would be delighted, and interested, in this letter – delighted to be going home early, and fascinated to hear that Daddy had left Wedgwood, an event as unlikely and as full of foreboding as it would be to hear that the ravens had left the Tower of London.

In fact, I read the letter with a thud of disappointment. I would be leaving two weeks early, two weeks that could have been spent in the art room with Miss Rich.

She was a phenomenon, who had arrived that term. Not only did I now want to visit the art room every day, and to be a painter when I grew up. I hung on every word she spoke, feasted on every minute in her company. She spoke of other worlds. She had lately been to Spain and met Salvador Dalí. She told me about Picasso. Loitering in the art room at the end of lessons, or during spare afternoons, offering to help her wash jam jars and brushes, or to lay out paper or craft materials for later lessons, I'd also hear what she had been reading. Unaware of the ban on books not written by Captain Johns or G. A. Henty, she lent me things to read. Yevtushenko's poems, in an English translation, the poems of e. e. cummings, *The Catcher in the Rye*.

I had not enjoyed reading for years, not since devouring Hugh Ross Williamson's series of Saints' Lives, and becoming obsessed by *The Imitation of Christ*, which Sister Mary Mark gave my mother. Now, I was truly drawn to reading. And my education began. Drawn, too, to an ironical way of looking at the world. When I gave her back a volume of Thurber cartoons and writings, I had learned that humour did not have to be 'jokes' or 'funny stories' with punchlines, such as Norman repeated. That irony, which had been displayed by Eric Woods in Marshall & Snelgrove over tea one day, was something that could colour a whole outlook on existence. Miss Rich was an ironist, and often things she said or quoted would only register after we had parted, and some turn of phrase would 'click' and I would 'get' what she had meant.

Short dark hair, cut in a fringe across her brow. Usually black T-shirts or roll-top sweaters. Black trousers and pumps. Her delicately freckled boyish face was framed by specs. I wanted to spend all my time with her. Not just school time. My life. Two weeks that might have been spent in the art room hearing about Salinger – she'd offered to lend me his latest, *Franny and Zooey* – were now to be spent 'at home', a place that no longer contained Blakie, and which was not even in Stone.

Curiosity was, nevertheless, excited by Jean's letter, and there was an undoubted joy in packing my trunk early and having it sent ahead. I was not to be fetched by car. I was to walk to the splendid Victorian railway station in Great Malvern and Jean would meet the train at Worcester Foregate Street.

In my boat on the Severn with Norman.

Kepax, the new (rented) house, was about four times the size of Stonefield Cottage. We – they – remained there little over a year, while they looked about for somewhere to settle down. They were unable to settle, of course, since Norman's roots were in Staffordshire, and his entire *raison d'être* was, on the one hand, designing and manufacturing ceramics and, on the other, being the friend, attendant and junior to Josiah. Without these two pillars to his existence, his life had no foundation or purpose. Where, or how, they lived could no longer be defined by what Norman did, because he had nothing to do. They would devote the rest of their days (in his case over twenty years of life) to moving house. Norman, who in my eyes at least had been a personage of power, even of glamour, returning from New York or Europe, or, when at the works, recounting the visits of royalty and politicians, was now a figure of lonely pathos. Jean, no doubt finding him as irritating as ever, nonetheless needed the help of a twelve-year-old boy to cope with what appeared to be a nervous breakdown.

The story of the debacle that led to his resignation as managing director, and his accepting a non-executive directorship on insultingly generous terms (insulting because it demonstrated that they could not wait to be rid of him), emerged, and was repeated, over and over again for the rest of his life as, year by year, inflation gnawed the pension to a pittance.

Josiah Wedgwood V, who had, with the help of his young cousins and of Norman, rescued the old family firm, had undergone the inevitable twentieth-century transformation: from the brilliant Marxist economist he had become a Hayek monetarist. Uncle Jos's career was a metaphor, really, of the politico-economic history of Britain in his lifetime. George Orwell with crystalline succinctness told the story of how the beautiful idea of socialism, as it dawned in the minds of the old shire horses on Animal Farm, turned by an inexorable series of events into the Stalinist horror story so that, by the end of the parable, the murderous pigs who had seized control were indistinguishable from the human beings who had once been their owners. No one, to my knowledge, has written the *Animal Farm* of capitalism, the story of how, to limit one's observations to Britain, the healthy desire for a small family business to be independent of the state, or the benign wish to preserve the workforce from the ruinous effects of hyper-inflation, could, within a couple of generations, bring about a transformation no less absolute, no less destructive, than the Russian Revolution. We associate this change with Margaret Thatcher in the 1980s, but the seeds of the thing were sown much earlier.

The paradoxes of political upheaval make the Muse of History appear to be the eternal satirist. Mrs Thatcher, who extolled the virtues of her father, Alderman Roberts, and his small corner shop in Grantham, ushered in an era when such shops would be cruelly bankrupted by supermarkets. The so-called Conservatives, far from conserving, carved up Britain with motorways, polluted its farmland with dangerous chemicals and, in their avarice, destroyed all that had made up Britain's wealth in the first two generations of the Industrial Revolution, namely technical skill, exercised in innumerable fields – in producing ships, textiles, steel, iron, pottery, glass, paper, bicycles, pianos, screws, lawnmowers, hats, umbrellas, etc., etc. These things had all been made well, and in abundance, in Britain before the 1980s. Now, they are all made badly, in China.

Uncle Jos, being the clever man he was, could see that Josiah Wedgwood and Sons, at the beginning of the 1960s, was a well-run family business. Wedgwood was a household name. The quality of the goods was consistently high. In America, where business had been ticking over satisfactorily since the war, profits had begun to soar. This was since the departure of the smoothypants charmer Hensleigh Wedgwood, who'd retired in order to write, with his umpteenth wife, Barbara, the history of the family. He had been replaced by a spiv called Arthur Bryan, a figure always spoken of by Norman with some loftiness, but who possessed the Midas touch.

Norman, in those last couple of years as managing director, would return from America with Jos astounded by how 'little Bryan' was making money for the firm. He knew nothing of ceramics, little Bryan. Had started as a bank clerk at Barclays in Stoke.

'He couldn't tell the difference between the Portland Vase and a packet of cornflakes!' Norman would laugh delightedly, and in those days, admiringly. 'But look at him! We're selling pots to the Yanks as if they *were* bloody cornflakes.'

'Why do they have to be "something" cornflakes, why not just cornflakes?' Jean would say crossly. 'It's so coarse, swearing all the time.'

Jos, who understood money – few better than the youngest ever board member of the Bank of England – began to see that the works at Barlaston, with their happy workforce of two thousand or so, their high global reputation and their respectable profits, were an 'asset', insufficiently exploited. But if Wedgwood were to be floated as a public company on the stock market? Imagine what wealth could accrue! Not least for the shareholders, the majority of whom, at that date, were a small number of members of the family.

At first, when he and Jos began to mull over these things over their evening tipple of gin with Noilly Prat, and their innumerable cigs, Norman did not realize that stock market flotation was a serious proposition. He thought it was the sort of dream that any householder might half entertain, mentally translating the cash value of a flat in a European city inhabited on a humdrum daily basis into some Shangri-La in the South Seas.

By 1961, however, the idea had come to possess Josiah very seriously indeed and, after Bryan joined the board, the matter was put to the vote at an AGM. Norman had imagined that the other directors would share his concerns. In fact, the vote was close, but the majority went along with the decision to become a public company. Once you had floated the company on the stock market, the short-term consequence was that a handful of Wedgwood cousins made a huge sum of money. But they were also laying themselves open to takeover.

Such a firm changed its very nature overnight. Vulnerable to takeover itself, it also felt tempted to take over other firms, and to make a conglomerate. Norman, before all this happened, argued with passion that this move would lead to a fall in production standards, as the prime motive came to be making money, not pots. It would destroy the Potteries as a district, as rival firms either went out of business or were taken over. The livelihoods of the workforce, not just at Wedgwood but in the entire region, would be jeopardized.

All his fears were justified. Wedgwood did indeed become a public company. The few original shareholders, Jos and his cousins, went from being moderately prosperous people to becoming, overnight, extremely rich. Arthur Bryan, who took over as managing director, and eventually became the chairman of the firm, went round the Potteries hoovering up the small firms, asset-stripping. The Wedgwood conglomerate now took possession of Coalport, Royal Doulton, Johnsons and so many other small firms. In every case, the pattern would be the same. Bryan, or one of his henchmen, would turn up at the little factory to address the workforce. Be assured! Although you have now become part of our great conglomerate, you are safe with us. You will still continue to come here to work. There are no plans to make anyone redundant.

Then the asset-stripping would begin. The little firm with its pot-banks would be shut down. In most cases demolished. Sometimes just left as a pathetic industrial ruin, nettle-blown and dusty. Some – most – of the potters would be made redundant. Those who had been taught how to paint cups or stick handles on to teapots by their mothers – mothers who had learned the same skills from their mothers and grandmothers and great-grandmothers – would be out of work, competing for jobs as checkout clerks in supermarkets and petrol stations. When Norman was forcibly retired in 1962, over 75,000 women and men worked in the Potteries. Now, as I write these words, fewer than 15,000 do so. Wedgwood was eventually taken over by Waterford Glass, and in 2009 it went into receivership. The pensions of former employees were at risk, and the judge who presided over the sorry debacle made the ruling that every discoverable asset of the ruined firm must be realized to help these people. Quite rightly so. It was discovered that a very small number of employees at the Wedgwood Museum had been put on the company pension scheme – which had always, since it started, been kept quite separate from the factory. This meant that the museum was now the firm's only remaining 'asset' and that, in order to pay the pensions, it must be broken up and sold.

Josiah I, Owd Wooden Leg, had started this museum, with his collection of minerals, his cabinets full of samples, his thousands of attempts at the perfect glaze, his many notebooks and letters, as a record of one of the great geniuses of the Enlightenment. The museum had been added to in each generation, coming down to our own times, with a glorious collection of some of the most beautiful objects ever made in the British Isles, including a whole glass cabinet devoted to pots by Norman Wilson.

As it happens, the museum was saved, through a combination of circumstances: inflation reducing the amount owed to the pensioners, the willingness of the public to contribute money and the enterprise and imagination of historian Tristram Hunt, biographer of Josiah I, at that stage MP for Stoke-on-Trent Central and now the director of the V&A Museum.

People matter more than pots. Sir Arthur Bryan's distinguished career as chairman of Wedgwood, and Lord Lieutenant of the County of Staffordshire, managed to destroy many of both – pots and people. It was no thanks to him that, after his demise, a Scandinavian firm bought the name of the company and took over the poor old factory built by Norman and Jos, demolished it and ruined the beautiful park with a housing estate.

The anti-capitalist parable here told could be replicated across the known world; and it could be argued that the Potteries would have been destroyed even if Sir Arthur Bryan had never been born. Nevertheless, I do sometimes feel sorry that I cannot share Dante Alighieri's belief in a literal, physical hell. I am not naturally vindictive, but it would be satisfying to know that somewhere in the Inferno's less comfortable circles Little Bryan was fixed, while some Dantean demons, mouthing appalling insults in the Stokey dialect, were perpetually cramming wet clay into his greedy chops, while some others, with even riper, crueller language, were shoving red-hot pokers up his arse.

22. Acqua Non Fizzimento

Now something really dramatic happened. They had moved to Malvern. From the Worcester house, which was much too large, they had lighted upon a tiny cottage called St Anne's, perched on a hill overlooking the town. Their approach on this, as on all subsequent, and frequent, house removals, was to hold on to the enormous lumps of brown furniture which had been suitable for the house in Burston.

Norman had the only sleeping quarters of reasonable proportions. My room was scarcely a room, more a cupboard. I was not fussed.

Norman's spirits had lifted a little with the thaw and the coming of spring. He had nothing else to do, so he was encouraged by his wife to go on solitary motoring holidays in Wales. Jean made friends with the mother of one of my Hillstone chums – they also lived in the town.

One day John, the friend, went to the Scripture and Latin master, boozy old Sir Conan Aske, and told him a story. John was in a state. Rudolph Barbour-Simpson had told him it was time he learned the facts of life. The headmaster suggested to this twelve-year-old that he should remove his trousers and underwear while he was instructed.

Sir Conan told the child to leave the school at once, and to run over the hills to his mother in West Malvern. The mother, as soon as she heard what had happened, telephoned my mother, and the two women came to the school to meet Sir Conan.

We'd always rather mocked Sir Conan, largely because he was so often visibly drunk and his lessons, which were supposed to teach us Caesar's *Gallic Wars* and the Bible, consisted of reminiscences, often rather interesting, of his army experiences in Palestine. On this occasion, however, he came up trumps. He summoned the very nice music teacher, Mr Taylor, a man we had all liked since his arrival in the school, and a young history teacher. This trio met the two mothers at the school gate.

Sir Conan said he had been waiting for an actual complaint to come from one of the boys before doing what he now proposed. To the two women, he spelt out what would happen if they called the police. Rudolph would deny the charge and my twelve-year-old friend would undoubtedly be put through a humiliating couple of days in court being accused by a clever barrister of telling malicious lies. The jury would be reminded that Rudolph was a Justice of the Peace and that Barbara's father was the headmaster of Harrow. In that town full of boarding schools, the Barbour-Simpsons were almost aristocracy. If, however, my friend's mother agreed, the three teachers would insist on Rudolph's resignation, with immediate effect, on the grounds of ill health.

This they did. And so came to an end, really, a part of my own inner nightmare. Norman and Jean did not *know* what had been happening to me for the previous five years. Jean, for all her capacity to bring misery into a harmless domestic scene, for all her manias and phobias, was also possessed of a paradoxical common sense. She was what the Germans call *bodenständig*. Norman, when he heard the news about what Rudolph had attempted to do, felt tricked. He insisted that Jean should type a letter on the Imperial portable, demanding the return of all the bowls and vases he had given them over the years. I doubt whether she wrote such a letter. He also told her it was not a subject he wished to hear mentioned ever again. He told her, however, that it was time that I was told the facts of life, and would she please do it.

The beginnings of such a conversation, about which my mother and I laughed when we recalled it in her old age, made me run out of the little Malvern house. I leapt on my bike and freewheeled through the steep main street of the town, only returning hours later. As the widow Jean laughingly agreed, choosing that moment of my personal life to tell me about sex was a bad case of closing the stable door after the horse had bolted. Hillstone boys had been confronted, in gruesome form, by evidences of sexual psychosis for years, and a few embarrassed remarks about the onset of puberty or the reproductive processes were unlikely to set matters to rights.

The remainder of my time at that school were happy and idle. It had been decided that I should be sent to Rugby, which specified, if you sat the scholarship exam, that you should know Greek. Sir Conan had left the school and married one of the matrons (who fascinated us because she had lost the index finger of her right hand). The baronet was replaced by a Congregationalist lay reader with a distressing tendency to tell us about his stamp collection. He knew no Greek, so taught me by puzzling over an elementary correspondence course in that language.

A new English master, replacing bald old Mephy, was a wonderful improvement. Major Manson was a bushy-eyebrowed, gentle figure who wore blue blazers and silken cravats, and read to us Saki short stories and essays by G. K. Chesterton. In one of my unwise fits of clearing out, perhaps when leaving my first marriage, I threw away all my old exercise books and all my early efforts at prose or rime, and all my diaries. They'd have no interest for anyone rather than myself, but there is one which I often recall, and which I wish I still owned.

We'd been given new notebooks for 'composition' and I'd written an essay bristling with supposedly Chestertonian paradoxes. The Major returned all our work when he had marked it, handing us each an exercise book as we sat at our desks. A very faint smile flickered as he placed my notebook down. When I opened it, I found he had pasted into the inside cover a watercolour. It was a chastely draped Greek lady, classicism of the era of Rex Whistler or Felix Kelly, exercised by the Major himself. Who was the lady? The inscription explained, 'This, the first volume of the works of A. N. Wilson, is dedicated to Clio, the Muse of History.' Very few presents have given me more pleasure.

Sister Mary Mark began my education. Then there was a Dark Age in which I do not believe I learned anything of use or value. I learned only to distrust authority, to fear the worst of grown-ups; and what I learned of sex and violence and their interconnection must have had a purely corrupting effect on my inner being. Major Manson and

Miss Rich represent the Renaissance, the coming of New Learning. Ragingly in love with Miss Rich, I spent as much time as I could in the art room. She suggested I paint a mural, and because I'd by now read Joyce Cary's *The Horse's Mouth*, another present from her, I doubtless imagined I was re-enacting the career of Gulley Jimson, the painter in that wonderful novel. A weird woman, clothed and with a hairstyle copied from the gyrating teenagers seen on *Top of the Pops*, bestrode the huge wall in the art room, the whole painting being a good eight by eight feet. In its colours and overcrowded composition it derived from *Les Demoiselles d'Avignon*. I knew that, in the course of the many hours I had spent painting it, during which she sat and spoke to me, I had grown up. Now that various things had happened to me, various aspects of my character had been determined.

The swooping ecstasy, the wrenching torment, of loving Miss Rich led my soul into a new world. My creative life feels as if it has been fed by the repeated experience of falling in love. At the age of seventy I am still in the same state of puzzlement over the matter as was felt by my twelve-year-old consciousness, i.e. not knowing, quite, what this condition is, what it means, why, at some moments, the very thought of another person can make me swoon. Very often, in fact I should say in the majority of cases, the other person has not even known that I was in love with them. My 'love life', if by that is meant sexual activity, has been extremely limited. Sometimes I have found my love reciprocated and there has been an affair, but such occasions have been very infrequent.

Being in love, however, is usually different. And I find that it is a feeling that never completely goes away. A chance encounter with an 'old friend', or the discovery of a letter used as a bookmark, or a dream of the once-beloved, will set off the mania all over again, so that for a week or so I am mad about them once more. This painful but stimulating habit of the inner being began when I fell in love with Miss Rich.

I knew something had happened to me when I saw my brother's face in the art room. He had returned to England for a short visit and, having heard of my mural, he came down to the school to see it. He turned to Miss Rich, who must have been about his age, and with a knowing smile, said, 'It's very good.' For this stylish young man, who had just come from Paris, to be meeting Miss Rich felt great. Hillstone was now seen for the little place it had always been. Art, and Miss Rich, had flung open the windows into the great world. She was sizing my brother up and thinking he was bohemian and groovy. *Incipit Vita Nuova.*

Some months earlier, in spring, Norman had taken me on my first visit abroad. In Paris we stayed in the rue des Beaux-Arts, on the opposite side of the street from the hotel where Oscar Wilde had died. Sharon Alexander, a beautiful American pianist studying at the Conservatoire, lived in that famous place, in those days still pleasingly shabby. This was supposedly the scene where the playwright gasped, 'This wallpaper and I are fighting a duel to the death. Either it goes, or I do' – before expiring.

Norman declared the young pianist to be an absolute Bobby Dazzler. Stephen, excitingly and visibly in love with Sharon, was a gentle, affable guide, revealing to us the Tuileries, the Louvre, the Luxembourg Gardens, the Île de la Cité, La Sainte-Chapelle and so much else.

Norman was so happy during that week. He loved being abroad. He loved showing me the galleries. In those days of innocence, I

Me, my brother and my future sister-in-law, Sharon Alexander, in Paris, 1962.

loved his fondness for the sunlit Impressionists in the Tuileries. (On my return to Hillstone, I discovered, from the expression on Miss Rich's face, that they were not quite the ticket. Cézanne was OK, but Renoir … !!!?) With my intellectually snobbish antennae, I could tell that Monet was for middlebrows, but while I was in Paris, this had never occurred to me, while Norman extolled the virtues of the bright skies and smudged visions of that painter.

Stephen was good at choosing restaurants. We went to a different one every day, but the one to which I wanted to return was Polish – it was called Chez Woja (spelling?). On our first visit I had been fascinated by an obese Polish workman forking in a large bowlful of radishes as his hors d'oeuvre.

Sharon tactfully spent each day at the Conservatoire. It was the first, and it would prove to be the only, time that Norman and his two sons spent together as a threesome. In the evenings we were joined by the Bobby Dazzler. It was agreed that one night we'd go to a grander type of restaurant – could it have been Maxim's itself? Sharon wanted us to meet a friend of hers from back home – home being Eldorado, Little Rock, Arkansas. It was the only evening when the sunny side of Norman's nature was obscured by awkwardness, bursting, when we had returned to our hotel *à deux*, into anger. The expressed reason was the bill: how could the friend from Arkansas – was his name Jack? – have had the effrontery to suggest this swanky place? Dinner for five of us! These were the days when English visitors to France were only allowed very limited resources, and could only take £50 abroad in currency.

As we lay on our single beds with their pale grey (I thought charming) repro Louis Quinze bedheads, Norman raged against the young man.

It was clear to me, even at the age of twelve, that Sharon was nuts about my brother and that Jack, or whatever his name was, if he had any aspirations, was simply wasting his time. Norman saw it as an assault on our family pride to have invited a rival to dinner. This awful oaf was trying to steal the Bobby Dazzler. Well, that was what was *said*. I wonder now whether one of the reasons for his anger was that the young man, whatever his name or intentions, had failed to recognize the conversational rules of a dinner table when Norman was in anecdotal mode. This young man had interrupted. Commented. Questioned. It was not what the audience was supposed to do when the gleeman had strummed his lyre and begun to unlock the word-hoard.

'I don't get it,' he had said amiably. 'Non fizzy menno?'

'Mento.'

'Menno's not an Italian word. I mean, for Chrissakes, he should've jus' stuck to English right, this Josh guy? Or maybe jus' said Acqua Minerale. Any fool could remember that.'

Some months later, when I was back at school, the news came that Stephen and the Bobby Dazzler were to be married, at Great Malvern Priory, one of the most beautiful churches in England.

The ceremony would be solemnized by the vicar, Canon Lunt, whose tiny ears had reduced all the confirmation candidates at Malvern Girls' College (my sister Jeannie among them) to cruel mirth. He asked Stephen how many were expected at the event, and when he learned that it was only going to be a dozen, he suggested a side chapel would be appropriate for such maimed rites. No, said Stephen, who has a sense of occasion: the high altar, beneath the huge medieval stained-glass window, which is in the same league as Chartres or York, would be the place where they plighted their troth.

So we found ourselves – the parents, Sharon's mother, who had flown in from the United States, and some aunts and uncles. Jeannie was in California. The best man was Edward Morris, later director of the Walker Art Gallery in Liverpool.

When they had been at Rugby together, Stephen and Morris both loathed being in the Combined Cadet Force. One day, the master who was in charge of this boy army let fall that they were all volunteers. The boys asked whether this was strictly true. Volunteers? Yes, said this master – Jack Baiss, the geography teacher, formerly a colonel in the Royal Artillery. They had volunteered to serve Her Majesty. At the end of their time at the school, they would collect Cert A, a certificate which proved that the class system was still alive and well in 1950s Britain. Cert A was what you clutched if a war broke out and you had to present yourself to a recruiting sergeant. Rather than having to do your Basic Training with the proletariat, you were whooshed straight into Officer Training.

'So, sir' – this was Morris – 'let's get this straight. The Corps is actually voluntary?'

'Technically, yeth.'

'So' – Stephen now – 'we could actually – just leave it?'

'Yeth,' said Jack Baiss with a harrumph, 'but only if you were bwave enough to tender your wethignation to RSM Bateth.'

Bates was a soldier of the old school. When inspecting rows of boy soldiers, he really did bellow the clichés expected of a sergeant major – 'You're an 'orrible little man, what are you?' ''Orrible little man, sir.' ''Orrible little man, SERGEANT MAJOR – SIR is only, for what is SIR only for?' 'Officers, sir.' 'Officers, Sergeant Major, you 'orrible little man.'

When, ten years later, I came to the school, Bates was still there. On all weekdays except Thursday he was the School Marshal, sitting in the Porter's Lodge wearing a black gown, already a parodic relic of a vanished class. On Corps Days, Thursdays, he would be clad in immaculate battle dress, with gleaming black boots and dazzling Blanco-ed spats. By now, the twentieth century had reached the stage of Bob Dylan and the Beatles. There was Bates, yelling at adolescents his old insults and instructing them in the art of dismantling and cleaning obsolete Lee-Enfield rifles, weaponry that had not been used in the British Army since 1957. I felt, and feel, for RSM Bates sentiments that are aroused in my heart by anyone whose very existence has been overtaken by the heartless movement of history – figures like Scott's 'Old Mortality'. Hatters. Glovers. Butlers. Welsh chapel-goers. Coal miners. There is apparently no place for them in the new world. I have an instinctive love for those whose spiritual home is the last ditch. An early review of one of my novels began, 'Here's one from the "They Don't Write Them Like That Any More" school'.

Morris and Wilson were the only two boys brave enough in the history of Rugby School to tell RSM Bates that they were going to resign from the CCF. I can imagine the incomprehension and the rage in his highly coloured, close-shaven bullet head as he heard these two clever boys snootily telling him the news. He chose his dismissal of the aesthetic duo with care, emphasizing the second syllable of his final withering word.

'Nearly all boys, having served in the CCF, leave Rugby School with honour and with Cert A. You leave with nothing but igNO-minny.'

And here, perhaps only five years after that painful conversation, were the two intellectuals in Great Malvern Priory, little more than boys really, participants in a grown-up marriage ceremony.

Sixty years later, Stephen and the Bobby Dazzler are still together, still perfectly matched.

Jean Dorothy prepared a wedding breakfast in St Anne's Cottage. She did not employ caterers and, given her usual lack of willingness to take care over cooking, the achievement seems all the more remarkable. Two whole salmon were poached. Salads were prepared. Norman had bought champagne and Riesling.

In the course of the jolly little party Edward Morris, who was bearing the brunt of my father's anecdotage, crossed the room for a breather and began to speak to Jean.

'Are you excited about the move to Wales?' he asked.

'How do you mean?' She stared at him first with astonishment, and then with darkening rage.

'The new house,' Morris blundered on. 'I gather you are moving house. To Llansteffan, the little village where you once had a holiday house?'

She was about to say that Edward was mistaken, but then she looked across the room to the pink-cheeked, blue-eyed spouse, his face flushed with Riesling and with amusement at his own reminiscences. Thelma Alexander, from Eldorado, Little Rock, was being initiated into some Wedgwood lore, and was hearing about the 'famous' drive through the Nevada desert when Norman accompanied Hensleigh to Reno to obtain a divorce.

'I'd often thought of divorce before,' the old, widowed Jean told me, thirty years later. 'But at that moment, I really *did* decide to divorce him.'

23. Journalistic Debut

'I'm so glad not to be a sixteen-year-old boy.'

The remark was made to me by my housemaster, Jack Llewellyn Rumbold Baiss – he who, a decade earlier, had told my brother and Morris that they could leave the Corps if they were brave enough to explain themselves to RSM Bates.

Retrospect tells me that it would have been impossible to have a housemaster who was kinder, wiser, odder, more emotionally intelligent. But how we mocked him at the time. Aged seventy, I still find myself, when alone, saying things in 'his' voice. Upper-class-sounding, lisping, slightly camp. All forty-five boys in his house thought we could imitate it.

We were allowed to order ourselves a Sunday newspaper. Naturally, the more spiritually elevated chose the *Observer*. I asked for the *News of the World*. He called me in and said, 'I'm dithappointed. That'th all. That you ordered that particular paper.'

He made the remark about the ghastliness of the adolescent condition sitting beside me in the school sanatorium. I wasn't ill. I had been confined there because I had become a journalist. Geoff Helliwell, a junior English master who put on wonderful school plays (I was Sir Politic Would-Be in his *Volpone*), was in charge of the school mag, *The Meteor*. I was the editor. It was 1967, the Summer of Love, but the corridors of Jack Baiss's house echoed to the noise of confused adolescents, unable to stop themselves writhing, as if in front of a microphone, and 'being' the Stones or Bob Dylan. 'How does it feee—eeel?'

Baiss was right. It felt awful. Being an adolescent is to be a sort of lunatic. The moodiness. The lurching from one strongly held tomfool opinion to its total opposite in a matter of days. The sex preoccupation. The capacity for self-pity, self-aggrandizement. If this is adolescence, then I remained locked in it until my mid-thirties, until my father died and my first marriage unravelled.

The reason I'd been confined to the San was that I had devoted my first issue of *The Meteor* to the Royal Visit, timed to commemorate the school's quatercentenary – 1567–1967. I'd written an editorial with which I am sure Geoff Helliwell disagreed. To commemorate the 400 years, the school had built some grandiose gates at the entrance to The Close (the sports ground), and my leader said that these gates, and by extension the school, should be thrown open to any pupil, regardless of their ability to pay.

Presumably, what made that issue of *The Meteor* noteworthy to outside observers was not so much the views (that children should be educated regardless of their parents' bank balance) as the setting and the timing. A royal visit.

The 'disappointing' choice of Sunday newspaper had given me a whiff of the old street of shame, taught me how to write half-truths in emotional journalese. Anyone under the age of twenty-five reading that last sentence would need reminding that all this took place half a century before there was a worldwide web. Fifty years before Twitter and Instagram would allow any sixteen-year-old to share his views with the rest of the world.

The *Daily Express* was in those days still a broadsheet, still owned by Michael Foot's hero Lord Beaverbrook. Presumably a local stringer alerted the paper to my article, and they sent along a reporter to investigate. Before long, several journalists wanted an interview with the Public School Red, the boy who'd 'insulted the Queen' by saying she should open the gates to all comers. This was the moment when the headmaster decided I must be locked up in the San until the Queen's visit was safely over.

The incident taught me something unwholesome about myself. I was aglow. For the previous ten years or so, I had been putting pen to paper, and despite Norman's proud exclamation – *This boy will be another Arnold Bennett!* – not a syllable had been published. A very tiny bit of myself thinks, better to have been Emily Dickinson or Kafka, a writer whose celebrated work was all done in secret and only discovered posthumously. But, in my fantasy about such a writing life, I am considering work that would be immortal – or at the very least what Penelope Betjeman called 'worth-whoile'.

The particular drug of which I'd partaken as editor of *The Meteor* was of a different order altogether. The stringer from the *Rugby Advertiser*, who'd tipped off the *Express*, had given me a buzz such as I'd never known in my life. I'd learned the speed with which some words on the printed page could be communicated to others. This still gives me a kick. I can labour for two years on a novel and believe, when it goes to press, that it is as good as anything I ever wrote. Of course, this is a satisfying experience. But it does not give that heady buzz which still comes upon me if a national paper has rung up for an article, and I see it in print the next morning.

If I had never written that article in *The Meteor*, and never understood the excitement of cheap journalism, I should probably have been a better person.

I recall my seven years on the *Evening Standard*, my stint as 'Lucy Fer', eviscerating ecclesiastics for *Private Eye*, my career as a purveyor of Why-oh-Why articles, as they used to be known in the trade, otherwise known as 'Op Ed pieces', for the *Sunday Telegraph*, the *Independent on Sunday* and the *Daily Mail*. None of this would have happened without that adrenalin rush to the puzzled nut of the Public School Red. And when I think with gratitude of my life as a journalist – a pleasure that has been deemed a dissipation of talent by both my wives, and probably by all my children – the recollection of the Queen's visit to my old school is inevitably tinged with a bit of shame.

———

'You have long days alone until this wretched business is all over,' Baiss said. We were in the sitting room of the San. 'I was wondering if you had read *The Lord of the Rings*.'

Such was the pattern of my childhood, most 'children's literature' remained unknown to me until I began to read aloud to my own children. So I had never even heard the name Tolkien. I'd never read *The Hobbit*, and the hippy cult of him – Gandalf-is-God T-shirts and similar – were a Californian phenomenon which had not reached Rugby.

When Baiss came to see me the next day to ask how far I'd got with *The Fellowship of the Ring*, it was with something like furtive shame that I gratefully seized *The Two Towers* (the second volume in the trilogy) from his hands.

When the whole palaver of the Queen's visit to Rugby was over, I confessed to the senior English master, T. D. Tosswill, that I had not noticed time pass in the San because I had been so absorbed by *The Lord of the Rings*.

Tosswill, who had himself taught in American universities and had experienced the hippyish cult of Tolkien at first hand, wrinkled his nose, that gesture which at one and the same time pushed his silver moustache towards his nostrils and made his horn-rimmed specs slightly jump towards his forehead.

Tosswill was a male Miss Jean Brodie. Those who were admitted to his little circle became aware that books and literature connected you not merely with the inner life of the mind but also with the world – a world of famous people, whose names one had seen on the spines of books. When we imitated his voice we created parody name-drops. 'Auden – yeair – and he said this sitting in that very chair where you are sitting now ...'

Because of Tosswill, we all believed, or professed to believe, that the greatest modern novel was Malcolm Lowry's *Under the Volcano*. He expressed amazement that anyone who was learning to appreciate Malcolm Lowry, or Auden, should so cheapen their palate as to read about elves. 'Yeair, but The Professor himself, of course, is great friends with my old tutor, Nevill.' He stared as if we did not catch his drift. 'Yeair – Nevill Coghill,' he would add, for the benefit of those who were slow on the uptake.

Though it was especially from Tosswill that there came these hints of a larger world, the school itself seems, to my adult mind looking

Rugby school play. Jonson's Volpone. *I played Sir Politic Would-Be, second from left.*

back on it, to have had an astonishing capacity to attract legendarily famous figures to visit us. I belonged to two choirs, the chapel choir and the school choir, and the Temple Speech Room doubled as a concert hall. Now, when I listen to *The Dream of Gerontius*, it seems unbelievable that we sang this piece before a public audience, with Dame Janet Baker singing the Angel. Michael Tippett himself came down to conduct us in *A Child of Our Time*. Richard Crossman, the Lord President of the Council, came and talked to us about politics, Lord Montgomery of Alamein – Monty – inspected the Corps.

Yet, though these visitants from the great world came and went, they did not convey to us, as did the teaching and conversation of Tosswill, that the world was something to which you could aspire to belong. It was from Tosswill that I learned that writing, in poetry or prose, was far from being an end in itself. It could be seen as a way of getting on, an instrument that could be manipulated in the will to power. To fast-forward to the point in the narrative where I began – about to be photographed as one of the Best of Young British Novelists – they were surely all figures who had learned this morally dubious message somewhere along the road.

Shortly before my arrival, the boarding house to which I'd been assigned underwent a thorough rebuild. This necessitated many of us being billeted in private houses. Christopher Mackenzie and I, two thirteen-year-olds, were assigned to a young biology master and his wife, John and Angela Price. I met them again not so long ago at a literary festival, and I was shocked by how young they were. They must be no more than a decade older than me. So, lodging with them was a bit like staying with an older brother and sister. Angela made us Ovaltine every night when we had changed into our pyjamas. Mackenzie and I knew how lucky we were. Mackenzie was the son of a doctor at Guy's Hospital, and I often used to stay with him in the holidays. His father taught us how to do the *Times* crossword, a harmless addiction which still occupies the first half-hour of every day. Pretty Mrs Mackenzie was much younger than Jean and used to appear at regular intervals in her little car and take us out for lunch. Mackenzie in turn would come and stay with me in Wales, and our friendship lasted to the end of schooldays – even slightly beyond – certainly to the time when we both had driving licences and could enjoy a fishing holiday together, bowling round County Kerry. At one of the guest houses in Kildare we enjoyed excellent rashers and eggs, as our eyes strayed to the photographs on the mantelpiece. One was of President Kennedy, and the other was of Hitler.

When our time as lodgers chez Price came to an end, Mackenzie and I shared a study, perfectly happily. There is no ideal way to bring up children, but the advantage of sticking them in a boarding school during the adolescent years, when they and their parents were likely to drive one another nuts, is that it enforces a sense of domestic tolerance. I enjoyed the companionship of Michell House, the gossip and the laughter. With another doctor's son, Gavin Young, himself later a GP in Cumbria, I had long discussions about the meaning of life, spilling into long, probably embarrassing, correspondence during the holidays. We went on to Oxford together.

Naturally, living cheek by jowl during those turbid years, we had crushes on one another and there was a limited amount of sex, though not with any of those named above! Partly because we were carefully policed. I only had one fully fledged love affair. It lasted nearly three years, and it was, I think, 'real love' on both sides. He chiefly comes to mind now if I see a painting of King Edward VI, whom he uncannily resembled – especially the portrait that hangs in the hall at Sherborne School. As far as I am aware, no one knew of our affair, and I would never have dreamed of mentioning it to regular friends, such as Young or Mackenzie, who would, I suspect, have viewed it with a strong degree of satire.

24. A Bit of a Ruin

Such was my mother's visceral detestation of my poor aunt, we never saw much of her, except when she would come to 'spoil Christmas' with her infernally delicious mince pies, and her reminiscence, repeated each year, that she had not been to midnight mass since attending this service in Amiens Cathedral in 1917. After the death of her father – she had kept house for him in Worcester in his widowhood – she moved to Malvern, where she had a job in a restaurant. She was the woman – they always were women – who sat beside the door in a small glass case and took payment for the meals when the diners departed.

By the time my aunt reached retirement age, my brother had married and Jeannie was still in America. I had had my first term at Rugby. Norman and Jean, who had not, of course, divorced, had moved to Hill House, Llansteffan, a substantial Dutch-gabled Victorian residence overlooking the village, the church, the headland with its medieval castle and the Towy estuary, all familiar from childhood holidays in Jean's cottage on the Green, but seen here to spectacular advantage.

Norman was proud of himself, having secured the purchase of the house, which included several acres of garden and a coach house, for £2,000. He was unwilling to admit that there was anything amiss with the property for fear of conceding, in their everlasting warfare, that his wife might have been right about anything. Nevertheless, as the car, which needed several 'goes' to squeeze between the narrow gateposts, slithered in its attempts to get a grip on the muddy track to the coach house, you could see why many potential purchasers had been put off. The house itself, a hundred yards further up beyond the coach house, is perched on a sheer hillside. 'Old Parnall' – my father explained, referring to the Victorian philanthropist who had built the house – 'never got round to building a drive through the top field. It was ra—ather naughty of Francis' – the estate agent in Carmarthen – 'not to tell us there wasn't a drive.'

'Only a mad person would have bought this place,' Jean said, as we staggered almost vertically up yards of wet grass with a school trunk, a tuck box and an already brimming artist's portfolio.

It was with absolute astonishment that, in the first days of the holiday, I heard my mother suggest that her sister-in-law should come to live with us in Llansteffan. Elizabeth could have her own kitchen garden, and occupy the ground floor of the house, with a large drawing room, a bedroom, bathroom and kitchen.

I think two things motivated the *volte-face*. One was, Jean was an observant Christian who fought battles with her demons. She genuinely tried to overcome her hatred of Elizabeth, and she clearly thought, when she came back from the early service each week, that she ought to offer a home to a woman who, had she retired in Malvern, would have had no money and would have had to reside in a small council flat. The other consideration, however – for Jean was a sensible person on some levels – was the alternative: life alone with Norman. She was just over fifty years old. Norman, ten years older, was well into his anecdotage, and with no friends. His obsessive regret about the fate of the Wedgwood company and the cooling of the relationship with Josiah in no way dampened his readiness, on any occasion, to recall the sayings and doings of that remarkable dynasty.

Jean must have thought it would help if a third party were present, to carry some of the burden, to be a buffer zone, even if that third party were someone she had spent the previous quarter century detesting.

Thus, after our first Christmas at Hill House – Norman, Jean, Elizabeth, me – the proposal was made and my aunt came to be part of the household until her death, an enhancement of my own life for which no words can express gratitude.

Jean had wanted to do the decent thing by an impoverished relative, but when confronted by the reality of my aunt's personality, she could not rise to the challenge.

To her sister-in-law, upon whom she'd attempted to confer a kindness, she turned out to be incapable even of common civility, and if I so much as spoke to my aunt, there would be complaints about my 'disloyalty'. Norman did not have it in him to say to his wife, 'You must take a grip and stop being beastly to Elizabeth. If Andrew wants to sit in the kitchen garden blathering to her about Shakespeare, why shouldn't he?' He couldn't do this. He didn't dare. He capitulated entirely to Jean's rules, even suggested to me it would be more tactful if I did not speak to my aunt more than absolutely necessary. He agreed with Jean that to discuss, for example, Jane Austen was verging on the pretentious.

Major Manson and Miss Rich had inspired me to read. Tosswill and other Rugby masters fed my hunger for books, but it was hearing Elizabeth enthuse about Shakespeare, and about the mainstream novelists writing in English, that made the light bulbs come on.

She read all the time and, without being an exhibitionist (as the other two sneeringly claimed), she enjoyed recitation. Norman had enjoyed it in the past. I think most people who read a poem or heard a song enjoyed repeating them, in those days. Cowper's 'Boadicea', Wolfe's 'The Burial of Sir John Moore after Corunna', Goldsmith's 'The Deserted Village', anthology pieces, were all favourites, and because she recited them, I came to know them also by heart. Many is the sleepless night, or solitary walk undertaken in times of sadness, which these words have consoled and appeased. But it was chiefly Shakespeare she loved. She told me she had never in her life sat down and tried to memorize a passage from one of the plays. Having seen Sir Johnston Forbes-Robertson at the Theatre Royal, Hanley, she found that the great speeches remained in her head. Oberon's 'I know a bank where the wild thyme blows', Shylock's 'You call me misbeliever, cutthroat dog, / and spit upon my Jewish gaberdine', Wolsey's farewell – 'I did not think to shed a tear.' Thanks to the vigour with which this tiny, humorous woman with beautiful thick, springy hair and a resonant voice performed these lines, I too came to know them, together with the great monologues from Macbeth and Hamlet. I knew them long before I 'did' Shakespeare at school.

Sir Johnston Forbes-Robertson had learned from Sir Henry Irving, who in turn had learned much of the stage business, intonations and mannerisms ('my Jewish gaberdine', for example, said while slapping the right hand against the left) from the actors of the Kean–Siddons–Kemble generation, who had themselves learned from Garrick. What Elizabeth Wilson was reciting in the cabbage patch in Llansteffan in 1964 was a stage tradition that stretched back through all the glory days of our national theatre in Britain.

When she was still working at the restaurant in Malvern, we would sometimes, on an outing from Hillstone, call at her flat. The door would open to thick Turkey carpets, heavy mahogany furniture and a nicotine-scented fug, for she liked cigarettes, which she sometimes called gaspers. When she opened the door, she would break into, 'If I'd known you were coming, I'd have baked a cake', a song that always had me in stitches. Before marriage, Norman would take his sister to music halls and they loved all the old songs: 'I'm a bit of a ruin Cromwell knocked abaht a bit', 'When we are married, we'll have sausage for tea', 'Two little girls in blue'.

25. Mme de Liencourt, Mr Lowry and Others

Norman was lonely, so of course he craved my company, took me to tailors in Swansea in the days when he could still afford it and kitted me out as a toy sixty-year-old. As I sat there, a teenager in tweed coats and flannel trousers of pre-Second World War cut, with a glass of sherry in my hand, I had a friendship with him, laughing at the so-often repeated examples of Josiah's eccentricity. But it was the sort of friendship a young man might have with a lonely old chap in the smoking room of a club.

It never appeared to cross Norman's mind that an adolescent, in a small Welsh village where he knew no one, might be bored by the strange way of life pursued at Hill House, at the ever earlier hours, for example, at which the world was literally locked out (my mother would shut the curtains, winter or summer, at five every afternoon, when a chain would be put on the front door).

Jean, however, could imagine the extent of my boredom, and she made efforts to assuage it. Two weeks of each summer when I was fifteen, sixteen and seventeen were spent in Brittany. Jean had found this French family for me in the advertisement columns of *The Lady*. Mme de Liencourt, who had a large house called La Clarté near Ploumanac'h, took in young lodgers for the summer, sent them to the local tennis club or sailing school during the day and conversed with them in French during the evenings. These weeks, with Madame, her daughter and grandchildren, were a wonderful lifeline, and although I did not mind sailing or playing tennis, and developed my first bout of heterosexual lust for our sailing instructor, a raven-haired gamine, it was a bit of a relief when, one evening, the old lady remarked, '*Andrew est beaucoup plus intellectuel que sportif,*' and asked me if I'd prefer church crawls and architectural exploration to tennis with my, chiefly American, fellow lodgers.

So began a wonderful friendship, based on irony, and a shared interest in the past.

Our first outing was to Ernest Renan's house at Tréguier. Mme de Liencourt was pious. The glove compartment of her battered 2CV was wedged with her missal, wrapped with a mantilla, and she heard mass each morning. This did not prevent her having an amused contempt for the clergy, and, even more, for the extreme right wing who had embraced high Catholic fervour and monarchism as a political weapon in the closing decades of the nineteenth century and, even more disastrously, in the first three decades of the twentieth. It was she who first told me of all this and who explained to me the subject of my brother's PhD thesis, *Action Française*. We stood beside the gigantic calvary near the railway station at Tréguier, erected as an act of reparation for Renan's sin, writing *Vie de Jésus*. He had studied for the priesthood, but lost his ability to believe. When a lady had asked him if he'd consider becoming a Protestant, he explained, '*Madame, c'était ma foi que j'ai perdu, pas ma raison.*' Mme de Liencourt told me that *Vie de Jésus* was harmless. Every person of faith carried within themselves seeds of doubt and none of us completely know how the Teacher of Galilee, described so sentimentally by Renan, had come to be revered as one and the same as the Most Holy Sacrament of the Altar. A much better book, however, was, she believed, his *Souvenirs d'enfance et de jeunesse*, and this she bought for me at the *librairie* in Tréguier. I still treasure my copy, with her inscription.

She was a very good language teacher, her technique being, especially at the dinner table (oh, the food at La Clarté! Proust, had humility been in the great novelist's nature, would have recognized that a greater gastronomic genius than Françoise was here!), was to

Mme de Liencourt.

make an observation in French, translate it at once into English and then to ask you to respond in French. My competence in her language has never been complete but in so far as I can speak it at all, it is largely owing to her, though Mr Schlick, a modern languages teacher at Rugby, had also been a help. He was a father of young children at the time, but without any complaint he accepted my monstrously selfish suggestion that I should call round in the evenings, so that he could prepare me for French A-level. (I had not opted for it in the sixth form, when I chose to do English and History.) I never told him, of course, that Mme de Liencourt had asked me, after a few days at La Clarté, whether my teacher came from Alsace, as he did. She told me it was better to speak 'Anthony Eden French', which was charming, rather than with the dreaded accent of *outre-Rhin*. She never expressed herself intemperately, so it was only during my second summer at La Clarté that I began to catch her ironies and that phrases such as '*nos invités qui n'étaient pas exactement invités*' referred to the invading Germans. Her brothers had been killed in the First World War. Her husband, a Gaullist diplomat, was shot by the Gestapo soon after the occupation of Paris.

She was not a snob, but some of her observations fed my subsequent *snobbismes*; for example, she told me that the usage 'Bon appétit!' and 'placement' were what waiters said. We, if referring to the seating arrangements for dinner, would speak of *place à table.* 'What would *we* say for "Bon appétit!"?' We wouldn't. I'd not yet read Proust.

I did not keep up with Madame's family, but, rather as happens in a *roman fleuve*, our paths occasionally crossed in later life. When my daughters Emily and Bee were about twelve and ten, and we were on holiday, I took them to La Clarté to peer through the gates, assuming Madame to have been long since dead. She was still alive, and came down the drive with her daughter, la Duchesse de Rohan, by then Mme Rodocanachi. We had a nice lunch together.

Years later, long after I'd married Ruth, the phone rang and it was Isabelle de Yturbe, one of Mme de Liencourt's grandchildren, with whom I'd played incompetent tennis at the sports club in Perros-Guirec, now married to Santiago de Mora-Figueroa, Marqués de Tamarón, the newly appointed Spanish ambassador in London. While Santiago was in post, 1999–2004, it was fun to catch up, over parties and dinners at the embassy, with Isabelle, who is a very amusing raconteuse. My favourite among her recollections was an unsuccessful attempt on her part to entertain V. S. Naipaul, whom they had invited to the embassy to celebrate his winning the Nobel Prize for Literature. Upon discovering that the ambassadress was in fact French, not Spanish, Sir Vidia advanced with full artillery blaring to execrate the land of her birth. Food, architecture, music, emanating from that benighted land were all defective. What about literature? Isabelle ventured. Might the great novelist concede that Balzac had written a few good books? Absolutely not! Flaubert? Stendhal? 'Are you trying to be funny?' he replied. She was on the verge of sending Proust in to bat when, shortly after pronouncing the specially prepared vegetarian dinner to be disgusting, the teetotalling Nobel laureate sank into a deep sleep. (He used to sleep fifteen hours a day.)

It was strange to think – and I thought it again when Isabelle asked me to a dinner for five, consisting of me, fellow journalist Matthew Parris, Santiago, herself and the Queen of Denmark – that none of these worldly acquaintances would have come my way had my mother not subscribed to *The Lady*, and recognized how bored I was in Llansteffan as a teenager.

The Queen of Denmark is notably tall, and smokes cigarettes seemingly without interruption. In both these respects she could not be less like Queen Victoria, her multiple-times-great grandmother, whom she resembles facially, especially when she smiles. She is an illustrator of books, and had asked to meet me because she knew I had written about C. S. Lewis and also that I knew the Tolkien family, about whom she quizzed me intensely. The Queen illustrated the Danish translations of both Lewis's Narnia tales and *The Lord of the Rings*. Meeting her was unlike meeting any of the other 'royals' I've come across. There was none of that fear that she might be so much the inhabitant of another planet that she would not catch one's drift. She is in fact disconcertingly intelligent and bookish, and when I came away from the Spanish Embassy that night, I was overpowered by a sense of sympathy. Being clever was a *sine qua non* for the absolute monarchs such as Queen Elizabeth I or Frederick the Great, but for constitutional monarchs, whose lives are extremely limited, it surely helps not to be too adventurous or intellectually curious. Queen Margrethe is a real reader. She has agonised about religion, and come out on the side of faith, persuaded largely by C. S. Lewis. She said to Matthew Parris and me that without this she was not sure she would have survived. I was very impressed by the detail with which she discussed Tolkien, and not merely Lewis's Narnia but also his academic and theological works.

There are people who pay money in order to have dinner with royalty. It would be ungracious to say that I would pay money not to do so, but there is almost always, in my experience, an element of the unsatisfactory about the experience. It is not so much that you have to be on good behaviour, as that both you and the royal personage are being put through your paces, rather than being truly yourself. If you want a monarchy to exist, the Royal Family have, by definition, to be different from the rest of us. Yet both they, poor things, and the rest of us wave across a great gulf at one another, and sometimes want to be friends.

The difficulty was expressed for me eloquently when I met the Queen Mother. She said she knew that the poet George Barker, bohemian, father of umpteen children by many different women, scruff and boozer, lived near Sandringham. She arranged to meet him in a nearby pub, and – he came, brushed, shaved and in a brand-new suit.

A commoner can't easily have a proper conversation with royal people because they are NOT like us, and, in the case of the older British royals you cannot be sure that they will understand even quite simple references to contemporary life. (One thinks of Prince Charles, when visiting the White House and offered a tea bag by the waiter, to put in his pot of hot water – 'What IS it? I mean, what does one DO with it?') I think that is why so many photographs of royal personages meeting commoners depict everyone having the giggles. It is the brittle banter that you find in hospital wards. In a rather similar way, people laugh at the remarks of the clergy, even when they are not even intended to be amusing.

Katherine, however, was best pals with a charming Byzantine historian named James Howard-Johnston at Oxford (stepson of Hugh Trevor-Roper) and he had married, as her third husband, the novelist Angela Huth, who was a friend of Princess Margaret. Once a term the Princess would come and stay with the Howard-Johnstons in their house in Headington for two or three days, and they'd round up Oxford dons, writers and similar, to come to dinner. Princess Margaret has had a bad posthumous press. The received wisdom, among those who did not know her, is that she must have been a nightmare, one minute the life and soul of the party, the next a haughty grande dame, that when she was in a good mood she stayed up all hours, selfishly ignoring the yawns and tired expressions of those who would have to rise betimes.

Probably there was a bit of truth in this impression, but as one of our friends, Jeremy Catto, remarked, when reading a posthumous hatchet job, 'That's not the Princess we knew.' She fitted into those Oxford dinners with remarkable ease, and without pomposity. A few years after my wife and I parted company, she rang Katherine – this was long before K's dementia had set in – and said, 'We missed you at dinner last night.' Katherine realized that she had simply forgotten the date.

'I'd so looked forward to seeing your new house'.

'Oh, well, I'm settling in'.

'Can I come and see it?'

'Of course', said Katherine, without thinking this meant, 'Can I come and see it today.'

Princess Margaret turned up outside the small terraced house in Jericho half an hour later and spent two hours drinking tea and catching up on gossip.

The sad thing about the Princess at this stage of her life was that she was intensely lonely. Elizabeth Cavendish, her lady-in-waiting, told me she dreaded being rung up on Sunday evenings by the Princess. Elizabeth's companion, John Betjeman, would beg her not to answer the telephone, since, inevitably, rather than settling down to a nice slump on the sofa and watching drivel on the television together, they would have to make scrambled eggs for the 'little friend', as he called her. And that cosy Sunday evening feeling, in their tiny terraced house in Radnor Walk, Chelsea, would all have been destroyed, and rather than having an early night after the ten o'clock news, they'd have to sit up as long as the little friend needed them, swigging The Famous Grouse with the certainty of a hangover next day. Her turning up to see Katherine was typical. And of course, poor thing, she was not really wanted, not because her friends and acquaintances disliked her, but because she was royal and when a royal person arrives at your perfectly ordinary house, where no staff are employed, an unnatural degree of effort is required.

Nevertheless – she gets full marks, in my memory, for good-humouredly trying to fit into the weird world of Oxford. She read the books we had written and commented on them. (She thought my best book was *Wise Virgin*, probably true when she said it.) She asked us to the theatre, and after the show we would go back to Kensington Palace for bacon and eggs. The apartment she occupied at Kensington Palace was the one occupied by the Marquess of Lorne and Princess Louise in the nineteenth century, and she said that in those days there had been French windows leading out into Kensington Gardens. Princess Louise had them made into an ordinary window, to make it more difficult for her husband to nip out into Kensington Gardens to meet guardsmen. Or I think of another outing she organized in which she showed us the dairy built by the Prince Consort at Windsor.

True, there could be moments where one inadvertently overstepped the mark. Once I told her that Dean Wellesley (of St George's Chapel, Windsor), the Duke of Wellington's brother, was cruel, and in an extempore prayer thanked the Almighty, at the end of the well-sung matins one day, upon the birth of the Prince of Wales, 'thereby averting the calamity of another female succession'. Queen Victoria was present.

'That was very tactless', said Princess Margaret.

'He WAS a very tactless man', I said.

'I meant YOU were very tactless to say it to ME', she said with a sudden burst of crossness.

She especially flourished in Jeremy Catto's company. It was a relationship which I suspect slightly echoed that of Disraeli with Queen Victoria. She played up to his Firbankian sense of humour, being by turns flirtatious and haughty. When he was showing her some medieval inscriptions in the Ashmolean, she asked him how many letters there were in the runic alphabet.

'Twenty-four, ma'am'.

'Not enough!' she retorted,

She revered the Queen, as well as loving her as a sister. I asked her if she was one of those who had dreams about the Queen (as I often do, for some reason). She did, and it was always the same one. She had done something wrong, and did not know, or remember, what it was. She only knew she was out of favour with her sister.

'When I wake in the morning after this dream, I have to ring her up. She is usually at work when I ring, so all I need to do is to hear her voice. "Hello." And I say, "Hello" and hang up. Then all's right with the world again.'

Once, when I asked her view of the ordination of women to the priesthood, she said that the Queen approved of the idea. (This was aeons before it happened.)

I made a remark implying that one person's opinion had to be weighed against another, but Princess Margaret replied, 'Yes, but the Queen is the representative of God in this realm.'

She meant this. It must have been weird, being on the one hand a member of the human race and, on the other, the sister of God's representative. On the whole she managed really well, and I now regret chattering about our conversations to others – with the inevitable result that garbled versions saw print. There were evenings when a lot was drunk, so it was unfair to single out her intake, when we were all drinking ourselves even sillier than when sober.

The convention is that you should not repeat things said to you at the dinner table by the Royal Family. I do not really know why not, so long as they are not state secrets or matters disclosed in strict confidence. When that lovable rogue Woodrow Wyatt – former Labour MP, subsequently high Tory peer and Chairman of the Tote – befriended us, he asked us to dinner with the Queen Mother. It was a merry evening, with stupendous wines, with about a dozen people present, including Peregrine Worsthorne and his first wife, Claudie. I was next to Queen Elizabeth (the Queen Mother) at table. She must have been about eighty at the time.

After we got home I wrote the conversation down. It was all harmless stuff, including an anecdote that the present Queen herself tells guests at Windsor Castle – she told it to Carol Ann Duffy when she became Poet Laureate. It concerned T. S. Eliot reading aloud to them from *The Waste Land,* and their all having the giggles, first the King, then the little Princesses and then Queen Elizabeth herself. She was a P. G. Wodehouse fan, and you can see that the lugubrious tone and unashamedly obscure modernism of Eliot's masterpiece would not have been to her taste.

When she was ninety, and the *Spectator* asked me to write an article to commemorate the fact, I quoted this story. For a couple of weeks there was a flurry in the press, with old Woodrow fulminating against my appalling disloyalty in repeating the sacred words of the last Queen Empress. He even accused me of having a secret tape recorder hidden under his dining table – a trick that would have been technically beyond me, though not beyond the reach of his employers at *News of the World*, where he wrote a column called THE VOICE OF COMMON SENSE. He himself had been busily writing down some of her more scandalous remarks and including them in his posthumously published diaries, so I felt there was an element of humbug in his fake indignation. Not that we truly fell out. He told me a few years later that the Queen Mother, alluding to this storm in a teacup, said, 'Shall we forgive him?' By that stage in history, other members of the Royal Family were briefing journalists about the most intimate details of their marital misfortunes. A few harmless anecdotes about dead poets were not to be compared with what some of the royals were leaking to my fellow journalists, and when the Prince of Wales and his wife were going on television, quite unnecessarily, to admit adultery.

The Queen Mother once wrote me a fan letter about something I'd written, but when I was sorting through my 'archive', I could not find it. Strangely enough, it was about my *Life of John Milton*, which she had read at Sandringham one Christmas. There were two famous fans of that book – Queen Elizabeth was one, and another, who praised it on a radio interview, was … the Revd Ian Paisley, a monster for whom I have always nursed a soft spot.

It was a mistake on my part to break the rules and quote the royal conversation, because it embarrassed K and upset people generally. Nigel Lawson told his son Dominic, while he was editing the *Spectator*, that commissioning and publishing that article was his only really big mistake, but I omitted anything that could have been seen as conceivably embarrassing. For example, Katherine and I had just been to an exhibition of portraits of the Queen, and I asked her mother why it was that, since Annigoni's masterpiece, now hanging in the Fishmongers' Hall, there was not a single picture of any merit.

'It's because she has no interest in the visual', said the Queen Mother. 'She was born without any aesthetic sense whatever. Princess Margaret and I look at all the designs for postage stamps, for example. They are sent to the Queen by the Postmaster General for approval. She admits, she can't tell the difference between a good and a bad design.'

Sure enough, since the deaths of the Queen Mother and Princess Margaret, the quality of British stamps has steadily declined.

I also censored, in my ninetieth birthday tribute, the Queen Mother's political reflections.

'I don't like Woy', she told me (referring to Roy Jenkins). 'What's this new party of his?'

'The Social Democrats, ma'am'.

'He'd like the "social" part of that. Underneath it all, though, he's still a socialist. This country is naturally conservative, and it's always happiest when there's a good old Conservative government.'

I was too polite to recall the landslide victory of Labour in 1945, or the acceptance by all three parties of the Labour idea of a properly functioning welfare state and a health service.

The judgement – that Britain is at its best when governed by Tories – scarcely surprised the Queen Mother's hearers, but I suspect her daughter the Queen has never said such a thing in her life. And, while acknowledging that it was cheap of me to write an article in which I blabbed, I do not believe that this spirited old lady could have been shocked. She had not met me at the table of some discreet courtier. She was quaffing gin followed by claret with me, Perry Worsthorne and Woodrow Wyatt – scarcely a journalistic trio well celebrated for tight-lipped discretion.

I am not a natural courtier. I realized this when my Oxford contemporary Stephen Oliver, a composer of wide range and seemingly effortless ability to write in many genres, asked me to collaborate with him on a masque, to be performed at a dinner given at Hampton Court, on 30 May 1984, for the 150th birthday of the Royal Institute of British Architects, in the presence of the Prince of Wales. Together with Adam Pollock, who designed stupendous sets and costumes, we invented something entitled *Britannia Preserv'd*, in which our country encountered, and tried to live in, a variety of architectural styles and settings, from medieval Gothic to modern brutalist. The moment Britannia emerged from the dome of St Paul's Cathedral was especially good.

It was an evening that the RIBA made into legend, since the Prince chose it to deliver a violent attack on them and their works, deploring the modern movement and the unimaginative way in which it had been imposed on British towns and cities. Naturally, having delivered this bombshell, he was not really in a receptive mode, and did not appear to have noticed the masque. But when we all lined up afterwards to have our hands shaken, Stephen, without sycophancy, seemed able to thank him simply for being there. Since the masque was broadly speaking in sympathy with the Prince's views on architectural vandalism, and since immense trouble had been taken – especially by Adam Pollock, producing Sir Christopher Wren's dome, among other things, and by Jane Glover, conducting Stephen's dazzling music, I thought the Prince could have been a bit more gracious.

Kind, sensible Stephen upbraided me for thinking like this. I'd missed the point of what it was like to be royal. Prince Charles was a well-meaning chap, hideously frustrated at having no real say in public life. One of the things he cared about passionately was architecture. Let him have his say. (Stephen, incidentally, could not have been more at variance with Prince Charles over this particular matter: he loved concrete and tower blocks. He was also a committed lefty who probably would not have minded, as I would, were the monarchy to be abolished.) But, argued he, the evening had not been OUR evening, still less that of the RIBA, even though it was their 150th anniversary. It had been the Prince's evening, and if he chose to turn up, insult his hosts and, flown with the emotion of his own fulminations, fail to say anything civil about our masque, that was his affair. I realized then that Stephen was right; but I also realized something about myself. Just as I am religious, but with more than half of myself incurably agnostic, so I am also a wistful monarchist, but with a very large degree of sympathy for Oliver Cromwell.

Just as it was Jean who saw I needed a life away from Wales in the summer, and arranged my visits to the Liencourts, so it was she, likewise, who recognized how serious was my ambition to become a painter and, way back in the days of Miss Rich and the art room at Hillstone, had sent me off to meet Mr Lowry. I've no idea how Clarrie, her father, knew L. S. Lowry. I once suggested to my brother that, since the celebrated painter, before becoming successful, had earned his living as a rent collector, maybe our grandparents had been aspirant rentiers and had owned some *Coronation Street*-style properties and employed him to go round to collect the accumulated ten bob notes which helped Jean attend Cheltenham Ladies'. This idea was dismissed as nonsense, and of course there is no evidence for it. I never heard, however, that Clarrie, or Mr Lowry come to that, moved in especially arty circles. Nor do I know whether my mother wrote, in advance, to Mr Lowry at Mottram in Longdendale to warn him that a twelve-year-old boy, who dreamed of becoming a painter, was coming to disturb his working routine. She *must* have done? She did not say so, nor did she give me a letter of introduction; merely put me on a bus in central Manchester and told me she'd be waiting at teatime in Marshall & Snelgrove. When I asked how I could possibly find the house, she said, truthfully, that the bus conductor would be bound to know it.

Bus conductors! Like butlers, hatters, glovers, a vanished breed. No reader under the age of forty would quite know what they were or why they were needed, but they were in fact a useful lot. A friend of mine when I was at Oxford was asked (I constantly hoped to be approached but no one ever did!) if she would be interested in a job in the 'Foreign Office', i.e. espionage. Fascinated, she agreed to go for an interview at a top secret location. She was told which bus to take, how many stops to count, after Elephant and Castle, before reaching the 'safe house' where the ultra-secret conversation would take place.

On no account was she to tell anyone – ANYONE AT ALL – where she was going. She sat on the bus, anxiously counting the stops and feeling like a minor character in Le Carré. She need not have worried since, when they had penetrated this obscure part of London, the helpful bus conductor called out, 'Next stop MI6, MI6, anyone?'

Anyway, conductors. The journey from central Manchester took inside of an hour. The conductor indeed told me when to alight and gave directions to Mr Lowry's house, a detached residence whose blackened bricks stood out against the misty-pale northern surroundings very much in the manner of one of his own, to my mind uncongenial, canvases.

The figure who opened the door wore a grey three-piece suit, pinstriped, an old-fashioned shirt with large collars of the kind that had been fashionable in the 1940s and a sober slightly frayed silk tie. Bright eyes. Silver hair *en brosse*, a prominent nose. The atmosphere of oil paint mingled with a whiff emanating from so many people in my youth and which you hardly ever smell nowadays, when most people take a daily shower, floss and polish their teeth and dry-clean their clothes. It was a sort of animal smell given off by people who had a bath once a week. It was not specific, not underarm or bad breath or any of the cruder odours, but a very mild version of what hits the nose when passing a butcher's shop. Most of the men in Llansteffan smelt like this. The only place where it lingers in my neck of the woods is in the very few remaining Irish pubs in Camden or Kentish Town, or at the back of the church of Our Lady of Hal, where very old Irishmen, dressed remarkably like Mr Lowry in suits, congregate.

I explained to Mr Lowry that I was the grandson of Mr Crowder, Clarrie, and, having an ambition to be a painter, felt so bold as to visit him. He invited me into the back room of the house, fitted out as a studio, with half- or three-quarter-squeezed tubes of Zinc White everywhere – on the floor, on tables, balanced on the easel. He appeared to be working on several paintings at once.

'Some years ago a friend took me to Sunderland. Have you ever been there?'

'No.'

'I have developed a great fondness for Sunderland. As you can see, I've started painting seascapes.'

I have never really taken to Lowry's signature works, streets, houses and the celebrated matchstick people. Men and women do *not* resemble matchsticks, and when you reduce them to matchstick status, what are you saying? There's no reason why an artist should go on aridly pursuing academic reproduction of the human form, but when violent distortion is at work, I want it, as in hundreds of Picasso's disturbing depictions of women, whose every orifice appears serrated or sharp, *to say something.*

Mr Lowry pointed appreciatively to the picture of a man lying on a brick wall.

'I really saw that, he was lying on top of a wall.'

So what? But the seascapes, the long, white misty horizon out beyond the Wear estuary, these were wonderful. There was something haunting about the face of a woman on one of the canvases. Years later, when I was at Oxford, I became obsessed by the beautiful face of Anna Fell. I realized the Lowry painting which had so arrested my twelve-year-old attention had been her mother, Sheila Fell. Anna and I went clubbing together at the Stage Club, and sometimes went fishing on Port Meadow. Aeons later, one of the friends we had in common said to her, 'You know, Andrew was madly in love with you at that time.' 'Really?' Anna replied, in her flutey, musical voice. 'Personally, I was madly in love with his wife.'

Mr Lowry had bought some of Sheila Fell's work at her first solo exhibition at the Beaux Arts Gallery in the '50s. Noting my interest in this face, he asked me what I thought.

The reply was a tactless question, for my eye had now been struck by the pictures that Mr Lowry had chosen to hang on the walls, rather than the works of his own which were propped up here and there. Most notably, there was the oil of Proserpine, modelled by Jane Morris, and painted by Dante Gabriel Rossetti, whose work Mr Lowry collected.

'Does the lady in the picture ...' I began.

'Yes?'

'Is the lady … well …'

'Yes?'

'Did you try to make her like the Victorian ladies?'

He was obviously displeased by the question.

'She's a friend of mine,' he said shortly.

His two principal Rossettis, both of Janie, must be among the most beautiful works of art in the British Isles. Even to my immature eyes, the contrast between the great Victorian masterpieces and Mr Lowry's daub was painful. Tactlessly, I could not stop staring at the Rossettis, nor could I stop jabbering about how much I liked them. I knew nothing of the Pre-Raphaelites and he told me about them, a group of young men who had formed a brotherhood to revive the painting techniques of the Italian Renaissance (of which I also, at that date, knew more or less nothing).

'He's always meant a lot to me, has Rossetti. But, now. You want to be a painter yourself?'

He gave me what was, presumably, advice given to thousands of young aspirants. Draw, draw, draw, draw.

'If you find you can't draw something, leave it. Draw something you can. I'll let you into a secret. You know why I do so many pictures of streets and houses and lamp posts? It's because I can't draw trees. Never could, couldn't I.'

He made me a cup of very weak tea, as milky as the Sunderland seascapes, as he said, 'I like to play music on the gramophone while I paint. Who is your favourite?'

'My favourite?'

'Ay. Your favourite composer.'

For a previous Christmas Stephen had given me an LP which had Mendelssohn's incidental music to *A Midsummer Night's Dream* on one side and Schubert's incidental music to *Rosamunde* on the other. I'd played the record a lot but was ashamed of the fact that I'd never checked which side I was playing, so did not know which composer was which.

I told Mr Lowry I liked Schubert.

'Well, you can't go wrong with Schubert,' and he went to his collection and put the Unfinished Symphony on the gramophone.

'You won't make much money as a painter,' he said. 'I sit here sometimes and I get so annoyed' – he laughed – 'so annoyed. I see a painting of mine has sold for tens of thousands of pounds, and it's often one I couldn't *give away*, or which I'd sold for a fiver.'

I was now settled in, and he clearly recognized that if he did not do something decisive he would be saddled with the daylong companionship of a twelve-year-old.

'If you like the Pre-Raphaelites,' he said, when the Schubert record had been heard and the weak tea consumed, 'you should go to the City Art Gallery. They've got some of the best ones. Holman Hunt. Millais. But for myself, Rossetti is the best of 'em. Now!'

He had reached a hat from the stand, an ordinary trilby which he was punching into the shape of a bowler. 'I think it's time for us to be going.'

'It's perfectly all right, Mr Lowry. I can stay as long as you like.'

'All the same, I'll take you back into Manchester.'

When we were on top of the bus – and again, he must have said all these things so often to visitors who had come to pester him – he went through the routines of pointing out where he had seen the man lying on the wall, where certain warehouses and factories, now demolished, had once stood. The industrial wasteland that he pointed out from the bus bore no resemblance whatever to his simplistic renditions of it, a fact which reinforces my distaste for the song about him and his matchstick people. Sentimentality about the rigours of life in industrial towns led the songwriter to suppose Lowry possessed a warm sympathy for the plight of the inhabitants, a schmaltzy version of events for which not a shred of biographical evidence exists. Far from the Lowry townscapes chronicling the felt life of the urban poor, they are surely, in their limited way, evidence of the callous way in which artists, with whatever degree of competence or originality, always possess the capacity to define the world entirely on their own terms – presumably one of the reasons why the majority of those who have chosen painters and sculptors as life partners have had such a miserable time.

On the bus he repeated his advice that I should do a drawing every day of my life. Several times a day, ideally. I was a polite little chap, though he was evidently relieved to be rid of me. We parted on cordial terms before I found my way to Marshall & Snelgrove and the café where the Palm Court Trio sawed and tinkled their way through the comforting repertoire of 'Indian Love Lyrics', and 'I'll Gather Lilacs in the Spring'. And there was Mummy, with her pot of tea.

To be a painter, then, always remained part of my self-image, and most of my spare time at Rugby was spent in the Art School, an impressive atelier above the Temple Reading Room on Barby Road, still, in the days before the vandalistic decision to sell its treasures, adorned with art works which had been bequeathed to the school in order to stimulate the imagination of its pupils: the Egyptian mummy on the landing, and, once inside, a fine selection of paintings, the best of which was a seascape by Turner.

Perched on a dais slightly higher than the floor level of the large hall was seated a small old man on whose bird-beak, jutting from a parchment-pale Irish face, balanced horn-rimmed specs. He always wore tweeds, usually of deepest russet. This was TK.

R. B. Talbot Kelly, one of the most accomplished watercolourists and ornithologists of his generation. At the Festival of Britain Exhibition on the South Bank of the Thames in 1951, he was commissioned to display an example of every extant British bird species. He managed to ensnare and stuff most of the required exhibits, but some either eluded him or were considered too rare to fall prey to the taxidermist. He made the substitutes out of paper. Apparently, however close you came to the glass, it was impossible to tell which birds were stuffed and which were made of paper by TK. He was later to do the same for the national museum in Uganda.

His father, an Irish painter and orientalist of note, was known for his paintings of Egypt. (In Betjeman's 'A Subaltern's Love Song', where 'the pictures of Egypt were bright on the walls' in Miss Joan Hunter Dunn's Aldershot, I wonder if they were watercolours by TK *père*.) TK himself, a boy at Rugby, had run across School Field to the recruiting sergeant at the beginning of the autumn term, 1914. His sketchbooks

and memories of the Western Front held us in thrall. Even there, it was
the bird life that fascinated him, hawks with their feet on discarded
helmets, crows pecking at human flesh. He was gassed, and spoke
thereafter in a high-pitched, flutey, upper-class Irish voice.

There is no single way of being a good teacher. The emphasis
nowadays, from early infancy, is to encourage and applaud, so that
a child rolling out a little piece of plasticine is given to believe, by
their teacher's smiles and the congratulations of their peers, that
it is a budding Donatello. Another way, however, is to make the
pupil realize from the first that they face a challenge, that there
are certain rules and standards which must be attained before any
progress is possible. Great artists such as Turner and Picasso, TK
would remind us, knew how to draw. Standing beside the Turner
in his school, he would say, 'This was by a man who had seen the
sea and knew how to convey what he saw. It isn't just a fluke by
someone making smudges.'

No one in TK's classes was allowed to attempt an oil painting
until they learned to draw and at least made rudimentary efforts to
become a watercolourist. He would walk up and down the rows of
desks with a moist sponge, rubbing out our efforts over and over
again until we began to get things right. Most of the boys did not stay
the course, and art was not on the syllabus after our first year; but I
was hooked and became an ardent admirer of this quietly humorous
genius. All my spare time was spent drawing and painting. On any
day when it was not raining too hard, I'd ride out with a sketchbook
and watercolour box to paint in fields and churchyards. After the
first term, I skipped winter games. No one seemed to mind. Summer
was different. One could sketch while watching cricket and, besides,
the senior boys, in the first cricket XI, wore not white but eau-de-Nil
shirts which enhanced their often considerable beauty.

TK left the school in my third year. It was a tradition that at
the last chapel service of term one of the leavers would read the
Parable of the Sower in the version of Mark's Gospel. As the last
day of term approached, TK came up to Holy Mo, the chaplain –
a scarlet-countenanced Old Rugbeian who had been converted
in a Japanese prisoner-of-war camp – to ask why he had not been

invited to read the lesson. 'Because, in fifty years, you have never set foot in the chapel,' was the answer. Major Talbot Kelly squawked back peremptorily, 'I do not see what difference that makes.'

The figure of TK, standing beside the brass eagle lectern in Rugby Chapel and reading that Gospel passage, is etched in my grateful mind. All the other masters, to attend chapel, wore black gowns, so he, who had no degree, no educational qualifications of any kind, stood there in his russet tweed coat, his Viyella shirt and woollen tie – to declaim, 'Behold, there went out a sower to sow, And it came to pass, as he sowed, some fell by the way side.'

It would have been a coarse-grained child, and of course there were some of those, to leave Rugby School without a Victorian sense that Life is a serious business. The Parable of the Sower, so unforgettably intoned by the presumably agnostic TK, enforced a sense that one way of judging one's life was the extent to which these words took root in one's day-to-day existence.

26. Galsworthy Scholar

TK had gone, but I continued to paint, largely under the guidance of an assistant teacher, Geoffrey Barraclough, the man who sculpted the giant stag in Stag Place, off Victoria Street in London. He was small, heavily bearded and, despite his name and upper-class English voice, seemed more Spanish than English. I think his mother was Spanish. He, and his beautiful wife, with whom We All were in love (she helped with the costumes and make-up in school plays, and we all yearned for her to be the one who adjusted our wigs or smoothed greasepaint onto our already greasy adolescent brows), spent as much time as they could in Spain. Like TK, while being at Rugby, Geoffrey managed to behave as if not only the school but the entire English establishment did not exist. He was a very good teacher, and with his help I assembled a portfolio of work, mainly oil paintings, but also sketchbooks and some gouache, which got me a place at St Martin's School of Art, which I intended to take up in the September following a 'gap year', in effect nine months.

How the gap year was to be spent was also settled. Jack Baiss was 'high', taking us, whenever possible to the Sung Eucharist in Coventry Cathedral to escape the tame liturgies on offer in the school chapel. It was presumably through some Anglo-Catholic chum that he received a request from the Community of the Resurrection, an Anglican monastery in Yorkshire, for a student-teacher in their school in Zimbabwe – still, in those days, called Rhodesia.

There is no point lamenting the door we never opened into the rose garden. Nevertheless, I do still very much regret not taking up the African offer – it was all arranged – just as I feel wistful to see my third daughter, even as I write these pages, attend the Royal College of Art, that I did not go to St Martin's, just to see if I could have become a painter. Anyone can do school work. Anyone. Anyone with my kind of privileges can do enough school work to get into university. To exercise creative gifts is another thing, and although I now know – partly from watching my daughter Georgie at work – that I did not have it in me to be an artist, it would have been worth the try.

Somehow, though, the whole plan for the two years following school unravelled. Norman, with his pronounced distaste for Christianity, was unimpressed by the idea of these monks. In vain did one beg him to read Trevor Huddleston CR's book *Naught for Your Comfort*, which explained how this band of dedicated Anglican Christians, the Community of the Resurrection, had encouraged resistance to the evils of apartheid in South Africa. Probably both my parents feared it would be dangerous to teach the poorest of the poor in Zimbabwe, and to risk disease and violence. Probably both of them shared alarm at the idea of monkery.

Tactlessly – worse than tactlessly, cruelly – I'd stopped going to church with my mother in the holidays. On the recommendation of one of the Rugby masters, I'd read John Henry Newman's *Apologia*, and it had swept me off my feet. On re-reading the book recently, I found it impossible to guess why: its preoccupation with long-dead ecclesiastical controversies of the 1830s appears cobwebby.

I think perhaps it was the lure of certainty – which my mature mind shows me is impossible on this side of the grave – that made Newman attractive: his claim that there were but two alternatives, the way to Rome and the way to atheism (which is obviously not true).

The one thing which in those days formed a bond between me and my mother – going together to the village church – came to an end. Instead, I began to attend the offering of the mass in a corrugated iron hut next to Dai Thomas's garage in the village. An

Irish Passionist monk came over once a week from Carmarthen to cater for the tiny handful of Llansteffan recusants. The old rite was still in use, such as we'd had in the convent at Stone. In old age, when we had formed our friendship, Jean Dorothy told me that every time she saw me going off to mass in the hut, she felt her heart cracking.

Worse than the idea of my planning to go to Africa to be among (albeit Anglican) monks was the prospect of my going to art school, rather than university. Jack Plumb, a Cambridge historian of the eighteenth century, had resurfaced. Destined to be Master of Christ's, my brother's college, he was one of the scarcely disguised characters in C. P. Snow's extraordinarily boring series of novels, which Norman read avidly. I tried one once and, with its adulation of those who advance themselves in 'the Corridors of Power' in both the academic and the political spheres, it seemed like a nightmare version of Powell's *A Dance to the Music of Time*, where the narrative role had been wrested from the ironical bohemian Nick Jenkins and taken over by the thrusting, power-worshipping bore Widmerpool.

As a schoolboy, one used to see C. P. Snow standing on the corner of Barby Road in Rugby with his brother, who was the school's bursar. Sometimes, inevitably, Tosswill would be with them. The Snow brothers, in Homburg hats, instantly recalled the sinister row of hatted monsters looking over the Kremlin wall to survey the May Day parade of tanks, field guns and other items of military hardware designed to crush their enemies in the West.

The internal hatreds and feuds of university folk, an endemic passion for these often bored souls with limited emotional resources, have never interested me in the slightest, but I confess to make one exception. F. R. Leavis's denunciation of Snow in his 1962 lecture debunking Snow's speech on the 'Two Cultures' is wonderful. 'As a novelist, he does not exist.' Leavis might well have been mad. He looks completely nutty from the photos. Nonetheless, he championed art against the philistines, a higher against a popular culture, and he questioned Snow's clumsy championing of 'science', by which was never meant a broad, sympathetic understanding of the universe in which we live with all its mystery and wonder, but the deluded materialist world view, in which the half-truths of Bentham and Herbert Spencer become the *dernier cri*.

For all I know, Snow and Plumb were sworn enemies (I never got far enough in Snow's books to find out), but they were both Fellows of the same college, which, of course (who could forget it?), was that of Charles Darwin, who might be famous in some eyes for having written *On the Origin of Species* but whose chief claim to fame was, of course, having been the grandson of Josiah Wedgwood. This made Cambridge a place of special significance in Norman's imaginative world. Who could forget that Ralph, father of Sir John and Veronica, had been at Trinity with G. E. Moore? Helen Pease, Jos's sister, has left interviews at the Imperial War Museum in which she describes house parties given by her grandparents, good Gladstonian liberals, at their large house in the Lake District to which the likes of Moore came, and with him, his acolytes in what became the Bloomsbury Group.

'We were the ruling caste of a ruling country,' she said, going on to explain how her father became first the Liberal, then the Labour, MP for Newcastle-under-Lyme (always a short 'a' for the word Newcastle, as for 'castle' itself). So much of what they stood for, these people, with their distrust of Conservatives and Empire, their self-belief, they – the liberal-minded, scientifically educated they – derived from their associations from Cambridge, even if Jos had in fact gone to the LSE, which is really Cambridge *in partibus*.

For Norman, who had never been to university, it was the secular equivalent of sacrilege for a spotty seventeen-year-old boy to say he'd spend six months with a lot of monks and then attend an art school, rather than tread in the footsteps of Darwin and so many other Wedgwoods. Moreover, a career among artists, or even among potters, was just what he didn't want for his sons.

He was impressed by Plumb, who has always, to me, sounded insufferable with his bow ties, cult of royalty, love of 'fine wines' etc., etc.; but Plumb could make us, Stephen and me, what Norman had only ever been in his fantasy life – gentlemen. What had it all been for, the expensive school fees, the rather snooty look on the faces of the Old Rugbeian fathers when they failed to respond to the declaration that they were Rag and Bone Men, if Andrew were to chuck it all up and spend six months with High Church emotional deviants educating Africans?

I now despise myself for giving in to his emotional blackmail.

Working with members of a religious community in a part of the world so different from my sheltered world of boarding schools and elderly parents would have placed me in touch with a theology that was tested and realized. One would have been working alongside those who had devoted their lives to God-in-Christ, finding the Incarnate God – or not – in a tough political situation and among lives where money and class and Plumb with his wine cellar would have been seen in their true perspective.

It would not have been a mistake to go to Africa, as Norman insisted. Nor would it have been a mistake to go to art school rather than university. Both choices would have enriched my life enormously. The wistful sense with which I began to write this book, that I have never been completely sure who A. N. Wilson was, my lack of any feeling of connect between my inward being and the activities in which I have found myself involved for the last half-century ... well, I do not know how that sentence is going to end, so I shall leave it trailing. Was I going to write that, by going to Africa, then art school, I might have found 'myself', the self who got mysteriously left behind in Stone, when I was packed off to Hillstone at the age of seven? No, that's too simple, and I know it is not true.

Any road up, as Blakie would say, the first intimations that my plans for the future were not going ahead came from the English master, T. D. Tosswill, standing on the corner of Barby Road and Hillmorton Road outside the Temple Speech Room, a ragged MA (Oxon) gown covering his baggy trousers and frayed tweed coat. With a nonchalant gesture, the slightest wave of his tobacco pipe, he indicated that I should pause for a few words.

'Yeair ...' I supposed that some sarky comment about my last essay on Chaucer or Shakespeare would be forthcoming. Instead, he drawled, 'Your father'.

It was cunning of Norman to have written to Tosswill, and not to my housemaster. More cunning than I'd have given him credit for. But, although by now all I saw, when I met him, was a slightly blotto, prematurely aged man repeating anecdotes, this was a person who had been a brigadier, built a factory, said to this one come and he cometh, go and he goeth. Or had it been Jean's idea, cleverer with people? Tosswill affected to believe that my rejection of an offer at Christ's (Plumb had most improperly simply told Norman I could go there, without so much as an interview) was a gesture of healthy anti-Cambridge prejudice.

'I *entirely* endorse your decision not to go to Cambridge,' he said, 'and – yeair – for what it's worth, I think you'd be much better off reading English, rather than History, at the University.'

He always said 'the University' when referring to Oxford. Though he had taught at Stanford, tried unsuccessfully to get a PhD at Warwick and ended his professional career as a professor at Walla Walla University, Washington State, there was for Tosswill only one University, its luminaries, from Samuel Johnson to Nevill Coghill, from John Ruskin to C. S. Lewis, being the equivalent of those English Worthies whose statues might adorn the gardens of eighteenth-century noblemen. While I tried to splutter out the plans (surely everything had been settled? Barraclough had got me into St Martin's, Baiss had arranged for me to go to Africa?), he spoke words quietly, which bit home.

'Your father has invested great hopes in you. I think – yeair – you owe it to him, at least to do the reading which would prepare you for entrance into the University. I'm afraid we've left it much too late to think of preparing you for a scholarship but – yeair – the scholarship set meet in my house several times a week. I want you to read what they are reading, to learn how to present an essay. They will be competing against candidates who will have read the complete works of Sh-yeair-kspeare, Milton and Chaucer – most of the great novelists. You owe it to your father to try. If, for some reason, you do not get an offer, well, then you have this – yeair. This. PLACE at an art school to fall back on.'

So it began, cramming for the University. We did read a great deal, and my sense was quickened, as it had been when first opening Tolstoy, that literature was not simply a craft that could be learned by immersion in the works of the great – George Eliot, Dickens, Milton – but also a calling, an engagement with truth. 'And, as Nevill, yeair – always insisted – with love.'

Elevated as this sounds, there was also the sly business of finding a college, among the many at the University, which would be more likely than others to give me a place. Years later, when he used to come to stay with Katherine and me, Tosswill would say that he had never expected me to get into university because I was one of the idlest boys he had ever taught. Tosswill the Oxford know-all, I suspect, like many teachers who sell themselves to pupils and parents as experts on colleges and universities, knew next to nothing about the contemporary scene. He managed to find out that one of the dons at New College was called Tolkien and assumed this was John Tolkien with whom he had done military service. He cannot have known John Tolkien very well or he would have known that he was by now a Catholic priest in the diocese of Birmingham, destined to be unmasked before he died as a paedophile.

Tosswill overlooked the fact that the senior English don at New College was a critic called John Bayley.

Nowadays, the situation at New College in 1968 is not imaginable; but in those days each college had to make sure it had enough applicants, and there was always the possibility that, while one place had a hundred applicants for ten places, another would not have enough. It was the year after the Summer of Love. Any young person wanting a cool time would apply to Sussex or the University of East Anglia, where my brother was now a lecturer. New College, Oxford, an offshoot of Winchester College, with its medieval cloisters and Georgian quadrangles, might have been beautiful, but it was scarcely cool.

For whatever reason, Bayley and colleagues found they only had a handful of applicants for the coming year. Of course they did not *tell* us this at the time, but half my year reading English at New College had been fished out of 'pools' from other colleges.

It was essential for Bayley to find at least eight, ideally ten, pupils before he set off on a world tour organized by the British Council in which he performed a double act of literary dialogue in four continents – Europe, Asia, Australia and North America – with his wife, the, in those days, prodigiously famous novelist Iris Murdoch.

Neither Tosswill nor I knew any of this at the time. It was astonishing to receive a letter from John Bayley asking me to attend an interview months in advance of the entrance exams, but I did so, after days of anxious cramming from Tosswill, days of watching him wince as I forgot whether John Donne was eighteenth-century or Victorian, and whether it was Spenser or Langland who wrote *Sir Gawain and the Green Whatever.*

The day dawned. I caught the train to Oxford and turned up at the college, where I would pass a decade of my life, and met two men who played so large a part in it, John Bayley and Christopher Tolkien.[3] Not priest John, but Christopher.

The porter directed me to Mr Bayley's rooms in the front quad, and, climbing the stairs, I tried to remember the differences between Ben Jonson and Dr Johnson, if there was one, and wondered whether I'd make a fool of myself if they gave me a passage to read 'blind' – a poem or a prose extract upon which I would then have to offer comments. The rambling conversation that followed was not, in fact, demanding on any such level. John, probably only in his forties but seeming older because of baldness, was a little imp, giggly, stammering, instantly charming. He explained about the world tour, his inability to be present when the entrance exams happened in December, the hope that I would put in for the scholarship. Obviously no doubt about their offering me a place. Thus, casually, was it let fall that, as far as they were concerned, my coming to Oxford was a *fait accompli.*

Christopher, son of *The Lord of the Rings* Tolkien, sat in his cloud of smoke, and asked my opinions about the current state of the Church. Nothing had prepared me for this. I subsequently discovered

---

[3] See my *Iris Murdoch As I Knew Her.*

that Jack Baiss had written them a letter of recommendation which contained the facetious prediction that I would one day become a bishop.

It is actually impossible for me to imagine anyone who would be less suited to the role, but I was involuntarily reminded of my housemaster's whimsy decades later when Rowan Williams, by then a friend, was Archbishop of Canterbury. He was on a Radio 4 arts programme called *Front Row*. He was talking about poetry, and then I came on, as it happened, to talk of some other subject – a recently published history of Christianity. When we had both finished, Mark Lawson, the presenter of the programme, said with a twinkle, 'I realized this evening, you both missed your calling. Rowan should have been the Man of Letters, and A. N. should have been an archbishop.' When I ask myself whether it would be possible for institutional Christianity to be in a worse mess than it now finds itself, I think of this joke and realize what an utter calamity it would have been if, in the manner of Baron Corvo's *Hadrian the Seventh*, I had found myself, by some grotesque prank of the fates, raised to the sacred purple.

Christopher Tolkien, who did have a developed sense of the ridiculous in all other areas of life, had a humour by-pass in the religious department.

My Oxford interview for a place to read English, before John had let fall that I would anyway be offered a place, began with Christopher tetchily and tormentedly asking me about the most notorious papal encyclical of modern times, *Humanae vitae*, in which the Pope denounced the use of the contraceptive pill.

Paul VI had been deemed by many a 'liberal', in terms of Catholic politics. Moreover, it really did seem, in the eyes of theologians and scientists, as if the Pill might offer a chink of hope to observant Catholic women that they could continue to have a sexual life without producing enormous families. We live on an overcrowded planet. Feminism was beginning to take hold of popular political consciousness, having previously, since the high days of Victorian feminism, been the preserve of the educated. The Pope's encyclical seemed totally illogical to many readers, since it allowed the use of the so-called safe period, thereby demonstrating that in papal eyes it was permissible to have sexual intercourse with the intention of avoiding conception. As the Duke of Norfolk said memorably at the time, the safe period 'doesn't bloody work'. In the past, the popes used to say that the only sexual acts that were not sinful were ones that might lead to conception, the 'point' of sex being, for them, simply the means of procreation. By suggesting the safe period, Paul VI appeared to be saying that one could have sex simply for pleasure, and in this case, why not do the responsible thing and prevent unwanted conceptions?

Humanae vitae led to an exodus of Catholics from the Church. Christopher, puffing his pipe in anguished fury, clearly considered my confused, incoherent, wishy-washy reflections on the matter to be less than satisfactory. He remarked sharply, 'If you join a club, you should either keep the rules, or' – puff puff, more clouds of aromatic nicotine – 'GET OUT.'

John Bayley broke the excruciating silence with a stammered smile, and the words 'D-dear old SSSSS C of E!'

So, my fate was sealed. When I came back to the college in December, following the entrance exam, it was simply a question of whether I'd be awarded a scholarship. I was welcomed as the John Galsworthy Scholar. Galsworthy, author of *The Forsyte Saga*, which I have always found completely unreadable, was an alumnus and benefactor of the college. I did once go to his play *Strife*, however, and admired it.

The drama that made most impression upon me in that momentous year of 1968 was *The Graduate*. A group from our house went to see the film, a few days before we left school.

There had been a sense, all term, of school, with its constraints and friendships, loosening its hold. The close friendships were in any case behind me. King Edward VI, about eighteen months older than me, had left ages ago. Those going to see Dustin Hoffman being seduced by Anne Bancroft were in no sense a group, not really, just a gang of coevals in a boarding house who would not bother to keep up with one another in the alarming thing called Life which was about to begin.

As soon as the Simon and Garfunkel songs began – 'Hello darkness, my old friend' – I tingled with the excited knowledge that childhood was at last over. I am about as far as possible from writers such as Wordsworth, or Dickens in a different way, who cherish their childish inner self. I never felt at home as a child, never liked being a child, after Blakie left, never enjoyed children's books or games or television programmes intended for a childhood audience. I was lucky throughout my schooldays; I was not bullied by other children and I did not lack for friendships, but none of them lasted, or meant anything to me. Bonds formed since the age of twenty, by contrast, have lasted ever since.

The Graduate, therefore, with its accompanying songs, was the most wonderfully liberating overture for the show that I had been waiting to start: Life Itself. Central to this film's story and, as it happened, to the life which I was about to begin, was that a very young man, little more than a boy, would find himself the object of a much older woman's desire. Quite how close this would be to my own story, and quite how soon, after leaving school, I would find myself not merely the partner of an older woman but the father of two children, could not possibly have been foreseen as, bleary-eyed, in fact gobsmacked, we emerged from the cinema, unable as yet to read the words of the prophet written on the subway wall.

27. Kibbutznik

I boarded the ship at Naples, Haifa-bound. The journey took several days, and there was time, as we stopped off at Palermo, Valetta, Nicosia, for a little Mediterranean sightseeing. I had never been alone before.

The idea of teaching in Rhodesia, along with the place at St Martin's, had been shelved. I'd capitulated. My sister had a flatmate called Judith who said that all young people these days wanted to work on a kibbutz. She had friends, perhaps family, at one called Kibbutz Beit Haemek. So it was all arranged. I was to go there until Easter. Thereafter, here I asserted myself, I signed on for a course at the British Institute in Florence in Italian Language and Culture. Norman said this was quite beyond his means. Inflation had by then shrunk what had begun as a lucrative pension, and he was too proud to ask Little Bryan for a rise. Jean revealed there was money left for me in trust by her father which would cover the cost of my studies in Florence.

So there I was, in a boat bound for Israel, very much a fish out of water, with Hebrew spoken at the table and everyone else in the dining room except myself knowing the songs that were sung. In Haifa, I climbed Mount Carmel, unforgettably beautiful, before the bus to Nahariya, a suburban little place not far from the Crusader fort/port of Acre, familiar to me from Runciman's *Crusades*.

It was true, as my sister's friend asserted. 'Everyone' from middle-class backgrounds was going to work on a kibbutz. I'd read that the kibbutz movement grew out of Tolstoyan communities in Russia, so the idea appealed. The kibbutzim were collectives in which farmers and craftsmen joined together and held all things in common. There was no servant class. Everyone took a hand in the most menial chores. All the work, tilling the land, keeping the place neat, cooking, tending for the children and the sick, was done by the collective.

At the Kibbutz Beit Haemek this worked pretty well; undoubtedly some of the older Dutch members of the community shared the unworldly ideals of early twentieth-century Zionists and when the day's work – picking bananas or citrus fruits – was done would return to their huts to read the great works of European literature, or practise the violin. The overwhelming atmosphere of the place, however, was of a lower-middle-class English suburb. Many of the men, some sporting handlebar moustaches, had been in the RAF. Only a year previously, in the Six Day War, the Israeli army and air force, armed by the USA, achieved a thumping victory over the combined forces of Egypt, Syria and Jordan. They had occupied the Sinai Peninsula, the old City of Jerusalem, including all the holy sites of Islam and Christianity, much of the so-called West Bank and, to the north, quite near the kibbutz, the Golan Heights. It was bizarre to sit in the branches of the orange groves, picking fruit, and to hear these NCOs from Bradford and Edgware chatting. You could have heard, if Kipling's stories are reliable, similar conversations in the hill stations of the Punjab in the days of the Raj, and I dare say, had I gone to Rhodesia, the farmers there would have spoken in comparable terms about their entitlement to land which they knew better how to cultivate than the indigenous population.

'Come back in five years,' one chap said to me, 'we'll have kibbutzim in the suburbs of Cairo.'

The exultant way in which they spoke of conquering the Arabs, whom they called 'wogs', was at extreme odds with the Tolstoyan dream of a world in which pacifism had brought about the stilling of aggression in the human heart. The more thoughtful members of the kibbutz were troubled by the fact that our little socialist community was built on someone else's village, but the majority were not. The Muslim cemetery behind the chicken sheds was a poignant spot.

The nearby town of Nahariya was a combination of *kleinbürgerlich* Germany and East Finchley with little delis and cafés, where older kibbutz ladies enjoyed shopping trips and nostalgic conversations about the department stores in Bradford and Manchester. The speculations about the Arab shopkeepers from whom they occasionally bought food – there was a Christian butcher who could ensure bacon and eggs for breakfast – were precisely of the sort that their coevals left behind in England were having about immigrant shopkeepers from Pakistan or the West Indies. The same lurid speculations about their sexual promiscuity and capacity for violence.

The kibbutz was largely secular, hence the bacon and eggs, but we kept the Shabbat, and sang the hymn to the Shabbat as the candles were lit with the first appearance of a star in the Friday skies. There was something wonderful about this, the more so since so many of us, including the residents, did not really follow the laws of Moses. A rabbi once told me that the Shabbat was the most beautiful of Yahweh's creations. God was there as we sang. (We all had basic Hebrew lessons, and I was grateful for these, though I have not kept it up.)

The kibbutz allowed for the religious observances of other faiths among the visitors. One of my fellow volunteers called Sandy, a thirty-something-year-old from Brighton who'd escaped a disastrous marriage and joined the Catholic Church, organized a large taxi to come each Sunday. It conveyed her, and some Anglican boys who'd been to Charterhouse and who were confirmed in Guildford Cathedral, to attend the Maronite rite in Acre. There was just room for me to squeeze in with them.

Acre is thought to be one of the oldest continuously inhabited spots on earth, so that, apart from its crusading history, its antiquities stretch back through the times of Alexander the Great and beyond. In 1947 the UN had designated it as a city in a future Arab state, its population being a mixture of Druse, Muslim, Bahá'i and Christian.

Then came the war of '48, the establishment of a state of Israel and all the subsequent troubled decades. In 1969 Acre was a totally Arab city, and the contrast between the kibbutz, with its *Daily Express*-reading flight sergeants and Finchley grannies, and this Levantine warren of old times and cultures could not have been more marked. We recusants from kibbutz life cherished these Sundays, the utterly mysterious, in all senses, Maronite liturgy, the packed church with its clanking incense-burners, its flickering candles, its rapt pious faces and, afterwards, Arab coffee on the harbour walls and sticky, honey-coated pastries.

Sandy was a troubled, lovable woman. She had realized there was something wrong in her marriage when, every evening as she came in from work, her husband put on the turntable a single by Engelbert Humperdinck – 'Please release me, let me go'. Her favourite novel, unsurprisingly given the town where she had embraced the Faith, was *Brighton Rock*. The final scene was Sandy's favourite, in which the old priest, thinking of what Rose, the waitress, has told him in the confessional, that she would prefer to be damned with the psychopathic Pinkie rather than receive absolution, tries to tell her about Charles Péguy, the poet who died at the very beginning of the First World War having returned to faith, but not the practice of the Faith. With Sandy one felt the excitement of spiritual adventure in her own journey. During the mass (the Maronites have their own liturgy in Syriac, the Aramaic spoken by Our Lord Himself) you felt two things that could never come to mind during an Anglican service: continuous antiquity and real Communion with universal Christendom. These Christians stretched back in time to Christ Himself, and they spoke His actual language. There was a continuous chain, stretching back into the first century itself and the extraordinary events that gave rise to the Christian religion. They were also in Communion with the majority of Christians round the world, and with the see of Rome, where, very old tradition asserts, Christians had first heard the Gospel from Peter himself. In the Gospel said to originate in Rome, that of Mark, in the passage describing Simon of Cyrene helping Christ to carry the cross, the author adds that Simon was the father of Rufus and Alexander, i.e. of two people who were actually known to the first hearers of this Gospel.

It was hard not to remember Newman being brought up short when a Roman Catholic bishop likened the Anglicans to the Donatists of the fourth century, go-it-alone Christians in North Africa who were cut off from the mainstream of Christendom, and on whom St Augustine had passed the judgement '*Securus judicat orbis terrarium.*' The judgement of the world is sure.

Most incongruously, for the rest of the week, perched in the orange groves. and half listening to the colonialist blather of the flight sergeants, I felt my heart tugged towards the old Faith. Later, when my months at Beit Haemek were over, I took a backpack and tramped round on my own, hitch-hiked to Eilat, which had not at that period been built as a tourist resort, camped with hippies overlooking the Gulf of Aqaba (memories of Peter O'Toole's capture of the place in David Lean's film *Lawrence of Arabia*!), hitched back in Arab vans through the Negev, explored the tourist sites of Galilee and finally alighted for two weeks in Jerusalem. Attending matins in St George's Cathedral, where I also stayed in their hostel, was a homesicky experience, with the words of The Book of Common Prayer being sung, together with school hymns. Even the architecture, pastiche English Gothic, was a candid admission of the Donatist/Anglican separateness from universal Christianity.

About ten days before, staying at a pilgrim's hostel on the shores of the Sea of Galilee, I fell in with a grey-bearded Franciscan priest who spoke fluent English with a Welsh accent but was by birth Portuguese. One of the whims he shared with Jean Dorothy and my Uncle Felix was that, since their mother came from the Christian family (surname Christian), they were descended from John of Gaunt.

The Portuguese friar, whose name I have forgotten, said I had 'a Plantagenet face' and so might well be one of those quarter of a million or so people who must by now descend from John of Gaunt. Having more or less nil interest in genealogy, and no belief in the John of Gaunt idea, I cannot now remember from which of the wives of John of Gaunt we are supposed to be descended.

It would either be Constance of Castile or Katherine Swynford, whose many children were born before wedlock but subsequently legitimized as Beaufort. The wife I'd like to have been descended from was the first, Blanche, the 'Duchess' in Chaucer's *Book of,* the mother of Henry IV. She died in my native Staffordshire at the age of twenty-two.

The conversations with the Portuguese friar made a great impression. He took me to Nazareth and showed me the excavations beneath the large modern basilica which suggested a church had been there since the first century. He expounded to me the idea, which I later heard on the lips of my friend Allan Maclean's father, Donald Maclean of Dochgarroch, that the first Christians were probably all of Founder's Kin, or at least close family friends. The cult which had grown up in Christ's lifetime, and its continuation after the Resurrection (first generation) and came to be written down (second generation), were not told about some imagined figures from storybooks. They were told about real people whose children and grandchildren were known to the small circle of the Jerusalem church and to the churches in exile, Antioch, Rome. Faith was something handed on by witnesses. I have found, in my life, when faith has vanished, that it is brought back by encounters with people. This is the essence of Catholicism – Joyce calls the Church HCE, or Here Comes Everybody – which is a realized sense of the people stretching back through two thousand years to the people who had actually known and experienced the friendship of Jesus and His mother when they walked this earth. The friar said to me that the fullness of faith could only be known when one was in communion with this cloud of witness, and that Anglicans, however well meaning, are forever outside it.

There is a bit of me which still understands this, and a bit that wishes to add: yes, but this argument would persuade me more to become an Orthodox than to embrace the preposterous claims of post-nineteenth-century Roman Catholicism, including papal infallibility, a religion in which authoritarian clericalism has so obviously helped to cover up, perhaps even to encourage, the abuse of children by priests. Also, in my old age, although I do accept that the fragmentation of Christendom is a grave scandal, I think that all churches have faults but all also have members whose lives shine with the life of Christ, and that this has been true in the C of E as it has in the other churches.

My eighteen-year-old mind, however, by the time I had got to Florence, was made up. Not long after I arrived to start my course in Italian there, I went to the great Dominican church of Santa Maria Novella and approached one of the priests, asking him to receive me into the Church. He was a youngish man of African descent. I have subsequently wondered whether he did not see that the impulsive young adolescent who made this request should be made to wait and consider the importance of the step. He told me he was about to go on a long visit to Lucca and directed me to the American priests at Gonzaga University, housed in one of the huge Renaissance palazzi near the city centre.

The priest who took on the task of instructing me had only recently emerged from a quarter of a century in a Carthusian monastery. I wish I had written down some of the things he said. He carried one of the most appalling moral burdens of any human being I ever met. In August 1945 he was a member of the crew aboard the plane which dropped a nuclear bomb on Nagasaki.

After a period of instruction, this gentle, deeply damaged man baptized me conditionally. A few weeks later I was confirmed by the bishop of Fiesole in his private chapel, together with the children of the American consul, who had booked in for the ceremony.

In her letters, frequent at this period, Sister Mary Mark, my old headmistress, worried about the effect all this would have on my mother, and suggested that I postponed being received until I came back to England. This was obviously good advice, but the truth is – and I cannot explain why this is the case – that the impulse to become a Roman Catholic during that period was absolutely overwhelming. To walk into one of the great churches in Florence and to know that I was not at one with what was going on was unbearable. I now think it was extremely selfish of me not to have waited.

Throughout this momentous inward journey a jolly student life was also in progress, in every way jollier than kibbutz life. Our Italian teacher, Luisa Rapaccini, was the author of the textbook we used for study, *Parlo Italiano!* All her class were reasonably fluent within a month or so and easily able to read a newspaper. After classes we would pour out to eat ice creams at Perchè No?

The cultural side of things, the story of the Renaissance, as seen through the pages of Vasari, Burckhardt, Ruskin – the history of the popes – and of the painters – was disclosed to us by the director of the British Institute, Ian Greenlees, and by his sidekick, Robin Chanter. People laughed at them, and they were indeed a throwback to a certain way of being English abroad, but they taught me a lot, and they awoke my Italophilia, which burns to this moment. I'd never have written my book *Dante in Love* had I not heard Greenlees's lectures on the great Florentine poet, and his reflections on the nature of love, as expressed in Plato's *Symposium*, the *Vita Nuova* and the works of J. A. Symonds.

Since my first day at the Institute I had been visited by the wound of falling in love, unaware that this particular obsession, lasting two decades, would sometimes threaten my sanity itself. It was her face which started it, very pale, framed with almost black short hair and the brightest blue-green stars for eyes and a broad laugh. My feelings about her were and are too strong to be described, but it would not be possible to tell the story of my life without mentioning them. She was destined to die in her early forties, thereby becoming a veritable Beatrice inside my head. She would go up to Somerville College, Oxford, and be my university contemporary for three years.

28. Lost Causes

Norman drove me, when the longed-for first week of October arrived. As always when it was just the two of us, and we were away from the psycho-dramas of home, I felt very fond of him. We drove round the Oxford ring road to the Slade Camp, where, as acting brigadier in the Oxford and Bucks Light Infantry, he'd organized the demobilization of thousands of men at the end of the war. The gulf between his forty-something self and the old man leaning on the fence and staring at his own past across the wasteland of the ring road was heart-tugging.

Unlike Jean, who 'could not see what was wrong with Cambridge' (Felix's university and that of Eric Woods), Norman was delighted that I was going to Oxford, and recalled pre-war trips with Jos to stay at the Mitre and attend concerts. The meeting with Rachmaninov was remembered and the Third Piano Concerto. But, oh the relief, the poignant relief, when, my belongings unpacked in my room in the New Buildings, we embraced, he parted – to stay with our cousins the Lewises in Headington, where Tony was a surgeon, at the Churchill Hospital – and the first day of Oxford life began.

It is well over thirty years since I left Oxford, and my marriage to Katherine Duncan-Jones. The power of the place never fails to overwhelm me, every time a train pulls up past John Lucas's church (St Thomas the Martyr, Becket Street). This dizzying sense of being in love with a place might be attributable to nostalgia, were it not for the fact that I had felt it the very first time I visited the town on a school trip, and for the stranger fact that I felt full-blast love of the place for all the years I actually lived there.

John Lucas (the clergyman, not the philosopher of that name) and I must have walked round it several times a week, every week, for a decade. There was not a corner of Christ Church Meadow or the Parks, not a college garden or chapel, not a side street, not a church, that we did not know: but these walks began in 1974, when I had already graduated and already acquired the obsessive love. The dome of the Radcliffe Camera, Hawksmoor's twin towers at All Souls, the cloisters in my own college and its walled garden exercise an hypnotic spell.

John Bayley once said to me, people should only become dons if they can't imaginably do anything else. Undoubtedly, apart from the knocking-you-for-six beauty of Radcliffe Square, and of so many of the colleges, one of the things that gives the place its powerful air of strangeness is the fact that so many of the heads you pass in the street or who are becoming pinker, then redder, then purpler in the candlelight of a high table, are stuffed with preoccupations unintelligible to any but a few: Husserl's phenomenology, the plausibility (or not) of string theory, new developments in neuroscience, the authenticity (or not) of some fragments from a Euripidean tragedy all but lost to knowledge.

When I was a college lecturer at St Hugh's, I clumsily asked Pamela Gradon, Reader in Middle English, whether she was looking forward to her retirement. She said the prospect terrified her.

'When I am talking to you, it seems perfectly normal to allude to the Lollards, the Wycliffe Bible or the fifteenth-century Church. You know what I am talking about. If I tried to talk about anything which has been going on in my head for the last forty years to a *normal* person' – she had bought a flat in north Oxford – 'what on earth do I talk to them about?'

Although I spent seven years as a lecturer at St Hugh's and at New College, I was never cut out to be an academic. I was never a scholar and, had my domestic circumstances been different, I should never have gone down this path. In the later years, London, literary journalism, books and bookmanship, a very different world from Academe, was where I belonged; but I do not regret for one moment my years beyond the Looking Glass, which began the moment I arrived at New College.

Of course, as far as the 'literary' side of things was concerned, I enjoyed revisiting Victorian and modern literature. John Bayley steered me through much of this stuff, and his company was delightful.

The rigours of Anglo-Saxon, or Old English as it is called in the trade – Anglo-Saxon being the people, and Old English being the language they spoke – was more of a challenge.

Christopher Tolkien. Where to begin?

The effete, upper-class-sounding voice. The calligraphic handwriting. The expression of agony on a fleshy face which broke into a cheeky-monkey smile, then a giggle. Humphrey Carpenter, who wrote the first biography of J. R. R. Tolkien and was a friend of mine, said his wife, Mari Pritchard, was alarmed, during the year he spent writing the book, that he, in a way, turned into

Christopher Tolkien with his second wife Baillie in a French cloister.

Christopher, such was the force of his personality. The high camp manner, the fastidiousness which appeared to find every aspect of life burdensome, the sense given that everything, beneath the surface, was hilarious. One of the old guard medievalists, C. L. Wrenn, crabby Fellow of Pembroke, who succeeded JRRT as Rawlinson and Bosworth Professor of Anglo-Saxon, snarled to a colleague, 'Tolkien brought his boy into dinner last night, posing as Oscar Wilde.' At that date Christopher affected blue cloaks, made at great cost at Halls', the tailor in the High; he was, to many in the faculty, an embarrassment.

The Professor had four children: John, who was a priest; Michael, a master at Ampleforth; Priscilla, a social worker; and Christopher, who was the father's darling. It was to Christopher, serving in the RAF in South Africa during the war, that the Professor had mailed out, chapter by chapter, fresh instalments of *The Lord of the Rings*. The letters to Christopher reveal the extent of their shared piety, JRRT urging Christopher, when he could not get to mass, to recite the entire Roman canon to himself (the long prayer of consecration starting *Te igitur, clementissime Pater*). If this proved impossible, Christopher was at least to say *Laudate Dominum*, one of the shorter psalms, or the *Magnificat*.

When the boy came back from the war, he was enthusiastically welcomed into his father's circle of chums, known as the Inklings (David Cecil, C. S. Lewis, Hugo Dyson and others), and because JRRT mumbled and was a shy reader, it was Christopher who entertained the group by reading the entire saga of the Ring, occasionally interrupted by Dyson's 'Not another fucking elf!'

Perhaps because he thought he Knew It All, perhaps because he was one of those who could not cope with exams, Christopher got a poor degree, and this in spite of his father, most improperly, imploring the examiners to mark his boy 'up'. Hyper-sensitive to the point of paranoia in whatever setting I encountered him – the Senior Common Room at New College, the various villages where he lived in Berkshire and the south of France – Christopher believed the dons had deliberately marked him harshly to punish his father because they were envious of his fame. (This theory was hard to sustain, since Christopher took his degree soon after the war, before *The Lord of the Rings* had been published, and although *The Hobbit* was popular among nicely brought-up children, its sales were scarcely of the order that would necessitate the engagement of tax lawyers, as happened with *The Lord of the Rings*.)

True, many in the faculty disliked the Inklings. It was felt the little clique was all male and exclusive and their Christianity, especially as popularized in C. S. Lewis's paperbacks, made many colleagues squirm. There were also members of the faculty who felt that Tolkien senior did not pull his weight in such matters as supervising graduate students. JRRT was one of those who found it difficult to bring a task to completion, and long-awaited learned work – an edition of Chaucer for Oxford University Press and of *The Exeter Book* for the Early English Text Society – remained just that, long awaited, while this group of pipe-smoking chaps sat around drinking heavily in bars and telling each other fairy stories. One of Lewis's worst poems, and that is saying something, begins, 'We were talking of dragons, Tolkien and I, in a Berkshire bar.'

When Christopher crashed in the Schools – a Third – the obvious thing to have done would be to give up any aspirations to an academic career, but the Professor insisted on his pushing ahead. He did a BLitt in Old Norse and published the results of his endeavours, *The Saga of Heidrek the Wise*, when he was thirty-six, in 1960. Then he began to pick up bits of teaching here and there as a college lecturer, first at Worcester College, then at New College.

This enabled him to join the English Faculty, though he had small hope of preferment, and to give university lectures. For the next ten years these lectures became legendary. It became necessary to stage them in larger and larger lecture halls until he was eventually filling the South School, the largest space within the enormous Tudorbethan halls on the High where students sit their final exams. The nickname given to these lectures was 'Sex and Violence in the Heroic Age'. He told the Old Tales of the North with prodigious eloquence, the Eddaic versions of Attila the Hun and Ermaneric, the feuds of the Volsungs, the story of Sigurd and Gudrún, as well as relaying the stories of the great Icelandic family sagas. Hundreds of undergraduates attended these lectures, most of whom were not studying Old Norse or Old English, simply because he told the stories so enthrallingly.

As a private tutor he was an attentive listener when one read out an essay, but unsatisfactory at supplying actual information. Inevitably, teaching the 'language' side of the English school requires an element of knowledge. The tutor always knows more than the student, which is not the case (or need not be) if all they are doing is discussing the novels of George Eliot.

If you're paranoid, as Christopher was, any student's question seemed designed to catch him out. If you asked reasonable questions such as 'Do we know if the inscriptions on the Ruthwell Cross are older than the Vercelli Book?' (these are the two sources for the famous *Dream of the Rood* poem in Old English) or 'What is the current state of play regarding the date of *Beowulf* – do scholars still think it dates from the age it describes, i.e. the pre-Christian north, or do people think it was now composed during the reign of Knut?', Christopher would look at you quizzically, light his pipe yet again with his lighter and let out huge billows of smoke. Then he'd go to a large bureau, open one of the drawers and, from a pile of papers, take out a yellowing script.

'This is something my father wrote about the subject,' he would say.

Quite often, it was not in fact directly relevant to one's question. How often I heard him say, whether discussing the *Laxdæla Saga* or the *Ormulum*, whether comparing the analogues of *Beowulf* or comparing the different dialects of Old English, 'Here's something my father once wrote.'

The obsession with the father was understandable, but there was something uneasy about his evident inferiority to The Professor. It was complicated by his pitiful yearning to belong to the smarter set of dons who, rather younger than himself, had friends in country houses or in London. This set revolved around the medieval history don Eric Christiansen and one of the modern languages dons, Alex de Jonge, and his film-star glamorous wife Judy, whose sophisticated style of talk set them apart from the average academic households in north Oxford. They were far too cool to enjoy *The Lord of the Rings*. They would hold up Iris Murdoch's love of the trilogy, and her willingness to spend hours with the Professor discussing the finer points of Elven lore, as a sign of her childish unworldliness. Tony and Marcelle Quinton likewise – Tony a philosophy don, Marcelle an American sculptor with a line in sub-Dorothy Parker wisecracks – were openly scornful of the masterpiece. These were the amusing people in the college. Moreover, these were those who might be able to persuade the Governing Body to overlook the bad degree and award him a fellowship.

In this company, when I first knew him, Christopher would disloyally pretend to understand, even if not totally to share, the Cool Cats' disdain for Frodo Baggins, Tom Bombadil and the Land of Mordor where the shadows lie. The first time I saw Christopher joining in the laughter as they mocked hobbits in the de Jonges' house, the cheerleader was an old New College man, now a London publisher, named Sebastian Walker, I was shocked. It was only hours since, in a tutorial, Christopher had been reverently reading to me what his father thought about *Sir Gawain and the Green Knight*. When the mega-bucks started to roll in, however, the balance of conversational power altered and the Cool Cats, awestruck by money, used to treat Christopher, especially when he had gone abroad to spend a lifetime editing his father's posthumous work, with some of the politeness accorded by unsophisticated people to royalty.

Behind the fear of hobbits and elves being uncool, there was class paranoia. Old Professor Tolkien's parents had been poor. In the infancy of himself and his brother, JRRT found himself in Birmingham living in lodgings with his mother. She had become a Catholic, and handed over JRRT like the Infant Samuel to the fathers of the Oratory in the Hagley Road. He was in effect brought up by Father Tristram, one of the last fathers who had known Cardinal Newman. Newman-obsessed as I was, I tried to pump Christopher about this, but he clearly found the whole subject of his father growing up in the poverty of mean boarding houses in Brum too painful. Moreover it reawoke the matter of Catholicism, which was something that scalded his soul.

Christopher was brought up not just Catholic but ultra-Catholic. As an undergraduate, he'd fallen in love with the granddaughter of the most ultra-Catholic apologist of the time, Hilaire Belloc. Bar Belloc, daughter of Peter, who was killed in the war, was the Zuleika

Dobson of her day. Christopher used to say he loved her so much he'd have been prepared to live in Swindon if she would marry him.

She was pure style. She married a man whose surname was Eustace and became an antiquaire-socialite in Chelsea. Christopher married a sculptor called Faith Faulconbridge, who was a hugely loved and admired art teacher at Notre Dame High School for Girls in the Woodstock Road. They had a son called Simon. It somehow all unravelled not because, but after, Faith had fallen in love with someone else – Elizabeth Mavor, author of a sublime book about the redoubtable Ladies of Llangollen.

Such was the unsophisticated world, male-dominated, in which they moved that Christopher felt bafflement and shame at what had happened. He sought the help of an old family friend, Douglas Carter, the parish priest at St Gregory and St Augustine in the Woodstock Road.

He bought Father Carter dinner at the Luna Caprese restaurant in North Parade and told him the whole situation. The very next morning Faith went to school as usual but, before lessons, she was summoned to the office of the headmistress and dismissed on the spot. Christopher's confidential conversation with a man he had trusted implicitly led to this appalling moment.

Professor Tolkien was desolated when Christopher left the Church. The Professor had engaged a young Canadian woman for secretarial help, and it was not long before Mrs Baillie Knapheis of Winnipeg and Christopher had become lovers, and the parents of two children. *The Lord of the Rings* was by now big business. As the second Mrs Christopher Tolkien, Baillie had pulled a lever on the fruit machine and could watch as the three cherries lined up and money cascaded. All Christopher's friends, especially the smart ones, were vile about her. One of the Cool Cats, a young man called Andrew Lever, once found himself opposite her on the London train. She was too shy to try to greet him, and hid her face behind an open newspaper. He got out his cigarette lighter and set fire to her paper, an act of malicious bravado worthy of Peter Verkhovensky in *The Possessed*. It was not surprising that she put such pressure on Christopher to leave England as soon as possible after his father died.

29. Angel Fluffs

One morning, Sub-Lieutenant M. W. G. Kerr, always known as Bim, Mark Blackett-Ord, Rick Stein (the future restaurateur and celebrity chef) and I left Christopher's class on *Beowulf* and wandered off for some coffee. Rick, who was older than most of us – he'd travelled to New Zealand and Mexico after a family tragedy – turned to us and asked in his slightly cockneyfied voice, 'So, why haven't you got any hang-ups?'

A good question. Mark and Bim certainly appeared to have no hang-ups and I don't think I did. This was in that uncomplicated first year at Oxford, when I was so absurdly happy. I think that Rick, who had made the choice to become an undergraduate in his early twenties, and had experienced grown-up life proper, assumed that the student life inevitably entailed depression, self-doubt, angst. Certainly, when I became a university teacher, I realized that the majority of my pupils, especially the female ones, were depressed or anxious much of the time. The huge proportion were homesick – in those days there were proportionately fewer privately educated students and the majority were coming away from home for the first time.

Neither Bim nor Mark had any doubts about their future. Mark was destined for the Bar, at which he subsequently was highly successful. Bim would end up as an admiral in the Royal Navy. What was there to have a hang-up about? Finding myself on the same staircase as an officer in the Royal Navy was a very happy chance. Many of my Tolstoyan pacifist notions were vigorously challenged by Bim in the college bar or over the dinner table. (Pre-Pot Noodle we ate all our meals in hall, which Oxford students do not seem to do so often these days.) Every now and then, Bim had an evening of what he called war games. It was not a phrase I'd heard. Senior officers would come down from wherever senior officers come from to join them, and Eliza Manningham-Buller, one of Bim's friends from Lady Margaret Hall, was of the party, so presumably she was already set on the career that would lead to her becoming the head of MI6. The 'game' was to ask: suppose the Russian fleet in the Baltic began to threaten one of our NATO allies, or suppose ... *Si vis pacem, para bellum* was one of Bim's favourite sayings – if you want peace, prepare for war.

My friendships were not confined to college. While still an undergraduate, I came to know Jeremy Catto, the medieval historian of Oriel College. He was Katherine's best friend, and it was she who first took me to his rooms in King Edward Street. The first thing that struck you when you came into the room was the superb David Hockney portrait of Jeremy, wearing evening dress and dark glasses and sprawled on his sofa. The artist who executed this crayon likeness was not in fact Hockney but Glynn Boyd Harte, who with his wife, Carrie Bullock, had been discovered on their honeymoon in Venice by Jeremy's pupil, and sometime lover, Colin McMordie, who was now at work on a PhD thesis supervised by Francis Haskell. In his unmistakable tones, half Ulster brogue and half Bloomsbury set, Colin would end a conversation with 'Well, I must be off now to the Art Library to translate my notes into Scott Moncrieff prose.' (Like Tosswill at Warwick, Colin failed his PhD.)

Jeremy Catto's funeral in 2019 was an astounding event, at which politicians, actors, the occasional rock star, men and women of letters mingled with medievalist scholars in the packed Oratory church in Oxford to hear Victoria's Requiem for Six Voices and to say goodbye to one of the truly great university teachers of the age, and, as we were reminded a few months later at the University Church at Jeremy's memorial service, to celebrate one of the great historians of the fifteenth-century church.

Alan Hollinghurst remarked to me after that service, as hundreds, literally hundreds, of Catto's friends spilled out on to the High, 'I'd no idea Jeremy ever did any work.' It is true that he kept his researches into the Lollards somewhat secret from those who attended his parties, where the beefier rowing hearties in Oriel would be welcomed as 'angel fluffs' and introduced to the aspirant Cabinet ministers down from London (William Hague and Alan Duncan among them) and where glasses of Wod would be thrust into the hands of the guests as they arrived. 'Or would you rather have ginwater?' Particularly if his hero the Regius (Hugh Trevor-Roper) was present, there would be some formulaic denunciation of their 'enemies' in the faculty, and the suggestion that some left-wing don was 'pure hellette on toastino', but Jeremy, unlike the Regius, was a fundamentally warm-hearted person, a rounded human being, and completely unsnobbish.

He and Katherine had literally bumped into one another on the corner of Broad Street and Magdalen Street on their first day as undergraduates in 1958. They had immediately gone off to play Poohsticks on the bridge at Magdalen on the edge of Addison's Walk and, deep into their seventies, they retained their childishness, their fondness for playing old singles on the record deck: 'American Pie' and Peter Sarstedt's 'Where Do You Go To (My Lovely)?', which was really 'their tune'. There were occasional spats. I never saw him angrier than when she described Colin McMordie as a pouter pigeon. But he was of a forgiving temperament, and if she had been seen round the King's Arms spreading some appallingly inaccurate gossip, he would indulgently describe her as 'Dame Rumour'.

It was in Jeremy's rooms that I made some of the friendships that lasted through life. The Boyd Hartes. Then there was a bearded redhead just down from St Andrews to study the architecture of James Wyatt, and resembling the young Swinburne – it was John Martin Robinson.

Once, drunk, looking for my coat among the crumpled mountains of macs and donkey jackets, I decided to lie down and recover from an unwonted intake of Wod, or was it ginwater? I discerned as I snuggled in that someone else had had the same idea as myself. It was a beautiful German boy. Second glance revealed Tanya Ledger, an aesthete about to embark on a study of Ruskin and the Arundel Society, destined to be one of the great historians of craft and design.

We began talking. She told me about being insanely in love with someone or another. Like me, she is usually in love. I told her about the beautiful Somervillian with whom I'd fallen in love in Florence, and at some point Jeremy appeared brandishing a bottle.

'But that's gin and you gave me vodka before.'

'Ginwater and Wod go well together.'

I think everyone in Oxford was in love with Tanya at that point. At a party in north Oxford, held in someone's garden, there were eighty or a hundred people on the lawn. The French windows opened and Tanya came out wearing a sailor's suit. There was a sort of collective gasp from everyone present. Oddly enough, much as I love her, I was never in love with Tanya nor she with me, and there was never the smallest hint of our having an affair. She had an affair with Jeremy though, perhaps the only woman so to do, although he did propose marriage to Char Bridgewater. Friendship in my experience is a deeper thing than 'love'. Fifty years since finding myself under the macs, drinking Wod – or was it ginwater? – I am still lucky enough to see Tanya and have her as a friend.

Tanya Ledger.

30. "Are they twa sweethearts?"

In one of those twists which make life aspire to the condition of a novel by Anthony Powell, Tanya would eventually become the sister-in-law of Christina Hobhouse, who had befriended Aunt Elizabeth at the mobile library in Llansteffan and who attended the recusant mass in Dai Thomas's tin hut. Tanya would marry Henry Harrod, a barrister in chambers with my old friend Mark Blackett-Ord. Henry's brother, Christina's husband, was the economist Dominick Harrod. They were related to Sir Johnston Forbes-Robertson, and when I see that legendary actor's portrait hanging in Henry and Tanya's house, I think of my aunt, in the Theatre Royal, Hanley, revelling in his interpretations of Cassius, Shylock and Hamlet.

When, on Christina's recommendation, I stepped into the Roman Catholic chapel at the Old Palace tucked off St Aldate's, I felt immediately at home. Of course, because it had been built on the cheap in the 1920s or 1930s on the instructions of converts from Anglo-Catholicism. The light fittings in the shape of cardinal's hats, with dusty old tassels hanging down, the plasterwork Edgware Road baroque candlesticks on the altar, this was the sort of 'tat' which High Anglican clergy liked in such shrines as St Mary's, Bourne Street, or the Annunciation, Bryanston Street, churches I'd sought out during the school holidays when staying with my sister, who lived more or less next door to another of them – T. S. Eliot's St Stephen's, Gloucester Road.

No wonder the military figure standing in the midst of this strange interior, wearing the modern floppy vestments of the anti-aesthete, was blind to its charm. After a term I would see the whole lot demolished and chucked in the skip. A characterless modern building containing a chapel which doubled as a meeting space for events took its place. In all the time I went to the Old Palace, building work was in progress and mass was offered in the sitting room, with students and homeless people squeezed in, sitting on window ledges or cross-legged on the carpet.

'The Lord be with you,' said a military voice.

And the congregation was replying 'And also with you', which to my ears sounds just about as numinous as 'The same to you with brass knobs on.'

It is probably foolish to make league tables of people in life, saying such and such a person was the cleverest, wittiest, prettiest etc., etc. ever known. Yet it must be true that Michael Hollings was the most remarkable, extraordinary man I ever knew.

It was the capacity for self-giving. It was utter. Self-giving to God, and to others. Hard to think of anyone less like myself in this respect. He was on fire with the Gospel of Jesus Christ. Anyone can see that the Gospel is an uncompromising call, for the death of self, for the transformation of every soul into God's likeness, for the bringing to pass of His Kingdom on earth. You can't get anything more revolutionary than that. Most of us are seeds scattered here and there, struggling to grow by the wayside. The seed which fell in good soil, bringing forth fruit a hundredfold, flourished not only because it was destined or lucky. Such souls are alive with the idea of spiritual adventure. Dorothy Day, Sister Mary Mark, Joan of Arc – they accepted the Call. They left their nets and followed, and expected others to do the same. Naturally enough, there were those who were unconvinced by Michael, seeing him as a mad officer who had presumably gone barmy in the Western Desert, fighting a gallant war and getting the MC.

When he was just twenty, in December 1942, he took part in a night attack on Longstop Hill, Tunis. He was shot in the throat, but made no effort to obtain medical treatment and continued to fight until morning. When he reported, with his platoon, at a Regimental Aid Post, he insisted upon the men being treated before himself, but when the medics unwound the scarf from his neck, they realized the extent of his injuries. The recklessness and bravery were always there in his peacetime self.

He was brought up as a Catholic, but he'd never attended mass with his fellow Catholics while on military service, and his friends were astonished that as soon as the war was over he began to train as a priest, at the Pontifical Beda College in Rome. He began his lifetime habit of sleeping on the floor or in deckchairs, presumably in part because of the discomfort of his wounds, in part in imitation of the Son of Man, who had nowhere to lay His head. He prayed half the night. Visits to Padre Pio, the Franciscan who had received the stigmata in his hands, helped Michael on his road to God. When he was chaplain at Oxford, many college tutors complained to him that their pupils were falling asleep in tutorials because they had been told to imitate Michael's nocturnal vigils of prayer.

Both at Oxford and, later, as a parish priest in Southall and Bayswater, he carried on a perpetual practice of the presence of God. His door was never locked. Any of his residences was always crammed with drifters, often quite smelly, who slept here and there, occasionally starting unintentional fires with their cigarettes, but usually shuffling in to hear him say mass.

I was so glad to be a bit late for his funeral in Westminster Cathedral, and not to be sitting in the main aisles among the Oxford graduates and the Catholic grandees. Being late, I was lucky to be able to squeeze into the side aisle by the Blessed Sacrament Chapel where an army of the homeless continued to edge in, much to the chagrin of the vergers or stewards. At the end of the service, when the coffin was lifted onto the shoulders of the bearers, this army of homeless men and women surged forward. They seemed like the holy ragamuffin pilgrims of Old Russia, or the followers of a medieval pilgrimage, these shaggy rough sleepers, fixing their tearful, intent gaze on that coffin. These were Michael's people. Jesus's people.

That first morning I attended his mass he stopped me at the door and asked me to breakfast. Sitting round the table at the Old Palace eating boiled eggs and drinking very strong coffee were his nice assistant chaplain Crispian Hollis – later a very kind friend to me – some undergraduates like myself, some graduates who appeared to be lodgers in the house and a number of ladies and gentlemen of the road. (Michael eschewed, and hated, the word 'tramp'.)

I had breakfast there every day for the next eighteen months whenever I was in Oxford.

Let me describe Michael's face, which was divided by an enormous, Cyrano de Bergerac nose. It was quite red. Even in those days he was a heavy whisky drinker. Very bright blue eyes. Sleeked-back, undyed dark hair, brushed in a military manner. The gash in the throat. Guards officer voice, broken by a lot of laughter. When I was lucky enough to work at the *Spectator* and was taken up by Algy Cluff, the proprietor, also Grenadier Guards, he had a very similar voice and manner.

The reader will by now have grasped my dithering temperament, doubting everything and inconstant in my affections. In Michael's company, it was quite clear that God was real. There was something completely real going on here, which was why, in later life, I kept out of his way. After I'd lapsed, I'd hear from time to time of those who had been to see him, that he had asked after me, suggested I came to visit. I fled him down the nights and down the days. But that funeral of his was one of the moments when, after years of leaving faith behind me, I realized I was on the way back.

He was amused by my Newmania: one of his geniuses as a priest was a capacity to meet people where they were, and, without compromising his own very clear set of values, to be all things to all people, whether it was Sheila Cassidy, who was there at that first breakfast table – who was tortured in the notorious Villa Grimaldi near Santiago for giving medical care to opponents of Chilean dictator General Pinochet – or conservative Catholics like Piers Paul Read, for whom Michael offered a Tridentine mass in his Bayswater church as an alternative to the Happy-Clappy version which was the chief morning service, and whether it was praying in the mosque in Southall with his Muslim brothers or conducting parish retreats for Anglicans.

Michael managed to put me in touch with priests at Newman's Oratory in Birmingham, who also owned and looked after the little row of cottages in Littlemore, just outside Oxford, where Newman and his closest disciples had spent two years agonizing before eventually submitting to Rome on 9 October 1845. One of these priests, Father Humphrey Crookenden, needed help with the garden there and I enjoyed my hours down there with him, weeding, and trying to make sure there was nothing growing in the garden that would not have been seen in English soil later than 1845. I eagerly accepted Father Humphrey's invitation to the house in Birmingham. It was clearly in his mind that I might one day become Father Andrew Wilson Cong. Orat. A part of myself (but even then, it was a diminishing part) was tempted. The chief draw, as I was aware, was not specifically religious, unless love of the past counts as a religion. The chief draw was that nothing appeared to have changed in that Birmingham house since the death of Newman, though I suppose there was electricity? (Or was there? The Pope who made Newman a cardinal, Leo XIII, had condemned the use of electricity, just as one of his predecessors saw railways as the work of the devil and called them *les chemins d'enfer*. This is the side of papal authoritarianism which I like – Pius X condemned the saxophone.)

Newman's room had been left unaltered, utterly, since the day he died in 1890. The cardinal's hat, as dusty as the lamps in the Old Palace, was slung over a hook on the corner of the wardrobe. The room was that of a bachelor don in the era of Lewis Carroll. Here were his yellowing old maps of Khartoum, cut out of *The Times*, so that the old man could follow Kitchener's progress. Here were the photos of St Mary's Oxford, in the High; here were his Trollope novels, his writing table, his sealing wax, his little truckle bed. There was really no sign that the twentieth century had dawned.

It seems natural to me to want to live in the past. Here was a genuine chance to do so. Were it not for my need for love, and for women in my life … But more than this, ever since becoming a Catholic, there had grown inside me the need to confront the certainties that Newman's *Apologia* seemed to offer. 'There are but two alternatives, the way to Rome and the way to Atheism. Anglicanism is the halfway house on the one side and Liberalism is the halfway house on the other.' (By Anglicanism Newman meant what was later called Anglo-Catholicism, and by Liberalism he meant that wishy-washy type of thought which has characterized most C of E bishops, such as the one I was unkind about earlier in this book, the one on the cruise.)

Old age has brought perspectives that were not visible to a younger self. On that very cruise, where the wishy-washy bishop was a lecturer, I had a profound sense of God – not in a Christian church but at the shrine of Apollo at Delphi. A similar sense, of a visitation outside oneself, of a quite definite Presence, came to me years later when visiting a Jain temple in Old Delhi. There was a palpable sense of holiness. A phrase in the Psalms comes back to me over and over – 'Thou that hearest prayer, unto thee shall ALL FLESH come.' Or again, I think of the day when Ruth and I were lucky enough to go to the Hay-on-Wye literary festival to hear Archbishop Desmond Tutu speak. One of the most memorable things he said, bursting into laughter as he said it, was, 'The thing people forget about God is – God is not a Christian.'

So, sorry, Newman, but the saying that there are only two alternatives, Rome or Atheism, is simply not true. Moreover, it is not merely untrue, it is irreligious. When I think of the lives of the majority of my many Roman Catholic friends and ask myself why the huge proportion of them have lapsed and decided to live without religion, is it not because they have been taught to believe a version of Newman's propaganda? Since common sense (apart from anything else) shows that so many of the claims of popes and Catholic apologists over the years have been *demonstrably* untrue, the 'only alternative' would appear to be atheism. So they live without what St Paul calls the unsearchable riches of Christ, as I myself did for about fifteen years of my adult life.

Moreover, as my beautiful Somervillian friend would ask, on our walks together across Port Meadow, or sometimes, after a bus ride, in Blenheim Park, what is wrong with halfway houses? She would remind me of my fondness for Rose Macaulay, whose witty novels had been a discovery during schooldays. The masterpiece is her last, *The Towers of Trebizond*, written when she was an old lady, after a long period of estrangement from the Church (an affair) and then a return. The theme of the book, comparable to that of *Brideshead Revisited*, is the operation of Divine Grace, but it is a better novel, for my money, not least because the narrator (a man or a woman? One is never told) ends up still wistfully gazing at the Towers of that Eastern citadel, which for her/him has become an emblem of faith. My beautiful friend liked to quote this narrator: 'Nothing in the world could be as true as the Roman Catholic Church thinks it is … I suppose this must be comforting and reassuring, but most of us know that nothing is as true as all that.'

Clearly, had I become a father of the Birmingham Oratory, I'd have had to come to terms with this, and whether I'd have stuck it out, become a man of deep prayer and developed a fuller sense of Catholic truth, and a more nuanced understanding of the human predicament, or whether I'd have joined the thousands of Catholic priests who, in my lifetime, felt faith draining out of them like sands in the hourglass, who knows? It was not to be. *Wyrd bith ful aræd.*

The girl I loved, and who was so well versed in Rose Macaulay, had a birthday. Was it a nineteenth? A twentieth? I had no idea at the time that her mother was dying, as she herself would do, in her forties. It was a lovely birthday party, two punts full of young people, some young men from Christ Church, one of whom she would marry, her friends from Somerville, and we punted up the Cherwell on a perfect sunny day and ate a picnic in a field, and were in Paradise. Because we never spoke of personal matters, and I did not know her mother was ill, her disappearance at the end of term was something I did not notice. I had my exams – Honour Moderations, they were rather pretentiously called. For me, Honour Mods means what my daughter Emily was to do later,

Latin and Greek, not writing about *Middlemarch*. The first year had whizzed by, as time does when one is happy.

Then Katherine asked me to spend a few days with her and a Cambridge friend on Osea Island, in the mouth of the River Blackwater in Essex, within sight of where the Battle of Maldon had been fought and, according to the poem, the proud old Anglo-Saxon warrior Byrhthnoth had attempted to hold the causeway against the Vikings.

Were Katherine and I beginning to wonder if we were in love? Later that summer she told me that she was painfully in love, had been for years, with a Fellow of my college. We went for long walks round Osea Island. The green corn was high. We both re-read *The Lord of the Rings* (one of those books which is better every time you read it). The talk was non-stop. There was so much to talk about, so many jokes. I liked her friend Vivien Stewart, destined, like others in this story, to die in her forties. Vivien suggested that later in the summer we should all have a holiday together in the Orkneys. If it seems to the reader strange that a nineteen-year-old boy should go on holiday with two women approaching their thirties, it never felt strange at the time.

I mentioned to Katherine that in the following week I was going to stay at the Birmingham Oratory. Katherine suddenly gave me her mother's telephone number in Brum. 'If you like, you could ring me, when you leave the Oratory.'

I was not sure about meeting the mother. It all seemed a bit sudden. And what if the Oratory *were* to be the future? Oddly enough, I had not thought about the vow of celibacy which would be involved. I suspect this is true for many who wonder if they have a vocation. If one had a vocation, would not God sort out the rest?

At the time of writing these words, it is the third decade of the twenty-first century. The Pope canonized Newman a few years ago. The Birmingham Oratory is apparently thriving. In 1970, however, it really appeared to be on its last legs. An Oratory is not a monastery. It is a community of priests who have agreed to live together and to serve the surrounding district of a city – the first of them having been started in Counter-Reformation Rome by St Philip Neri.

I was greeted by Father Philip Lynch, formerly the Superior, now well over ninety years old. It was he who could remember Father Tristram, the last of the fathers who had known Newman himself. Not all the memories cast Newman in a favourable light. Lynch told me of a priest who had joined the Oratory in about 1870. All went swimmingly for a few weeks and then, without explanation, Newman stopped speaking to him. Ice descended. The young man never knew how he had offended, but for twenty years Newman swept past him on the landing without giving him a glance, and any remark he made at the hour called recreation was received in silence. Is this the behaviour of a saint?

The household that I experienced in 1970 was fairly rum. There were, I seem to recall, seven priests still hanging on. Keeping up the uncharitable Newman tradition of No Speakers to a colleague they disliked, five of them had sent Father John Challoner to Coventry. He had written a perfectly sensible article in the *Birmingham Post* questioning both the theology and the science of *Humanae vitae*. Only my friend Father Humphrey Crookenden was Christian enough to speak to this colleague, who, after a year of being isolated and snubbed, left the priesthood and married.

Those who remained (except Lynch) had all been Anglican clergymen. They were all dismayed by the changes howling through the Church. They were doing their gallant best to uphold the spirit of the First Vatican Council, while utterly ignoring the implications of the Second. They continued to mutter private masses at the side altars in their vast church. (One of these altars contained the body of St Valentine, but not, they told me, *the* St Valentine.) They spent hours sitting in the confessionals, which in those days were still frequented by the laity. One of them did so with the scores of Italian operas on his knee, and while the penitents muttered their wrongdoings, he was reading *La Traviata* or *Un Ballo in Maschera*. He took seriously the Vatican I ban on priests going to the theatre, and, when he became RC, it had been a bitter blow to him to give up the opera.

Aeons after my stay in the Oratory, I was in Palermo on holiday with Ruth and we visited the Catacombs. Rather than burying the dead, the Capuchin fathers clothed them, propped them up or suspended them from coat-hangers. You walk through chamber after chamber of dead Sicilians, whose skeletal forms are still clad in the nankeen trousers and epauletted uniforms of the Napoleonic era, or in the bonnets and flounces of the later nineteenth century. There are many priests, their skulls grinning beneath lopsided birettas, their bone-fingers grasping rosaries beneath lacy sleeves. When I reached this macabre section of the Catacombs, memory instantly transported me to the Hagley Road, Birmingham, in 1970.

Meals, taken in the panelled dining room, were served in silence. One of the Palermo skullheads would bolt down his food ten minutes before the others and then read aloud to them as they munched the boarding-school food. In that particular week it was Antonia Fraser's *Mary Queen of Scots*.

After the evening meal there was a gruesome hour called recreation. They sat in a semicircle round the hearth in a parlour designed to remind Newman of the achingly and everlastingly missed Senior Common Room at Oriel. The fathers quizzed me for news of Oxford, but in this company it seemed a cruelty to reveal that the twentieth century was in full blast: the Mitre was a Berni Inn; there was talk of the colleges going mixed, or, as Warden Sparrow called it, bisexual; the Cornmarket and the Westgate were now shopping centres; and the old Oxford shops – Elliston & Cavell, Capes, Knights – were dying, and being replaced by chain stores.

What they really wanted, though, was Oxford *church* news; not, of course, news of Roman Catholic places of worship. They had, doubtless, all gone over to the Dark Side and had embraced the Council. The Oratorians, homesick C of E converts, wanted news of the proper churches. Was St Mary Magdalen still using the Prayer Book, as in the days of the redoubtable Father Hack, or had it, as rumour suggested, now gone over to using the English Missal? Was the maniple still worn at St Barnabas? And what about St Paul's, Walton Street? Kind old Father Humphrey looked at me sadly. 'You tell them,' he murmured. After his innumerable gardening trips to Oxford, he had not had the heart to inform them that their favourite church, the Greek Revival *Ecclesia Sancti Pauli* in Walton

Street, a teetering bulwark of advanced Anglo-papalism, had been closed down. The diocesan authorities wanted to demolish it and develop the site. (Later, it would reopen, but this time as a café. The words ECCLESIA SANCTI PAULI over the door were replaced with the single word, FREUD.)

The optimism with which the Birmingham Struldbruggs surveyed their nineteen-year-old recruit was touching. Next day they made me promise to return before the end of the Long Vacation. We trooped into the refectory for another dose of Lady Antonia. The odour of fish pie appalled, but, having spent a decade of my earthly existence at boarding schools, I did not take the rank pong as a warning.

To stand on the pavement of the Hagley Road forty minutes later was to realize one had shockingly stepped back into the twentieth century. Well, almost. There was the old Plough and Harrow inn, looking much as it had done when George Eliot and George Lewes stayed there, having come to Birmingham to hear Newman preach. Gladstone had refreshed himself with a glass of claret in the coffee room there, having called on his old friend and sat in the very room, the ecclesiastical equivalent of Miss Havisham's wedding breakfast, which now gathered its sacred cobwebs. To this inn, too, had hastened Lord Rosebery, Gladstone's successor as Prime Minister. Rosebery had rushed to Brum by train to see Newman lying in his open coffin. 'This was the end of the young Calvinist, the Oxford don, the austere vicar of St Mary's. It seemed as if a whole cycle of human life and thought was concentrated in that august repose. That was my overwhelming thought. Kindly Light had led and guided Newman to this strange, brilliant end.'

That was it. More, really, than the end itself, or the narrower claims made in the *Apologia*, it was the 'whole cycle' which explained Newman's hold on the imagination. His life journey represents a whole cycle of human thought. That was what captivated his contemporaries, especially those who, like Matthew Arnold and George Eliot, felt themselves being swept, on their life cycle, in a completely opposite direction, towards agnosticism and a heaven left empty of its gods.

As the buses roared by towards the centre of Brum, I asked myself whether I should leap aboard one of them to revisit the dear old Pre-Raphaelites in the City Art Gallery, Millais's *The Blind Girl* being the favourite, or whether I was brave enough to telephone Miss Duncan-Jones, as I still half thought of her. As I pushed my way into the nearest kiosk and dialled the number, a slight queasiness overcame me, possibly attributable to the urinary atmosphere, possibly to nervousness. Then came her breathy attempt to stammer 'Hello', and I pressed Button B.

The house was not far away, near the university. She had not explained about her mother, a pretty woman in her sixties, dressed in a little crimson suit with a velvet collar. I did not, therefore, know that the person offering me the cup of Earl Grey was a distinguished scholar of the seventeenth century and an expert in Andrew Marvell. I guessed, from the only half-convincing upper-class tones and the histrionic mannerisms – closed eyes as the head nodded for emphasis – that she might be on the stage. Sipping the tea, I realized that to consume anything at this juncture was going to be a mistake and that if acute embarrassment was to be avoided, I needed to get out of the house fast. Luckily, I got to a lavatory in time.

The Oratorian fish pie was Fate's Instrument. The worst food poisoning ever suffered before or since in my life was starting. Some days later, as delirium receded, I awoke in the Duncan-Joneses' spare bedroom. An earnest young medic from the University Health Centre was telling the two women that I should have been in hospital. Turning to me with some severity, he pointed at a glass next to the bed and said, 'You should not even think of drinking that.'

Not realizing that I was a mere refugee from the nineteenth century, who had never taken anything more injurious than the opium of the people – of Victorian people at that – he had falsely guessed I was a modern student, with an unwise narcotic dependency. I was showing all the signs of Hepatitis A. Even in delirium I had been drinking red wine – so he supposed from looking at the Ribena on the bedside table. Bed rest was necessary for at least another day or two, and then I should have blood tests.

So, there I lay, gradually regaining strength, while in her actressy voice Mrs Duncan-Jones read aloud (very well). We had *Sanditon* and *The Watsons*. To be able, in a stranger's house, to have what Charles Darwin called a stomachic catastrophe without feeling shy is a great test of the practical kindness and common sense of your hosts. By the end of three days, a strange intimacy had grown up between the three of us, me and her mother, and Kate, as her mother called her. (I came to do so and have now reverted to calling her Kate when we are *à deux*. From the time of our estrangement, she became Katherine.)

On what was to be my last day, K looked at her mother, went slightly red, and blurted out that she and I were thinking of going together to Orkney.

Three years or so before this, knowing of my Romanizing mindset, my kind housemaster had shown me a newspaper interview with the Orcadian poet George Mackay Brown. In answer to the question why he had become a Catholic, he had replied, 'The Church o' Scotland's awfu' dull.'

The remark appealed, as did Brown's work when I tried it. It was one of the reasons I wanted to go to the Orkneys. Despite her anti-Catholic prejudices, Katherine also admired him. We had read his poetry together on Osea Island, though neither her mother nor I could persuade her to read Sir Walter Scott, whose Orkney novel *The Pirate* is a good one.

We had a week together, in the company of Vivien Stewart, starting in the Standing Stones hotel, recommended by the Regius and Catto, who had had a fishing holiday there quite lately. We moved to a more modest establishment in Stromness and, in a hired car, we explored most of the sites: the Neolithic (2000 BC) chambered cairn at Maeshowe with its runic inscriptions scrawled by Vikings circa AD 900; the cathedral of St Magnus in Kirkwall; the Italian chapel at Scapa Flow, built by prisoners of war out of Nissen huts. If Newman's corpse had made Lord Rosebery aware of a whole cycle of human life, the

Orkneys in a different way compel awestruck awareness of the past, and of the many lives, so different from our own, that have left their impact on landscape and seascape. Almost the most haunting memory for me is, at low tide, the remaining shards of the German fleet jutting from the waters of Scapa. The great High Seas Fleet had been held in the enclosed harbour after the Armistice in 1918, awaiting the outcome of the peace negotiations at Versailles. If, like me, you always find defeat more attractive than victory, the ruins of Troy more poignant than the wily triumphs of Odysseus, then Scapa Flow will exercise its magic on you. Admiral Ludwig von Reuter, doughty old Prussian hero, faced the knowledge that the fleet would either fall into the possession of the Royal Navy or be commandeered by the Bolshevik desperadoes who looked poised to run the revolutionary government back in Berlin.

In a desperate gesture which would surely have been saluted by the Teutonic poets who first chanted the *Edda* or *The Battle of Maldon*, he saw there was more honour in catastrophic *Götterdämmerung* than in sensible compromise. He ordered the scuttling of the fleet. The British managed to nab about twenty of the vessels before they went down, but over seventy saved their honour and sank beneath the ocean deep: except at low tide, when now a rusty prow, now a broken mast, can be seen as defiant reminders of an heroic age, poking through the gunmetal grey of the northern waters.

On Sunday I took a bus to Kirkwall for mass, and I was in luck. When it was over, I saw the emaciated figure of the poet George Mackay Brown. His face was so sunken as to appear hollow. He was about fifty but could have been any age. Years later, reading Maggie Fergusson's superb biography, I realized I had been right to feel reverence, not because he was without blemishes but because, as a writer, he had concentrated on all the things that mattered, making the poetry better and better, honing the prose and not sharing the preoccupations of us smaller fry as we hurried to one another's launch parties, and clutched our warm white plonk at the backs of bookshops. The kindly priest, Father Herbert Bamber SJ, who stood at the door of the little church saluting visitors, offered to introduce me to Brown, but this would have been wrong. For a moment I milled about with the other mass-goers. On my way out, I shuffled near him. He could see a fan approaching, and I could read the embarrassment on his face as I tried to think of just one line to splutter out before running away. 'I so admire ...' But probably better to say nothing. I smiled at him weakly and ran off.

'Ah, did you once see Shelley plain?' Yes I did. 'And did he stop and speak with you?' No, actually.

K and I left Stromness a few days later. Vivien Stewart was enjoying the place so much that she stayed on a little longer. When Mrs Bremner, the proprietress of our hotel, brought her plate in the evening and laid before Vivien the meat and two veg, she inquired, 'Are they twa sweethearts?'

When she returned south, Vivien repeated the inquiry, perhaps as a delicate way of making it her own.

'What did you say to Vivien?' I asked K, when we were back in Oxford together.

'I said we might be.'

We were still five months away from attending the meeting of the Tennyson Society in Lincoln. After our Orcadian holiday, however, I realized that any thought of following in Newman's footsteps as a celibate had been discarded.

31. St Trinian's

The arrival of Helen Gardner at Woodcock Cottage, our little wooden bungalow on Boar's Hill, was a frequent occurrence. She came at least once a week even though at this date she was still Merton Professor of English Literature, and she was always in the middle of a vast amount of work, meetings of the Delegates of the Oxford University Press, meetings at the British Council in London, faculty business. She was the butt of many misogynistic jokes, but I had become very fond of this silver-haired, chain-smoking five-foot-tall dynamo, who took her position as Kate's godmother extremely seriously. She had views on all aspects of our lives, and she expressed them freely. It was crazy, for example, for us to be living out on Boar's Hill with a baby, rather than having a place near the centre of town where I could cycle to college and libraries.

K had taken a year's sabbatical leave while she had the baby, whose name was Emily. Emily Rose, after Emilie Rose Macaulay. In this period K had also undertaken to produce a paperback selection of the works of Philip Sidney. It was not an especially onerous task for someone who had become one of the world's experts in the field, and who had been working on Sidney for a decade. It was this paperback, however, that Helen wanted to discuss. I offered to make them tea while they spoke of it, but this was rejected. The Dame wanted her habitual gin and it. The fact that I was standing there – this was 1971 – with a baby in my arms by no means suggested that anyone present should extinguish their cigarettes. Helen's second or third Embassy was ablaze, as were her eyes behind the glinty specs.

'And when Andrew has brought the drinks, I want him to stay and hear what I have to say.'

Ominous words. I put Emily back in her cot – she was the easiest baby you could imagine, and would have won baby competitions had we put her in for them: cherubic, pink, apparently always contented. I'd soon returned to the little drawing room, which we'd papered with Sanderson's William Morris Michaelmas Daisies – carrying a tray with ashtrays, ice, vermouth and the all-important dark green bottle of gin.

'Now, Kate. There was a meeting of the Delegates this afternoon, and we were all astonished that you have written to the Press announcing your intention to submit your Sidney edition this year.'

'Well, it's not a very difficult ...'

Ignoring K's attempts to reply, Helen continued, 'As I have told you already, I should never have recommended you, even for so small a job, had I known you were expecting a child. Now the baby has come.'

'Helen, I really think it is for me to decide if ...'

'When I heard about the baby, I of course immediately told the Press that we should delay publication of your Sidney for at least two years, to give you time ...'

'But I don't need the time ...'

'... and now the Delegates learn that you have gone behind my back and told your editor that you can hand in a completed typescript next summer.'

'Which I can do, easily.'

'Which happens to be the summer when Andrew takes his Schools.'

She squidged her Embassy in the saucer and immediately lit another. 'Which is what I have come to talk to you about.'

As she often reminded us, Helen belonged to the generation of women who had been obliged to choose between marriage and a career. Katherine's mother, upon marriage, was immediately required to resign her job as a lecturer at Southampton University. This was a regular thing.

'Kate, I just think you are being extremely selfish. You do not have time to do this book and look after a baby and, while you are doing so, you expect Andrew to help domestically, to live out of college, miles from the libraries. What I have come to propose is that he should move back into New College at once and ...'

'I don't think that's going to ...'

'Now, I've had a word – just a little, dear, thank you, no, no more vermouth, just top it up with gin, thank you – I've had a word with William Hayter [Warden of New College] and he is perfectly prepared to let Andrew delay taking Schools for a year, to give him time to prepare properly. Gabriel Turville-Petre was supposed to be teaching Andrew Old Norse this term, and he has been in hospital for at least two weeks. Christopher Tolkien has not arranged any alternative teaching. He ought to do it himself, of course, but asking any member of the Tolkien family to do any work – thank you, dear, just a little more, but I must remember I am driving – I always remember when Ronald Tolkien was supposed to be examining a thesis on the *Ancrene Wisse* [Advice for Anchoresses, a medieval text] with poor Pamela Gradon ...'

When the little car had jerked and lurched out of the drive and into the wooded suburban lane, K was understandably furious. So was I, but for different reasons.

K's line was, How *dare* she? This was the line which I feebly echoed too. Until our last year together, over sixteen years later, we never went in for speaking our minds. I should have said, 'She's a bossy old woman but Helen is *right*. I'm *not* getting enough time to work, and, actually, you know, I really resented "having to get married" in the middle of my student life. It's all been on *your* terms ...'

But I never did say this and this was entirely my fault for being so bloody wet. I suppose I was conceited enough to think, when it came to taking the exams, I could wing it. I'd got a First in Mods and would surely do so again in Schools. Had I been doing simply

English Literature, from Chaucer to Walter Scott, this might have been true. But, to avoid the impression I was a student in the same faculty where my wife was a lecturer and college Fellow, I opted for a different course, specializing entirely in medieval languages – Old English, Germanic Philology, Old Norse, Medieval Latin. This stuff required concentrated study which, in the next eighteen months of my student life, I did not give to it. I was lucky to get a Second, though as it happens I think the grades I got in Schools summed up my intellectual qualities with complete accuracy. They were marked Alpha Gamma. Some of the essays were deemed to be very good, straight A. Others, where I was trying to bluff a competence in a difficult language, Icelandic, which at that stage I did not possess, were an embarrassment.

When we married, Norman and Jean had written to Katherine saying, broadly speaking, what Helen Gardner later put so forcefully: that I should be given space and time to continue my studies; surely, as a university teacher, K found this obvious. Instead, she and her mother, both university teachers, cooked up an intolerable reply to my poor parents, inquiring why the retired manager of a pottery came to know more about preparing for university exams than two scholars of their eminence.

Looking back now, through the miasma of resentment which the matter caused me for most of my middle life, the perspective is clear. I am just so grateful that a not especially glorious degree result made it unlikely I'd ever pursue the career of an academic. There is a true difference between the Scholar and the Person of Letters, and it is obvious which of these two I am.

By the time I took my degree, I'd already finished my first novel, a detective story, never published. Thank God.

Until Success as a Person of Letters came my way, what was I supposed to do? I joined the Inner Temple, thinking I might pursue a career at the Bar, but my heart was not in it and there was no chance of my father ever having enough money to subsidize me while I studied the law. He had inherited his father's financial incapacity. Hill House was apparently costing him more money than was now covered by the pension, which inflation had devoured. He had impulsively sold the house for £20,000 and he now found himself with nowhere to live, with two women who were not on speaking terms.

Then, one day, the phone rang and his cheery voice announced that they had moved. They'd found a house in Malvern. Well, Malvern Link. An easy journey from Oxford by rail.

I leapt on a train and found them. The euphoria of the telephone call had crashed to abject misery.

'That estate agent really wants shooting.'

'But it's a lovely house,' I lied.

'Not to *tell* us that it was semi-detached,' he moaned.

My poor aunt was squidged at the end of a narrow landing with a small gas ring her only means of cooking. There seemed to be no light in the house. The huge hills weighed over it like gigantic burial cairns. The suburban, dogshit-strewn park which the semi overlooked had never been beautiful. The lumpy brown furniture from Burston and Bramhall did more than fill the small rooms. They were not so much rooms as repositories. This seemed no place to break the putative news that I'd made a step towards finding a career.

When I'd considered the Bar, John Bayley had laughingly sung,

In other professions in which men engage
(Said I to myself said I),
The Army, the Navy, the Church and the Stage ...

Iris had been especially keen on the idea of the Church, and so had K, who came, on her father's side, from a long line of scholar-parsons, mainly Welsh. When it became clear that we 'had to get married', she would not countenance accepting the requirements then expected by the Roman Catholic Church when one partner was C of E, one RC. She refused to promise to bring up the child as a Catholic, and she would not have any RC priest involved in the wedding service, so that I was by now an apostate, excommunicated.

I ask myself what would have happened had Michael Hollings still been in Oxford when all this happened. I suspect I would still be RC to this day, but the truth is, I do not regret my fifty years of religious muddle, being for the most part a practising Anglican with periodic waves of Doubt or Roman fever, when I feel tempted either to give up Christianity altogether or to find some way back into the arms of Rome. Anglicanism actually suits me on many levels. Crispian Hollis had become the Catholic chaplain after Michael, and he took a more relaxed attitude to my lapse. When I said to him, 'My wife wants me to go back to the C of E,' he replied, 'Are you sure you ever really left it?'

Not that either K or I took a frivolous view of these things. Quite the reverse. I was astounded, a few years ago, when one of my contemporaries told me that in the first year or so of my marriage Jeremy Catto and his friends regarded us as exemplars of perfect love together. In fact, in the first two years we were married we spent hours and hours weeping, and wishing we had not married. K could not stop loving (carnally) the Other Man. I could not stop loving (hopelessly, platonically) the beautiful Somervillian. But we believed that we had been married, and in the eyes of God, with a full nuptial mass at St Mary Magdalen's church. John Gilling, soon to be vicar of St Mary's, Graham Street, said to Katherine one day after the Sung Eucharist at Christ Church, 'Your knot has been firmly tied – there'll be no putting asunder there.' Only months later – I can still hear her moaning, gulping with sorrow, 'Oh, we should *never* have married! I'd n-never have insisted, if it had not been for .... *Mother!*'

The deepest bond between us was our child, but running this a close second was the fact that we went to church together, and after a few months of being married I actually started to receive the Anglican sacraments once more. After graduating, I took a job at Thornton's, the second-hand bookshop in Broad Street. In my walks with the beautiful Somervillian, and our shared conversations about Rose Macaulay, I could actually see why there were those who felt that the Catholicism to be found in the C of E, without the nonsense of papal infallibility, was a purer, older form of the Faith than was being offered in Rome. Rose Macaulay, K and the Somervillian Muse all led me to become an Anglican almost by conviction and wholeheartedly from an emotional point of view. The rose-scented waters of Anglo-Catholicism splashed from their holy water stoups.

Ordination was something else. Can I really have thought this was a viable career move? I now find it difficult to reconstruct the mental processes that could have persuaded me, ever, that it was on the cards. Calling to mind the incredulity on my father's face when I told him, in that miserable little house in Malvern Link, that his son was going to train for the priesthood in the Church of England, I empathize with him completely. The forget-me-not blue eyes filled with tears.

Having been accepted, at a selection conference, it became necessary to find a theological college. The obvious one was Cuddesdon, a training ground for future college chaplains, deans and bishops. Situated in a hill village just outside Oxford ('The Hill of the Lord', as its Victorian founders had called it), Cuddesdon had a reputation for intellectual seriousness, based on that of the Tractarians. (That is, the High-Church clergy of the Newman generation who, together with Newman, had written the series of *Tracts for the Times*, devoted to returning England to a more Catholic form of Anglicanism.)

The interview with the Principal, the Revd Leslie Houlden, was rigorous. He told me that while I was a student at the Hill of the Lord I should be expected to lead a bachelor life, living in college.

It was clear that I could not possibly accept his terms and come to Cuddesdon as a bachelor. He was perfectly polite both to me and to Katherine, whom I think he knew slightly. Before we went into dinner in the rather fine refectory (G. E. Street is the architect of Cuddesdon, he who designed the Law Courts in the Strand) we were approached by a fresh-cheeked Highlander who said that he believed Dean Duncan-Jones of Chichester, and the Revd Andrew Duncan-Jones, his son, were friends with his father, Donald Maclean of Dochgarroch.

The young man was Allan Maclean. The conversation he began that evening, even by my ecclesiastically obsessed standards, was a trifle esoteric. It was about the brand of English Catholicism favoured by Katherine's grandfather and Allan's father, known to some as the Mass and Maypoles religion, pioneered at St Mary's, Primrose Hill, in London. (It meant emphasizing the forms of Catholicism that had been extant in Tudor times, that is, Gothic vestments, not baroque fiddleback chasubles; Roman regalia such as the biretta were scorned.)

The conversation that began with Mass and Maypoles has been going on between me and Allan ever since. He conveyed instantly what had been lacking in Leslie Houlden's conversation, a sense of amusement, and a sense of life having large social and aesthetic boundaries. He had a car. He had not lived in the south since he was a boarder at the Dragon School in north Oxford. He asked if we'd like to accompany him on outings.

We became friends that evening, and half a century later we remain so. Allan always accompanied K and the children on our Scottish holidays and he has been the well-informed companion on countless church crawls and London walks and explorations in the English and Scottish countryside. We had a memorable fortnight in America together. All that sprang from one evening at Cuddesdon.

Since I was not to pursue my studies on the Hill of the Lord, this left only the St Trinian's of theological seminaries, St Stephen's House.

Oh, my.

Whereas the interview at Cuddesdon had been prickly, austere, even rather pompous, nothing could have been friendlier than an afternoon with the Principal of Staggers, the unworldly, blinking, myopic, probably rather saintly Father Derek Allen. Before becoming a Staggers Bag (as students at St Stephen's House were called) myself, I did not realize that Father Allen was more correctly referred to as Nora, sometimes Big N. Unlike Leslie Houlden at Cuddesdon, Nora saw no objections to my remaining at home with K, who was by now pregnant with our second child (later the historian and genius food writer). Since I was a member of New College, the plan was that I should read for a BA in theology at the university, beginning in October 1974, and come in to Staggers for religious services and to learn the practical sides to the job.

I have never been on a blind date, but I imagine that on some such occasions you know within thirty seconds of meeting the other person, perched on their bar stool, that this isn't going to work. Probably the best thing, in these circumstances, would be to make your apologies and catch the next bus home. It was like that for me, beginning at Staggers. I knew with total certainty as I walked through the door that this was a tremendous mistake.

There were probably forty-five of us, no more than half a dozen of whom were perverts. The perverts, of course, were those, like myself, who lived with a woman, and the usual sign of being a pervert was that you were not given a name in religion, as they were called. The only exception to this was Mae West, a nice American from Keble College who was married to my friend Sara Maitland. Before she married Mae West, aka Donald Lee, Sara had dated a beefy American graduate student at University College called Bill Clinton. Then she'd married Donald. In later life, both became Roman Catholics and Sara devoted herself to the Solitary Life of prayer.

Decades passed before I found myself at a literary festival, and saw that the afternoon when I was 'on', promoting something or another I'd written, Sara was peddling a book of hers called *Silence*. Before I make a speech or do a public interview, I like, as do most people, half an hour or so of silence to collect my thoughts and calm my nerves. On this occasion, as I sat in the Green Room, all concentration became impossible as the unmistakable corncrake tones of Sara could be heard from the other side of the room, loudly asking her publicist about future gigs, radio interviews and the like, to promote the virtues of silence. It was a moment of unconscious comedy comparable to the time Lord Longford went into Hatchards bookshop in Piccadilly to complain that they were not displaying his latest book in the window. The title of the book was *Humility*.

Anyhow. Mae West and I and the handful of other perverts were in the distinct minority. The other Bags were unlikely ever to perpetrate what was called the sin of matrimony. Half of them, beneath the ridiculous manner, were serious men who would go on to become devoted priests, often in rough inner-city parishes. It was difficult to know how the others had ever got past a selection conference, until you learned that they had not done so. They had taken the simpler course of asking the Bishop of Southwark to sponsor their applications. Merv the Perv (the Rt Revd Mervyn Stockwood) was a self-tormenting, alcoholic figure who possibly thought he was helping these individuals by urging them to take holy orders. Even he, however, was compelled by the Governors of St Stephen's House, when that year came to an end, to delay their ordination at least until they had paid their bar bills, which in some cases ran to thousands of pounds.

The term began with a Solemn High Mass. The air was thick with the mingled scent of thirty different cheap colognes. Sometimes, walking into a large department store, and through the *parfumerie*, my mind takes me back to that chapel. Only at Staggers, the scent of aftershave was mingled with incense smoke, which billowed over the permed and coiffed heads of my fellow collegians: Pearl, Frankie, Clarissa, Tawdry Audrey, Plum Tart and the others. The trouble is, I never did master all their names, so that, in subsequent decades, if I find myself being reintroduced to a figure who is by now a revered rural dean or archdeacon, I have to fall back on addressing them as 'Father', since I could only recall the 'name in religion'. One does not want to embarrass a prebendary or a suffragan bishop by saluting them as Deirdre or Maud.

The high proportion, as I say, were set to continue the admirable old traditions of the Biretta Belt in churches which had always seen it as their function to find Christ in the lives of the poor. Others, who had so eagerly looked forward to the laying on of Merv the Perv's apostolically consecrated hands, should really have been directed not to a theological college but to a psychiatric ward, as their subsequent lives demonstrated, some of them named on lists as unsuitable for work with minors, others in trouble with the law for kleptomania. More than one committed suicide. Alcoholism, not just the traditional booziness of the high wing of the C of E but problem drinking, was rife. And the sheer weirdness of it all was unlike anything experienced before or since. I think of Pearl, whose wardrobe was stuffed with elaborate doctoral robes – DMus, DD, PhD – from various universities. As far as we know, Pearl did not have a degree at any place of learning but managed to get more than one academic post on the strength of the fantasy that the gowns in the wardrobe represented actual academic achievements.

Of the forty or so who lived in, most, in that pre-HIV/AIDS time, had had sexual relations with one another. That is a high number of permutations. Even among those who were not fully fledged alcoholics, the intake of booze was phenomenal. Despite the best efforts of Nora and of the faithful Senior Tutor, Clarissa Cobb, it was seemingly impossible to keep the young ladies under control. They tried the ploy of making Compline compulsory at 9 p.m., to make sure that everyone came in from the Stage Club in George Street for at least part of the evening, but however you stretch it out, the service of Compline is quite short, and the *Salve Regina* had no sooner been sung than they were off again to the thump, thump, thump of Village People singing 'YMCA' and 'In the Navy'.

Nora was an innocent, a holy idiot who had, I am convinced, never 'stepped aside'. Most of the trouble at St Stephen's House stemmed from Nora's crazy habit of hearing the confessions of students at the college. In the canon law of the Roman Catholic Church such an arrangement would be absolutely forbidden, for the obvious reason that if a student comes to the head of college and confesses to behaviour for which he should be sacked, his sins are hidden by the seal and it is impossible to sack him. It was eventually the Vice Principal, John Halliburton, a very nice, rather learned, scatterbrained clergyman who had recently 'poped' for a couple of years, then fallen in love with a beautiful woman and returned to the C of E, who blew the whistle. The Halliburtons were loathed by the Bags for being spoilsports, but the fun really did have to stop. Poor Nora was sent into the C of E's equivalent of internal exile, Eastbourne, where he became the vicar of a high church and was much loved by the parishioners. He was replaced by the more austere, disciplinarian figure of David Hope, later

Archbishop of York, whose decision to put a stop to the everlasting Mardi Gras earned him the soubriquet Ena the Cruel.

After my first few weeks at Staggers, I actually stopped going into the place. Partly, things were difficult at home. After K gave birth to our second child, Beatrice – always known as Bee – she suffered severe post-natal depression. So it was a sad, confused year, lit up partly by the fascination of studying theology. I still read the New Testament in Greek each year. In my copy I have inscribed Dr Johnson's words, 'The most difficult book in the world, for which the study of a life is required'.

I was lucky that year in my friendships. Allan Maclean has been mentioned, and it was when he took us to Argyllshire, and found us a cottage near Poltalloch in the parish of K's uncle Andrew, that some of the gloom began to lift. Another great friendship was with Canon John Lucas.

Every theological student was supposed to find a 'placement', and following a recommendation I knocked on the door of his vicarage in Becket Street, near the railway station. It was opened by a small, silver-haired figure, very neat, with wire-framed spectacles. He was then sixty-five years old and he lived to be very nearly 101, so it was a good, long friendship.

When I had remarried and moved to London in the 1990s, John was clever at finding bargain breaks in hotels, and in particular in a spectacularly placed, ugly modern hotel on Tower Bridge with views of the Tower and the Thames. From here we could walk through his old stamping ground – Wapping High Street, when he had been a curate at St Peter's, London Docks, established by the saintly Charles Lowder in the 1860s. Even in the twentieth century, when John had worked there, the poverty was of a level which to us in our twenty-first-century comfort is all but unimaginable, the lack of sanitation or privacy, the sheer pathos and fear of it all. This was the core of the great Anglo-Catholic tradition which the best of my friends at St Stephen's House would follow. Of course, the Movement was hopelessly, irrecoverably split by the ordination of women to the priesthood. This was not because the old-fashioned Anglo-Catholics were misogynist necessarily, but because their entire *raison d'être* was that the episcopate of the Church of England was essentially the same as the episcopate of Roman, Russian, Greek, Coptic and Syriac churches. The churches might all be split for sad, historical reasons, but they shared not only baptism but also the order of bishops, priests and deacons. The Orthodox and the Roman Catholics, i.e. the majority of Christians throughout the world, do not accept that women are bishops. It may be unenlightened of them, but in this case that is not the point. The point is, the Anglo-Catholics are now in a position where the majority of historic Christendom does not recognize their episcopate. So the Church of England is not in this sense a church. Perhaps it had always been a fantasy to suppose that it was. Had not the Pope, as long ago as the 1890s, declared Anglican orders utterly null and void? But – until the ordination of women, it was possible to sustain the hope that, one day, some form of reunion might be possible, and the dream of One Holy Catholic and Apostolic Church would become not just an item in the creed but a visible reality.

When John Lucas became vicar of St Thomas the Martyr, Oxford, in 1947, it was a flourishing Anglo-Catholic concern with a large convent, full of nuns, who ran the parish school. The streets were lined with tenements where workers on the Great Western Railway and college servants lived. Little by little all that part of Oxford was demolished. The old marmalade factory of Frank Cooper, which abutted the churchyard, was moved. The nuns dwindled to single figures, and the few remaining sisters went to live with the Community of St Mary the Virgin at Wantage. Most of the tenements were pulled down. The school closed. The parishioners were moved to Blackbird Leys or Botley.

John possessed what for the good parish priest, as for the good novelist, is a *sine qua non*, an obsession with the lives of other people. He would discuss the marriages, illnesses and family relationships of his parishioners with the same absorption with which Proust might analyse the lives of the Guermantes, though in our conversations we were talking of the widows of stokers on the

Great Western Railway or of impoverished piano teachers living in small terraced cottages on Osney Island.

It always seemed highly appropriate that John's most celebrated predecessor as vicar of St Thomas's was Robert Burton, author of *The Anatomy of Melancholy*, since at the bottom of his hilarious take on life there was melancholy without limit, and a depressive temperament which bordered on despair. I do not think he was gay. As a boy at King William's School on the Isle of Man, he had been badly abused by a teacher and he was one of those many damaged souls who could not recover from the experience and had no desire for sex in his life. But he craved love.

In his day-to-day conversation, melancholy was kept at bay by his sense of the absurd, and if you have been an Anglo-Catholic for half a century and more, there was plenty of absurdity to observe. One day when we were walking down Walton Street past the Birmingham Oratorian's favourite church, *Ecclesia Sancti Pauli*, he suddenly began to laugh. He remembered one of the curates there, Alex Lawson, always known as the LGC or Lowest of God's Creatures. The LGC spent a whole winter embroidering a lacy cloth to put on the altar in front of the Blessed Sacrament, so that those who came to worship could read, in scarlet Gothic characters, the words A GREATER THAN JONAS IS HERE. Unfortunately, the LGC had forgotten to measure the Holy Table, which was much smaller than the cloth on which he had been so laboriously engaged. All the faithful were able to read as they knelt was the puzzling motto TER THAN JO.

He was full of such memories, alternating between a sense of the ridiculous and a reverence for his heroes – Warden Kidd of Keble College, or Darwell Stone, Principal of Pusey House, who, when told by an undergraduate he'd been to see the Dolly Sisters during the vacation, was silent for a space. The Darwell, as he was often called, replied seriously, 'That is a religious order of which I had not heard.'

When John retired from St Thomas's he spent about twenty years going every day to Ritchie Russell House, a centre at the Churchill Hospital for those suffering from paraplegic conditions, multiple sclerosis, etc.; feeding them, cleaning them, holding and lighting their cigs. He used to say it was this activity alone which lifted his blinding depressions. Deep cynicism had always existed side by side with his piety. When I was first attached to the parish on my placement, I was shocked to hear an exchange between him and one of the parishioners. A woman asked him to pray for her sick child. 'Of course I shall do so,' he replied, 'but I am bound to tell you that after fifty years in the priesthood I have never known prayer to be of the slightest efficacy.' He was *not* bound to say this, and one could have compounded a cynic's manual from his utterances ('That God doesn't know the meaning of the word *kindness*' – after a friend developed cancer).

Some time after his ninetieth birthday he felt that the Church of England he had known and loved no longer existed, and he became a Roman Catholic. Despite the extreme kindness of his new co-religionists, especially the Holy Child nuns who put on a splendid celebration of mass followed by lunch for his hundredth birthday, he was not happy in the new church. I think I could best explain this to myself by contrasting a funeral at St Thomas's in which I took part, and the perfunctory rite which the monks put on for John's own obsequies. In St Thomas's, where there were many rough sleepers in the parish, the police found the corpse of a youngish woman in the gutter. No one ever identified her, as far as I am aware, and when the coroner's permission had been granted, John conducted her funeral. There were requiem candles. A catafalque. The coffin was draped with a splendid purple and black pall. And when he had said a requiem for the soul of 'this our sister', we went to the crematorium where he read the Book of Common Prayer funeral service. We were the only two people present, but all had been conducted with the solemnity and seriousness of a state funeral. When John died, the few who gathered at St Benet's, the Benedictine house in St Giles', were given a perfunctory little service. My children have taken more trouble when burying their hamsters. And a look of some surprise came over one of the monks' faces when Frank Robson, one of John's oldest friends, suggested the monk might accompany us to the crematorium with the coffin.

'Won't the undertaker do that?' asked this Ampleforth Benedictine. Frank, former Registrar of the Province of Canterbury, quietly said, 'I think you should come with us to the crematorium.'

Frank, who like me had been John's friend for a very long time, was the last of us to visit him in St Luke's Hospital. As he was leaving the room, he heard a frail voice from the bed saying, 'Oh, Frank.'

He turned. 'Yes, John?'

'There's something I want you to know.'

'Oh?'

'Yes.'

Though frail, the voice was emphatic.

'I've given up religion.'

Frank, though a part of church officialdom, was also pious, and he did not know how to respond to this remark. In his gruff Geordie voice, he said, 'Well, goodbye, John.'

He knew it really was goodbye.

As he turned the doorknob to leave the room, he heard the voice coming once more from the bed. This time the frailty had left his tone and he spoke quite loudly. 'I mean – ENTIRELY.'

A few hours later the old canon drifted into troubled sleep. A pretty Chinese nurse, recognizing the unmistakable signs of the End, held his hand and said the Lord's Prayer. He died as she was saying the words 'Thy will be done'. *The Anatomy of Melancholy.* Dear John.

32. Superficial Journey

Francesca Wilson had got to know the Duncan-Joneses in Birmingham, while working as a schoolmistress there during the war. Ever since their teenage years, K and her brother Richard had spent a week or two at Walberswick, on the Suffolk coast, where Francesca had a number of small houses. Francesca, no relation, came of canny Yorkshire stock, and one of her rules of life was 'Never spend more than £1,000 on a house'. Her palatial house in Fellows Road, Primrose Hill, was bought the morning after an air raid, for £850. The owner was glad to be rid of it, after it suffered minor bomb damage. The disastrous sea floods of the 1950s drew Francesca to Suffolk, where she bought a number of waterlogged properties for a few hundred pounds each. By now a Mother Teresa lookalike, antique, headscarved, she had the appearance of a Balkan peasant.

Her bread-and-butter money was earned as a schoolteacher. Her very first job had been at Bedales, where she taught Jos Wedgwood in the sixth form together with Dorothy Winser, who later became Jos's much-detested wife. Francesca had been at Newnham College, Cambridge, with Ka Cox, Rupert Brooke's lover, and remembered naked bathing with the pair at Grantchester.

All but communist – she would not join the Party simply because she wasn't a joiner – she nonetheless retained a fondness for the old days of privilege, largely on aesthetic grounds. She used to say it was impossible for those who grew up after the First World War to imagine the beauty of the privileged classes in Edwardian England, their skin, their hair, their clothes, all exquisite.

Francesca had first become involved in relief work in 1913, when she went to the Balkans to assist Serbian refugees. For the next fifty years she devoted herself tirelessly to the rescue or betterment of the lives of refugees. Nikolaus Pevsner was only one of many who first found free board and lodgings, when he escaped Nazi Germany, at Francesca's house. One of my fancies is that humanity will only be perfect when we all learn to practise the Beatitudes. In the unsatisfactory meantime, most of us can only manage to practise a few of them. *Blessed are those who hunger and thirst after righteousness.* The two individuals I have known whose lives were an everlasting hunger for righteousness, or justice, as the Greek word means, were both atheists: Francesca Wilson and Paul Foot – who used to spend weeks and weeks of his life following up miscarriages of justice and trying to set things right for the victims.

Francesca's various shabby residences were crammed to the rafters with the needy. The wooden house on stilts in Walberswick was reserved for women and children dumped by unfaithful husbands. Creek Cottage, where Francesca spent three or four months each year, was now partially occupied by a crazy architect who had replied to an ad, placed in the *New Statesman*, offering free accommodation to a poet for eight months of the year when Francesca was not there. Every time she came back in the spring, she would find some alteration made to the building by this madman, culminating in an extra floor which lasted only a few weeks before collapsing through what was left of the house. When Francesca had guests, he lived in a tea chest on the beach, still returning to Creek Cottage to use the bathroom: not for lavatorial purposes, but to fill the bath with muddy seedlings. 'Don't use the bath,' Francesca would say in her rasping voice. 'We can wash in the sea if need be.' The croaking, cigarette-deepened pre-1914 upper-class voice used to grate on Katherine, as did Francesca's entire character, the leftiness and the misogyny (which often go together). It was always expected that Katherine did all the cooking, for example, while I sat at Francesca's feet, and although she was kind to offer the forsaken wives refuge in the house on stilts, she always made it clear that she did not blame the men for deserting them.

With the exception of Malcolm Muggeridge (whom Francesca despised for blowing the whistle on the Soviet Union in 1931 and in her view exaggerating the extent of the Ukrainian famines – history has vindicated him and shown he actually *underestimated* the numbers who died), Francesca was the best talker I ever knew. The conversations ranged from memories of war, to books, to theology. She had been one of the first to arrive when British troops entered Bergen-Belsen in April 1945. I literally sat at her feet, chain-smoking away the small hours. Katherine, with her strong distaste for bohemianism, and her natural Toryism, found that a little of Francesca went a very long way, and was in bed with a good novel by the time Francesca was wistfully recalling her love affair in Paris with Mikhail Bakhtin. She fondly recollected his making scenes in bistros, hurling plates and yelling, '*Moi je déteste la vie quotidienne.*' 'I L-L-LOVE it,' K's voice would come from the bedroom. She usually made an excuse to drive home early with the children.

In that year, 1974, I won the Ellerton Theological Prize at Oxford. I was seriously drawn to the idea of becoming a professional academic theologian, but I knew that it was going to be impossible to go back to Staggers, even under the, presumably saner, supervision of Ena the Cruel. Sitting up with Francesca night after night, I admitted to myself that, fascinating as it all is, I did not believe a word of it, and I could never bring myself to be a clergyman and pretend. (As so many of them, evidently, did.)

Francesca urged me to get a job as a teacher. To my protests – that I had done no training, that no decent school would want me – she said, You Can But Try.

'Go to the village shop in the morning and see if there any posts advertised in the small ads of *The Times.*'

It was like the first chapter of a comic novel: for, there it was, just as she had predicted. Merchant Taylors' School, Northwood, an unforeseen vacancy, an English master required at once. My referees were Helen Gardner and Christopher Tolkien, whom I rang from the phone box on Walberswick village green. Francesca helped me draft the letter of application. A second-class degree was perfectly OK for these purposes, and I could swank about the First in Mods, and the university prizes – the Chancellor's English Essay Prize as well as the Ellerton. I bunged off the application, and in no time I was being summoned for an interview, haring back to Oxford to find a suit, a clean shirt and a tie.

One aspect of the story which made it appear like a well-turned slice of fiction is that, while I was to spend two (very happy) years at that school, and although my fellow English teachers seemed to exercise no obvious conversational constraints, I never did find out the reason for my predecessor's hasty departure. He had not been sacked. When I asked one of the other masters, John Steane, an eminent music critic and the editor of the Penguin edition of Christopher Marlowe's plays, he simply laughed. Robert Hunter, our head of department, was a good, published, poet and would simply shake his head when my predecessor was mentioned. We spent many hours together in the pub. Robert, aged sixty, had recently been widowed. At sixteen years old, he and his wife had eloped in order to be married at Gretna Green, and they had remained devotedly together until her death.

Merchant Taylors' was scarcely a blackboard jungle. I wasn't much of a teacher but I liked the boys, who were much more polite than we had been at Rugby, presumably because the high proportion were day boys, who retained the gentle manners of home. In their charcoal grey suits they seemed like child and teenage versions of lawyers, investment managers, dentists and doctors, which is what most of them would become when they left. They would be like their fathers, also in grey suits, catching the commuter trains in Chorleywood, Pinner and Northwood. It was to accommodate them and their mothers and fathers that the Metropolitan Line had been built. Two of the boys who did not conform entirely to these Betjemanic stereotypes were Alan Duncan, an aspirant politician even then destined for a knighthood, and a seat in Parliament, and another boy, even then the scourge of everything Duncan stood for, Martin Rowson, much the most original person I ever taught at school or university, whose political cartoons make some of the most satisfyingly scabrous commentary on our times, and whose graphic novel version of *Tristram Shandy* is a masterpiece.

Apart from the 'six heures', as John Steane always called our regular hour in the pub before dinner, there was not much to do in the evening, and I could not commute to Oxford every day. Those evenings when I did not go into London to visit Francesca, or Allan Maclean – then working with homeless drug dependants at Centre Point – I stayed in my bedroom and wrote a novel called *The Sweets of Pimlico*.

It was a friend of Katherine's, John Cornwell, who got me into print. The title of his first novel, *The Spoiled Priest*, described his own position, though he had never in fact been ordained. Leaving his seminary, he'd studied at Oxford, written some fiction and then become a journalist on the *Observer*. He became something of a Vaticanologist, and it is for this he is probably best known, and for his work as an academic specializing in the relationship between religion and science.

Katherine had always considered fiction to be my métier. She read all my novels as I wrote them, chapter by chapter, often making invaluable improvements. It was she who gave the typescript of *The Sweets of Pimlico* to John, who passed it on to his agent. Within a few weeks it had been accepted by Secker & Warburg. John and Katherine were the ambulance drivers, but the novel would never have been the success it became had it not been for the midwife, my editor John Blackwell.

Chain-smoking, alcoholic, doomed to die in his early forties, he was the most helpful editor I ever had until, much later in life, I met Margaret Stead, who edited my best novel, *The Potter's Hand*, and my second-best work of non-fiction, *Dante in Love*. (My best, surely, is the one about Victorian doubters, *God's Funeral*.) What Blackwell and Stead have in common is the uncanny ability to see what the slave boy should look like before he is hacked out of the marble.

Blackwell, clad in blue denim, filling his Soho eyrie with the fumes of Gauloises and sipping alternate swigs of canned beer, vodka and black coffee, could see, as he read through a typescript, the sort of book it might be.

I know with total certainty that *The Sweets of Pimlico* would not have had such success without John's crafting. He was not, however, someone who made pointless changes. Some of my subsequent novels, notably *The Healing Art* and *Wise Virgin*, needed very little editing. My second book, *Unguarded Hours*, was a farce based on Staggers. It is a much cruder work, which I think owes something to the fact that its midwife also edited the novels of Tom Sharpe, but it still has a cult following in the ever-diminishing circles of Anglo-Catholics, or Walsingham Matildas, as John Osborne unforgettably called them.

Unguarded Hours had depicted the Firbankian world of a theological college, but it did so without Firbank's subtlety or edge. *Kindly Light* was a sequel, relying on a plot theft from Evelyn Waugh's *Vile Bodies*. Three or four months passed after I had delivered the typescript, and from Blackwell I had heard not a sausage.

By this stage my head had been swollen with good reviews and prizes, and I felt I was entitled to better treatment than this. Returning to the smoke-filled eyrie, I found John even more drunk than usual, but he suggested we repair to the Venezia, a restaurant round the corner in Chapel Street, famous less for its (run-of-the-mill Italian) food than for the fact that it had a room at the back, rentable by the hour if you asked the waiter nicely.

In those days I did not eat. My mind/soul, whatever you call it, was unable to recognize my marital sadness.

I simply refused to articulate any such thoughts. Bottling it all up must have been the chief reason why I was anorexic, and suffered from a number of illnesses, in my early to mid-twenties – two bouts of pneumonia, one of pleurisy, weight loss down to seven stone. From the end of my marriage to K, I have scarcely ever been to the doctor, whereas when I was living with her and trying to make the best of it, I suffered from levels of anorexia and illness which seemed to reproduce those of my mother, Jean Dorothy. When asked to dinner, I would either outright refuse, or ring up at the last minute to feign excuses, pretend that something had gone wrong with babysitting arrangements, and suggest I come to see the friends after dinner for a cup of coffee when the meal was safely over. If it had not been for a local GP near Oxford, who cured me by hypnotherapy, I think my eating disorder would probably have killed me.

So – Blackwell and I in the Venezia, and all I could do was to push bits of pasta round a plate. Two horrors always happened if I did find myself in a restaurant, with food on a plate in front of me. First, the food multiplied. There seemed to be mountains more tagliatelle on my plate than there had been when the waiter had brought it. And the second horror was when the waiter returned, stared at the uneaten food and asked if there was something the matter. Maybe signor like to see the menu? Maybe there something wrong widda da pasta?

While I was undergoing all these neurotic, unspoken fears and horrors, John drank the bottle of Soave which he had ordered for both of us. When I dared mention the novel which he had received four months earlier, he ordered a couple of grappas.

We blinked our way out into the afternoon sunshine. In those days licensing laws still insisted that pubs closed after lunch, not to open again until 6 p.m. For those who wanted to drink in the afternoons a private club was required. John rang a doorbell in Dean Street and we were soon clambering up a dirty linoleum staircase to the Colony Room. I was to go there a few times in the 1980s, having been befriended by a Soho 'character' called Dan Farson, but by then afternoon drinking was permitted in every pub in London, the legendary proprietor of the Colony, Muriel Belcher, was dead, and the place had lost its *raison d'être*. On this occasion in the mid-'70s we had the full experience. Muriel greeted John, 'Who've you brought to see us today, cunty?' Francis Bacon was in the corner of the room with Peter Ackroyd, and – this is why I mention this afternoon – there, perched on a bar stool, wearing dark glasses, was a lower-middle-class imitation of Jacqueline Onassis. It was Christine Keeler, still only in her thirties, but looking like a ruin. There was Dantean horror in the scene. After a few more drinks, I gave up any hope of discovering what had happened to my novel, and I lurched towards the tube to catch the next Oxford train.

Katherine formed the impression that John Blackwell, on his precarious bike ride home to Clapham one evening, had taken the typescript with him, possibly stopped in some bar and was too shy to admit that he had inadvertently lost it. The truth was sadder and gentler. He had read the book, and one reason, when I materialized to discuss it, for his even-heavier-than-usual drinking in the Venezia and the Colony Room was that he could not bring himself to tell me that it was crap. Some days later he sent me two closely typed pages, accurately outlining the novel's defects. It was a noble letter. It said that he, the firm, wanted to go on publishing me, and would certainly like to read the novel I wrote next. If I insisted, they would publish *Kindly Light*, but they strongly advised against. I wrote back furiously, asking them to publish it as soon as possible.

Inwardly, I knew that Blackwell was right. Not for the first time in my life, I heard good advice, knew it was good advice and stubbornly ignored it. The bad novel came out and received deservedly sniffy reviews. The following year, however, I wrote one of my best novels, *The Healing Art*, which won three prizes and golden opinions.

An unforeseen consequence of all this came about three days after reading a glowing notice in the *Sunday Telegraph* by a novelist who had once been famous, John Braine. His first book, *Room at the Top*, made into a memorable film starring Simone Signoret, was a Yorkshire version of Maupassant's *Bel-Ami*, and placed Braine, along with Kingsley Amis, Colin Wilson and others, in the category of Angry Young Men. John Osborne was perhaps the chief of them, with his play *Look Back in Anger*. They weren't left-wing exactly, but they were angry about the class system. Chippy Young Men would probably have been a more accurate name for them. After success they lurched definitely to the right, and used to meet at Bertorelli's in Charlotte Street for what they proudly called the Fascist Beasts' Lunching Club.

As I say, a few days after the publication of his nice review of my book, Braine rang me up. It was the first of dozens, probably hundreds, of telephone calls, few of which took place when he was completely sober. The rasping Yorkshire voice began, 'Now, I know what you're doing. Your gorgeous mistress, who has amazing breasts, as a matter of fact, is serving you breakfast in bed, you lucky sod, and you are reading the sodding *Guardian*, for Chrissakes – you are what Stalin – no – let me finish – you are what Stalin would call a Useful Idiot, reading the sodding *Guardian*, boot – BOOT – this is why I am ringing – BOOT – your novel – the *Healing* – I am telling you, this is a sodding Cresta Run of a novel, and what I should like to know is this. How does a sodding left-wing bastard, and I don't mean that unkindly ...'

The telephone call was made from the commuter town of Woking in Surrey. Kingsley Amis, a fund of John Braine anecdotes, recalled being rung up and hearing the sandpaper Bingley tones – 'Hello, Kingers! You'll never guess! I live in London now.'

'Oh, that's nice, John.' (Thinking, Oh Christ.) 'Whereabouts, John?' (Hoping it was nowhere near him.)

Then came the triumphant – 'I live in WOKING!'

Braine was the most tragi-comic case I ever came across of the terrible unwisdom, for a writer, of giving up the day job. As a librarian in Bingley, he could have written books if and when he had a good idea, and when inspiration flagged he could have continued to provide a livelihood for his children. He was widely read in world literature in translation. He was intelligent enough to see that most of what he wrote after *Room at the Top* was catastrophically bad. The knowledge was intolerable. That is how I interpret the need, in so many writers, not merely to drink but to drink to oblivion.

Religion stopped being a consolation.

'I am NOT working-class. I am lace curtains Irish,' he would say with emphasis, his fingers shaking as with both hands he tried to flick his lighter into action and hold it reasonably still and reasonably near the end of the quivering cig. 'I'm lace curtains Irish for Chrissakes. What the Church doesn't realize ... Andrew, what the Church. Doesn't realize. We go to mass – no, listen – we go to mass to lay down our burdens, not to hear sodding PACIFISM and Communism from Monsignor Sodding Kent.'

There was no accounting for Katherine's taste in people. Though herself the reverse of coarse, and usually deploring coarseness in others, she overlooked it in John Braine and we had several happy evenings together. She even drove us – Braine, his girlfriend Janet and me – to see a revival of *Room at the Top* at the Nottingham playhouse.

Sadly, our friendship lasted only a few years. He died, in wretched poverty, of a stomach haemorrhage. His last Christmas dinner had been taken among the homeless and destitute of Hampstead at a Salvation Army hostel. At the funeral, in the huge domed church of the Passionist Fathers just behind the Whittington Hospital, we sang 'Faith of Our Fathers'. His choice.

About this time I was getting to know Richard Ingrams and the *Private Eye* crowd. Ingrams was puritanical about booze, having drunk too much whisky in his twenties and been warned off the stuff by his doctors. In the five decades I knew him he took nothing stronger than Diet Coke. When I told him about Braine's melancholy end, we fell to meditating the other sad examples of writers who had wrecked themselves or (as I suggested a little earlier) numbed their sense of their own inadequacy with drink.

Even now, when we meet, Ingrams urges me to write the book which, when we first planned it, we were going to write together, with the title *Bin Ends*.

Not that alcohol is the only cause of writers' strange behaviour. The name of teetotalling A. L. Rowse comes to mind. When I had published a few books, the great Cornish chronicler of the Elizabethan age took me up and was endlessly kind, inviting me to stay at his large house near St Austell or giving me dinner at the Athenaeum. (Incidentally, should any reader suppose he had improper intentions towards me, such thoughts can be dismissed. As he hooted out loudly once, causing heads in the club to turn, he had no time for sex. He only once had sex in his whole life, with a policeman in the blackout during the Blitz.)

Rowse's own book on *Homosexuals in History* is one of the best treatments of the subject, but if you wished to have a conversation on the subject, it was wise to choose your time and place. Once he was buying me dinner at the small Cornish fishing port where his parents had been married, Charlestown. Some allusion must have been made to the 1890s, because I allowed the phrase 'Poor old Oscar' to escape my lips.

Rowse began to shout – really to shout. 'Typical exhibitionistic IRISHMAN! Why didn't he THINK before suing Queensberry? Bloody fool. The Channel steamers were packed with utterly harmless men, during those stupid trials. Schoolmasters. Clergymen. Men who had led secret lives. The Victorians were very good at double standards, at turning a blind eye. But Oscar had to flaunt himself. TYPICAL IRISH, you see.'

Assuming the noise level was the result of drink, the head waiter hurried to our table and murmured to me that, if I could not control my friend, we would be asked to leave.

It was never possible to know whether Rowse was aware of how absurd such antics appeared. A nurse at Treliske Hospital, Truro, when I visited him after a small stroke, remarked to me how sad it was to see a man in such a condition.

'And they do say 'e were a professor at Oxford, but now look at 'im.'

I tried to reassure her that he was always like this. The behaviour she regarded to be a sign that he had lost his wits was what the Fellows of All Souls had witnessed most evenings for half a century. He was propped against his pillows speaking unstoppably and at a high volume about his discovery of the Dark Lady of Shakespeare's Sonnets. To the Cornish nurse, this was a raving madman.

Yet when I think of expeditions with him to see all the great houses and the few beautiful churches of Cornwall, or when I think of how vividly and intelligently he could speak about the courtiers of Henry VIII or Elizabeth I, I feel nothing but gratitude for having known him. Maybe, then, Ingrams and I are wrong to attribute the self-destructive behaviour of writers to drink. The mismatch between the 'world of all of us', the 'real world' and what is going on inside a writer's head is what makes interesting writers distinctive. All children, especially the illiterate, live inside their own fantasy worlds. Their dolls and animals and imaginary friends have voices which to the child are perfectly real, and it is the loss of the capacity to believe in them that *constitutes* the process usually called 'growing up'. For writers, this process can never fully happen. The voices inside their heads, their imagined

Me and the great Cornishman, A. L. Rowse, outside Truro Cathedral.

inner worlds, retain a reality more vivid than the world of what Forster called telegrams and anger.

These thoughts had predominated in the mind of a young schoolboy poet in the late 1920s and early 1930s when he, Peter Quennell, had been considered one of the rising stars of English literature. His coeval Evelyn Waugh was in some particulars afraid of Quennell: his success as a social climber matched Waugh's own, and his disregard for the bourgeois norms of sexual propriety disturbed Waugh's inner Puritan. Waugh referred to Quennell as Fuddy Duddy Fishface, and used to say that he wrote better than anyone of his generation, with the disadvantage that he had nothing to write about. He only had style. Quennell was aware of this. It was what drew him to Baudelaire and the Symbolist poets, about whom he wrote an elegant book.

I'd been dimly aware of him since schooldays since he joint-edited a magazine called *History Today* and before that the *Cornhill*

Magazine. When, having written a few novels, I began to be asked
to review books, I wrote about *The Marble Foot*, the first volume of
Quennell's memoirs. I was carried away by the book.

Chiefly by the style. He modelled his prose on that of John
Ruskin, on whom he was an expert. Ever since reading Lytton
Strachey's *Eminent Victorians* at Rugby, I had felt an inner passion,
a desire to craft words into well-made sentences. Even if one could
not write poems (and this must be the aim of any real writer), one
could at least shape beautiful prose. This was something to which
Quennell devoted his life, and both volumes of autobiography, *The
Marble Foot* and *The Wanton Chase*, are models of how to write the
English language. If I taught English as a foreign language, I'd hold
them up as exemplars to imitate.

At the same time, Quennell, the only child of middle-class
parents, felt the world in which he had grown up to be tame beside
the possibilities that early fame and publication brought with them,
echoes of a world where more 'interesting' people could be met. In
Quennell's case, this meant the Sitwells. The thorns in the Parable
of the Sower would, had he been a Christian, have choked his faith.

Not that he was a Christian, not at all. He described to me how
he had once spent Friday to Monday (he was careful to employ
upper-class usages and to eschew such Americanisms as the word
'weekend') with the Betjemans in their freezing farmhouse at
Uffington in the Vale of the White Horse. (Betjeman was Q's exact
Oxford contemporary.) A big lunch, he'd have said 'luncheon', had
been consumed. Q had decided to sleep off some of the effects of
this repast, and the best way of getting warm seemed to be to go
back to bed, wearing all his clothes. As sleep began to descend,
however, he became aware that the covers were being drawn back
and Penelope Betjeman, heavily swathed in jumpers, was snuggling
in beside him. He felt flattered, being one of those men (a majority?)
who was always 'on' for any approach from the opposite sex. Carnal
love was not, however, on this occasion on Penelope Betjeman's
mind. Q had failed to accompany Penelope and John to church
that morning and during the lunch(eon) some allusion had been
made to Q's agnosticism. Now, the heavily cardied Penelope was

prodding Q awake and demanding, in her strange cockneyfied voice, 'Naow, Peter, what IZ ORL this nonsense about yew not believing in the Divinity of Our Lord?'

She had brought up to the bedroom for his edification a book called *The Elements of the Spiritual Life* by the vicar of a nearby parish, F. P. Harton. Alas, the book failed to convince him. He told me this story over one of our own bibulous lunches or dinners, for my review of his books had touched the old man and he became a frequent companion. Only as I write this book does it occur to me to ask whether my close friendships such as John Lucas and Peter Quennell suggest a need for a father substitute. In Q's case, there was an added ingredient. I admired his life as a *roué*, and a part of me would like to have followed this path.

His own determination to make of life a Rake's Progress had begun at Balliol College, Oxford. Schooldays in Berkhamsted, where he was contemporary of the son of the headmaster, Graham Greene, had been strait-laced and emotionally repressed. To cure him of the habit of weeping, his parents sent him to board at Mr Greene (senior)'s school, and when they found him weeping at home, they boarded him out with the local doctor during the holidays until the tiresome habit could be controlled. Meanwhile, his parents were hard at work on their history books for children – *A History of Everyday Things in England* (four volumes) and *Everyday Life in Roman Britain*. When Q was knighted, the monarch remarked, 'STILL writing books, Mr Quennell?' with some astonishment, and it was only when he came home that he realized she had read *A History of Everyday Things* in her own schoolroom, and, being neither particularly literary nor very observant, she had assumed that, in 1980, he had been scribbling these books for sixty years.

The lack of tears was emblematic of the lack of a lot else.

'I'm weeping inwardly,' he told me at a restaurant in Chelsea. He had just had one of his appalling rows with his wife Marilyn, his fifth wife, known inevitably as Quennell Number Five.

It was John Betjeman, by then his near neighbour in Chelsea, who told me of Q in earlier days. He was sent down from Oxford for the, in those days, relatively unusual crime of active heterosexuality, which had been discovered by the proctors. Betjeman had also been sent down, but for idleness. The two young men decided to travel to Italy together. They flirted with girls. They spent more than they could afford. They drank too much. At Venice they swam in the Lido and luxuriated in the architecture. Once, when Q had left their table at Florian's, Betjeman saw on his plate the letter collected that morning from the poste restante. A quick peep. It was written by his mother, Marjorie, and Betjeman had time to read the sentence, 'If it had not been for your irresponsible behaviour, you could by now be enjoying a bracing holiday with your father and myself. We are exploring the Norman castles of Wales.'

Q was a charming old throwback to a vanished literary age, but he should have been a warning signal to me. One of his early books, an exquisite slim volume, produced after a visit to pre-war Tokyo and Beijing with Harold Acton, was entitled, all too aptly, *A Superficial Journey.* He was affronted by the references to himself in Virginia Woolf's diaries – 'I don't like that young man's clever, agile, thin-blooded mind', or 'Peter Quennell – whom I don't warm to – exiguous worm'.

If I were writing a journey through the afterlife, with Dante, not Virgil, as my guide, I think the vatic bard might lead me towards old Q in the infernal shades. Even there, he would not be able to see what Virginia Woolf had meant. And, as happens so often in the *Commedia,* one would shudder, both with pity for the sinner in torment and for the fact that his story held up a mirror to one's own sinful soul.

33. St Andrew's by the Northern Sea

I'd never meant to publish works of non-fiction – meaning, popular history books, biographies and such. If I'd stayed in the academic world, I might have tried to write articles for learned journals, suggesting emendations to two lines in *The Clerk's Tale* or possibly even tackling an edition of some Middle English text, with apparatus, notes, etc. If I ever believed myself capable of such a task, of course, I was kidding myself. Although I'd studied medieval literature with Christopher Tolkien, and although it was my job to teach it for seven years, it was obvious to everyone, including me, that this was never going to be a serious proposition – me as medieval scholar. I had a very good working knowledge of all the major texts in Old English and Middle English, and a grasp of the grammar, and enough knowledge of the history to be able to see these works in context; but that was it.

When I moved back to Oxford, after school-teaching, and resumed full-time life in the marital home, I fell gravely ill with pneumonia. After my marriage fell apart, several friends suggested to me that these bouts of illness were physical expressions of inner malaise and they're probably right. During the second bout of pneumonia, Katherine was taken aside by the doctors and told to expect me to die. I recovered, but for weeks I was exhausted and led a sofa existence.

Starting with *Waverley* and reading my way through all the novels until I'd finished *Count Robert of Paris*, I read the entire works of

Sir Walter Scott. Of course, there are other novelists in the world, and as an incurable bookworm I have enjoyed very many reading experiences in a long life; but I do not think there is any pleasure to match that of reading Scott, and even today, if I reach for one of the novels to look up a reference, I find myself lost to the world for hours. He combines so many qualities – compelling narratives; Shakespearean breadth of character creation, with hundreds of unforgettable figures crammed into the pages; vivid historical reconstruction; and not just that, but historical imagination, the ability to make you see why people in that foreign country, the past, behaved as they did.

If my self-diagnosis is right, and I was led to the fantasy of wanting to live in Cardinal Newman's Oratory as a means of inhabiting the past, then reading Scott was the corrective to this. He was an antiquary without rival, and in one sense, both in his books and in his life, he lived in the past. But he is the most intelligent conservative thinker known to me, because he realizes that history only moves forward. Some of the most tragic, and also the most ridiculous, figures in his novels think you can go on fighting battles that were lost years ago. He, by contrast, had Hegel's sense that we move inexorably onwards, strong as our affection might be for the Last Ditch.

He was also unrivalled in his ability to describe landscapes, and to describe why human societies are shaped by the landscapes in which they grew up. Reading him during that sofa phase of convalescence in my mid-twenties restored me, saved me really, body and soul. I began to doodle in notebooks, observations which arose from reading him. The nineteenth century, not merely its literary history but its aesthetic, its cult of the medieval, its Gothic revivals, its use of history in opera, its wistful hope that it could return to an Age of Faith and its discovery that it, or the Faith, had mysteriously altered – all these things go back to Scott. Europe learned from him. Pushkin, Goethe, Weber, Verdi, Hugo, they would none of them have composed as they did without Scott as the forerunner. I found myself writing a book that would eventually be published as *The Laird of Abbotsford* – Abbotsford being the house on the banks of the Tweed which he built, and which some have called a Waverley novel in stone.

It certainly would not have been the same book had not Allan Maclean taken me to all the Scott sites, to his grave in Dryburgh Abbey, to Smailholm Tower, to Kelso, as well as to every cranny of Edinburgh which he described so unforgettably. Allan liked the anecdote told by Scott's son-in-law Lockhart, of his dining, as a very young man, with Sir William Menzies at his residence in George Street and Sir William's complaint that from where he sat he could see through a window in North Castle Street, where 'a confounded hand' was perpetually at work. 'Since we sat down', he said, 'I have been watching it – it fascinates my eyes – it never stops – page after page is finished and thrown upon that heap of MS., and still it goes on unwearied.' It was Scott, secretly penning *Waverley*, but Allan used to apply it jestingly to my own prolific habits of composition, which were already getting out of control.

One of the paradoxes about my friendship with Allan is that it gave me back my lost youth. Although as twenty-something-year-olds we must have seemed fogeyish to our friends, visiting ancient monuments, discussing architecture and church politics, Allan was also at the hub of a circle of Edinburgh coevals, some his cousins, others university contemporaries, whose idea of a good time was racier than squinting at the hearth of Archbishop Sharpe in the hall at Abbotsford, or comparing people we knew to figures in *The Antiquary*.

So it was I entered Bannerman's Bar in Cowgate, a place where I passed some of the happiest and most irresponsible hours of my life, laughing, boozing and flirting. The bar took its name from the proprietor, Julian Bannerman, a curly-headed Byron, a little older than the rest of us, who had all the gifts necessary for a good host in bar or nightclub – socially voracious, reckless, funny, a bit of a snob, piratical. The Lord of Misrule. Some of the friends first met there had lives cut very short by drugs, drink, motor accidents. Many are still alive. One of the rowdiest evenings, when Bannerman announced that drinks were on the house, was when he announced his engagement to a student called Isabel Eustace.

This was none other than the daughter of Bar Eustace, born Belloc, the Zuleika Dobson of Christopher Tolkien's Oxford, with whom everyone had been besottedly in love.

Isabel is no less striking than her mother. Forty years later, she and her husband are the parents of three extremely handsome men, and the creators of some of the finest gardens in England, at Highgrove, Arundel – where not? Although the joint is still named Bannerman's Bar, Julian's own proprietorship came to an end when he discovered there was something called VAT. HM Customs and Excise would have closed the place down. Years later, he told me that Allan Maclean, whom he always calls 'the vicar', had given quite a lot of money to get him out of that particular financial crisis.

Presumably my abandoned behaviour at Bannerman's Bar embarrassed Allan, but if so, he never said so. He continued to be a good friend to Katherine, even though I must have put him in the awkward position of having witnessed indiscretions. I was nuts about a young woman who, herself coming out of an unhappy marriage, served behind the bar. She was a Bardot lookalike, but even more beautiful. I have just (as I write these words) heard the news of her death.

It was during this phase that I was summoned to an interview for a lectureship at the University of St Andrews. To be given a proper job at a prestigious university would have cancelled out what I still acutely felt – the disgrace of a mediocre degree. My Scott book had been published by OUP. It had won a prize – the John Llewellyn Rhys – and it would have provided a dignified excuse for what Katherine and I both really wanted by this stage, marital separation, without it being given so formal a name. If I were to spend half the year in Fife, we could lead lives that one of her colleagues termed 'telegamous': i.e. still married but living in separate places. The strain of living together all the time would be lifted. Who knows? Perhaps some new way of living could be found without divorce.

The interview panel at St Andrews consisted of three people, and I had prepared for the experience carefully, boning up on Scottish literature, trying to imagine which writers they'd expect me to have read, in Andrew Lang's university. Dear Andrew with the brindled hair, Robert Louis Stevenson had called him. Would I grow old in this stupendously beautiful place, pacing along Lade Braes walk or among the ruins of the Priory and Castle as the winds blew in from the crashing North Sea? The idea was appealing. I was in love not only with my new Bardot-esque friend from Bannerman's Bar in Edinburgh but with the whole place.

The first question, posed by a breezy middle-aged woman, took me by surprise. Rather than expecting knowledge of Henryson or Stevenson, she inquired, 'What's your handicap?'

A second member of the panel reassuringly murmured, 'You'll find it easier if you play.'

The Professor of English, Peter Bayley, concluded the twenty minutes or so with a further piece of advice. 'Only one thing to say. We are not a writing faculty. If you were to be offered this post, it would be on condition that the writing stopped.'

If great things may be to small compared, Allan's joke about the unstoppable hand in North Castle Street was a fair one; not because I am worthy to touch the hem of Scott's plaid, but because I too have a writing compulsion. If a restful existence on the links were to be forced on me, might I not go barmy? I mulled these things over with my beautiful friend, who had come with me for the interview. As I told her, truthfully, I had two reasons for applying for this job: one was to prove myself capable of getting a university job, and the other was to be near her; but I found it impossible to envisage a life without writing.

Peter Bayley, with his navy blue blazer, his stripy tie, possibly signalling a boyhood spent at some minor public school, and his cavalry twill trousers, had been the English don at University College, Oxford, before taking the Chair of English at St Andrews. He was reassuringly unmodern and looked like, indeed was, the sort of man you might meet at the bar of a golf club in the Home Counties.

It was tense, waiting for his phone call. He'd told me he would let me know within twenty-four hours. In fact, my friend and I were having breakfast in bed when he rang to offer me the job.

'You'd like St Andrews,' he told me. And I am sure he spoke the truth. 'There are no shits here. No queers. No pinkoes.'

In his time as a member of the English Faculty at Oxford, he would have been aware of the high preponderance of such colleagues, many of them able to score three out of three of the supposedly undesirable characteristics. I expressed rapturous gratitude, and said I'd ring him back soonest, but that – a shy look at the Bardot lookalike – I would have to consult my wife.

Many's the time, when boarding a train to Scotland, or even simply walking through King's Cross Station and hearing the announcement of the Scottish trains, that I have asked myself whether I made the right decision to turn down Peter Bayley's offer.

Wistful is a light-sounding word. But if wistfulness can be strong, I feel an overpowering wistfulness whenever I so much as see the name of 'the little city worn and grey' as my brindled namesake called it, 'St Andrews by the Northern Sea'.

34. Prosaic and Drivelling

What I had at Oxford, after all, was not a proper job but two temporary college lectureships. One of the secretaries in the Bursary at New College left me in no doubt of my status when I ventured into the office with the impertinent request to be paid for the term's work. (I was paid by the hour, and for some reason, meagre as the expected cheque would be, it had not been given to me. 'But what are you?' she asked me, supplying the answer at once, 'A temporary college lecturer – less than the dust!')

During my stint as a schoolmaster, the Principal of St Hugh's approached me and asked if I'd take over the medieval and language teaching at her college for the foreseeable future. Rachel Trickett was a good friend, who was doing her best to get me an academic post in Oxford. It happened that, at about this time, Christopher Tolkien invited me to his house in Berkshire to discuss a scheme. He had applied for a term's leave to finish *The Silmarillion*, the book on which his father, recently dead, had been labouring for decades. (Touchy Christopher stopped speaking to a friend for nicknaming it *The Sellamillion*, a joke taken up by *Private Eye*.) It is actually JRRT's masterpiece, telling of the Creation, of the wars in the First Age of the World, fought over three magic jewels, the Silmarils, and of the downfall of Númenor.

Christopher confided in me that, although he had assured his new colleague Anne Barton (John Bayley had become a professor and moved to St Catherine's – Catz) that he would be back soon after Christmas, he and his wife were in fact going to do a bunk to France, sell their Berkshire house and emigrate to the village of La Garde-Freinet, not far from St-Tropez. He could not guarantee that Anne would simply let me step into his shoes, but he felt that if he told her with no notice, she would be more or less bound to accept the arrangement.

Thus it was that for the next seven years of my life I taught undergraduates at both New College and St Hugh's. I took them though the compulsory papers in Old English and Middle English and taught them for another compulsory paper, the History of the English Language. Ashamed at the hash I'd made of Icelandic in my exams, I'd by now mastered it sufficiently to teach Norse when needed, ditto medieval Latin, when, as occasionally happened, an undergraduate opted to do a special paper on one of these languages. It now seems presumptuous of me since, although I had a goodish working mastery of both subjects, I was in no sense an expert.

I was extremely lucky with my pupils. In the whole seven years I never met one I disliked. I am also grateful for the fact that, by dint of seven annual repetitions, so much of this stuff is still lodged in my by now forgetful old nut. But a don I was not, nor was meant to be. K, by total contrast, was through and through a don and more wedded to Oxford than she ever was to me. Every so often I'd beg her to move with me to London, but, although we'd considered taking a flat near the British Museum to enable her to work in the manuscript room, the idea of leaving Oxford was always vehemently rejected. She was right. She knew where her spiritual home was.

Only once did a move away from the Home of Lost Causes (no cause more seemingly lost than our marriage) seem feasible. A recently made friend, Father Brocard Sewell of the Order of Carmelites, told us that Capel-y-ffin, the farmhouse near Hay-on-Wye that had once been the home of Eric Gill, David Jones et al., was up for sale. The price, £70,000, was affordable. We went to view it.

Long since, when still an undergraduate, K had won a prize for her essay on Giraldus Cambrensis, archdeacon of Brecon in the early thirteenth century, who in his 'Description of Wales' left accounts of that beautiful bit of mountainous country between Hay and Abergavenny. The medieval abbey had long been a ruin, when an eccentric Anglican deacon, Joseph Leycester Lyne, styling himself Father Ignatius, founded a monastery at Capel-y-ffin, where there were some rum goings-on, including an appearance of Our Lady over the rhubarb patch. There is an annual pilgrimage to commemorate the event, led by a Salvation Army Band. Father Brocard, matchless chronicler of the 1890s and editor of a good 'little magazine' called the *Aylesford Review*, thought we'd be the ideal occupants, and I saw what he meant. When we got there, K saw what he meant too. It is a chunkily built, whitewashed house. The kitchen has murals by David Jones from his 1930s occupancy. The attic floor is a chapel, decorated by Jones and Gill. There are enough outlying cottages and stables to allow the owners to have a letting income from walkers and pony-trekkers. It is a part of the country of which we are both very fond. Both avid readers of *Kilvert's Diary*, K and I enjoyed the entries when he walked over from his nearby parish of Clyro to visit Father Ignatius.

But we both knew that we could not live there together. It was not imaginable that we could have a future there together, because it was not imaginable that we had a future together anywhere. In Oxford we had developed a way of life in which we could conceal from one another, and from our friends, the extent to which we already led separate lives and were already estranged. In the mountains of Breconshire, with no Bodleian Library, no Somerville College, no London, to which we could nip for refuge, we would presumably have gone mad. There was infinite sadness in our driving away from Capel-y-ffin. We knew that, if we had a future together, this would have been an ideal place to make a fresh start.

We and the children drove on to west Wales. Norman and Jean had moved yet again, this time to the railway village of Ferryside, on the Towy estuary, looking across the water to their former house at Llansteffan. Visiting them with K was always a strain. She made no effort to laugh at Norman's ancient jokes, and mercilessly cut short his anecdotes with reminders that she had heard them before. He had lately been over to Cresselly and photographed the house for Hensleigh's book *The Wedgwood Circle*, written with his wife, Barbara. Cresselly is the seat of the Allens, a family who had provided more than one spouse for the Wedgwoods. It was also a family from which K descended, so it would have been kind of her to pretend an interest in Norman's snaps; but such kindness was by now impossible for her.

Jean, for her part, made no effort to conceal her loathing of K. Huge sighs were heaved when some excuse was invented to drive the children back to Oxford after only a day or two. I stayed on for a bit longer.

'Slightly naughtily,' Norman confided, 'Francis [the auctioneer and estate agent in Carmarthen] did not mention the railway.'

He said it as we watched the little diesel rattle beneath us on its way to Llanelli.

'But you get used to it.'

'Tell him not to complain about the children,' said Jean.

'My children?'

'How do you mean?'

'She means the neighbours' brats. We can't spend any time in the garden.'

It was a perfectly decent house, quite a substantial villa in fact. The lumpy brown furniture looked good in it. There was space for my unfortunate aunt to be kept out of sight on a higher floor.

'It's far too large for us, but we had to buy a bigger place for Liz. *She's bleeding us dry.*' This from my mother.

'Don't go up and see her,' Norman begged, knowing that I would do so and that there would be the predictable jealous explosion, followed by a sulk. I found Aunt Elizabeth unchanged, unflappably absorbed in an umpteenth re-read of *The Portrait of a Lady*, a Craven A smouldering in the ashtray.

'Katherine didn't stay long,' she remarked as I was leaving. She did so with a laugh, and I realized for the first time that all the laughter I'd known in her company had been self-protective banter, not actual mirth. I realized that when I was a young boy at Hillstone and she had made me laugh with 'If I'd known you were coming, I'd have baked a cake', it was because she was aware of Jean's hatred and was trying to put a brave, humorous face on things.

'Watch out for your father's guns. He's getting too fond of them,' she said darkly.

Jean also adverted to this subject when we were alone together. My father had taken to daily drives to Carmarthen. A chat with the repair man. No harm to ask him to look under the bonnet to make sure the old car was in working order. On market days Norman would take a cup of coffee in the market. It was usually possible, on crowded Wednesdays, to find an occupied table and a captive audience for some of the anecdotes. So for an hour or two, my mother and I were left alone together.

'I'm afraid he's going to shoot one of those children,' she said.

'What sort of guns are they?'

'He's still got his old service revolver. And then there's an air rifle. He's taken to shooting over the children's heads. He says they make too much noise with their bikes, riding up and down the lane.'

Some time later – when I'd gone home to Oxford – there was an 'incident'. The police were called by the children's mother. Not only had he been firing the gun, but he had told this woman that a few air pellets up her son's backside might teach him to be less noisy. Or less Something noisy, as Jean related the exchange. Norman got away with a caution, but I was worried about them.

He was probably getting on for eighty by now. His visits to Oxford were less frequent than in the early days of our marriage. His intense loneliness was painful. Apart from the hours when I was teaching, he wanted to be with me all the time, talking, talking, talking. He had aged well: his moustache was now silver and the well-cut clothes looked none the worse for being frayed. When he and they decayed further, he took to buying second-hand clothes, paying a local dressmaker to remove the tailors' labels from his old suits and sew them into these cheaper garments. If he were ever taken into hospital, the nurse who hung up his clothes might enjoy the delusion that he was a gentleman.

He loved it in Oxford when we were asked to parties. Tanya Harrod remembers bringing him to drinks with the Waterfield brothers, and his holding Julian Barnes with his sky-blue eyes with memories of Josiah, who had been dead for a few years now, or with assurances that my favourite painters were the Impressionists. The Bayleys, who had perfect manners, seemed as if they genuinely did find him delightful. John liked quizzing him about ack-ack guns. In my case, however, with delight in Norman's company there was also aching, paralysing, boredom.

Perhaps those who throw themselves wholeheartedly into marriage do not have time to cultivate friendships. Perhaps, after his rift with Josiah, no friendship would quite do. I have known other men, intensely married, who had no friends. Without mine, I suppose I'd have gone mad. K and I saw a lot of friends, both in Oxford and in London.

Of the London contingent, one of the dearest was Selina Hastings. She often came up to Oxford to stay with her sister. Selina had been at St Hugh's so, now I was teaching there, we had endless gossip about the characters of the dons. Her capacity to enjoy the foibles of others and to empathize, not only with charming people but with semi-monsters, surely explains why she has been so astute a biographer of such alarming figures as Evelyn Waugh and Somerset Maugham.

She was a good friend of us both, Katherine having taught her for a term or two. Inevitably, though – she has now been a near neighbour of mine in London for decades – she came to see more of me than of K. On a day when I know I am going to see Selina I wake up like a child on Christmas morning. For half a century we have shared reflections about our friends, swapped views of books or recipes, or memories. Her store of recollections and imitations always makes me laugh. There is no relationship happier than friendship between a man and a woman. Friendship between two men seldom involves the sharing of confidences. With Selina I have shared almost everything, including those writer problems which no non-writer wishes to hear about. She is a brilliant listener as well as talker. And although, for both of us, our chorus line of friends provides an unintended *opera buffa*, I do not think we are really unkind about them.

Logan Pearsall Smith's aphorism fits her exactly – 'Hearts that are delicate and kind and tongues that are neither – these make the finest company in the world.'

Selina Hastings.

Apart from being grateful for fifty years of friendship, I also owe her a professional debt. For a short while, after leaving the *Daily Telegraph*, where she helped David Holloway edit the Books Pages, she worked for our friend Sebastian Walker, who had left Chatto & Windus to set up an independent children's book publishing firm, Walker Books.

We both cherished the fact that, when he was starting out as a publisher, Sebastian's cleaning woman in Islington said, 'You oughta read your neighbour's book what he wrote for his kids.'

Sebastian's glancing, contemptuous eyes glazed over.

'Ever so good, them little girls say it is.'

Eventually the neighbour himself shoved the typescript through Sebbie's door and he refused even to look at it. He put the typescript immediately into the waste paper basket. Sebbie was chagrined when the cleaner said one day, 'Seein' as 'ow you was so snooty, 'e sent it to some other publisher.'

'Who did? What?'

'Mr Adams. You know I clean Mr Adams's house next door as well as yours. 'E sent 'is book about rabbits to someone else seeing as you wasn't interested.'

A year later, the whole world was reading *Watership Down*.

Selina said she was hoping for comparable success when she asked me to write an animal story for Walker Books and she accepted the idea that I should try to do for stray cats what Richard Adams had done for the rabbits of Berkshire. Alas, *Stray* never sold as well as *Watership Down*, but I think I am right in saying that it has been continuously in print since I wrote it.

———

The closest I ever got to doing medieval research was to write a novel called *Wise Virgin*, which won the W. H. Smith award and was my best early novel. A lot had been poured into the mixture. The central character, a blind scholar, though living in the twentieth century, is obviously based on John Milton. For years and years he has been trying to edit a manual of spiritual teaching, written in Middle English, for a small community of nuns. I was – am – interested in medieval devotional writing, and had to teach the *Ancrene Wisse*, which is a bit like the text in my book, *A Treatis of Loue hevenliche* – though my treatise was also a bit like Julian of Norwich and a bit like an anonymous text called *Hali Meithhad* (Holy Maidenhood). My story reduced Milton's three long-suffering daughters to just one, Tibba, whom I based on a student of mine who, that year, all innocently and with nothing said on either side, filled all my waking and some of my sleeping thoughts.

The resultant mixture was *Wise Virgin*. It only now occurs to me, as I write these paragraphs, that a learned Oxford medievalist (Kiwi by birth) called E. J. Dobson might have supposed that he was in some ways being depicted in the book. One of the novelist's occupational hazards is meeting those who believe themselves, nearly always wrongly, to be the models for characters one has invented (or half-based on someone quite other). I revered Eric Dobson for his scholarship. His mighty two-volume history of

English Pronunciation, 1500–1700 is a hefty but necessary purchase for anyone, such as myself, paid to teach the History of the English Language. A smaller, much more charming piece of academic detective work by Dobson is *The Origins of Ancrene Wisse*, in which he identified the actual village, the actual religious house, where the text was composed.

Dobson took a fatherly interest in my career, or, rather, would have done if I'd had one. After five or six years teaching this esoteric stuff, I was clearly one of the small number of medievalists in the faculty, and since I took any work I was offered, I had pupils at colleges other than St Hugh's or my own. But when was I going to write the learned article, or start work on the PhD thesis on some obscure medieval subject?

Anne Barton, in effect my boss at New College, gave out contrary messages about my likely chances of being offered a Fellowship, hence tenure. Since it was obvious that her feelings about me vacillated, and since she had the power to hire and fire, I never dared ask her directly about this. Anne, once a beautiful American, was now a strange, twitching, blinking, obese figure who made (to those who complained about the habit to me) embarrassing advances to the undergraduates. She was sleeping with the English don from St Catz, Michael Gearin-Tosh. With his high-pitched Bloomsbury giggle, his flamboyant clothes (fur coats, silk scarves) and his shock of long curly silver hair, he seemed an unlikely lover for Anne, particularly as he shared her weakness for chasing his male students round the room, rather than teaching them. Nevertheless, a pair they were. Tosh lived in the lodgings at St Hugh's, having more than once proposed marriage to the Principal, Rachel Trickett, but there was more in their relationship of Betsey Trotwood and Mr Dick than there was of romance.

So, Tosh would tell Rachel when my shares were in the ascendant, and she would pass on the news to me. For a year or two Anne would say, via this bush telegraph, that she liked me enormously, but gossip in Oxford's febrile world passed rapidly up and down the line, and because I was great friends with the Quintons I was an object of mistrust. This was because Marcelle,

Anne (in those days Bobbyann Roesen) and Gaby Annan – as she became – had been three college girls together at Bryn Mawr and one seldom saw either Gaby or Marcelle without their wishing to dwell on the amorous adventures or, very occasionally, other aspects of Anne's character, such as her intellectual mediocrity, or her marriages, first to American academic Bill Righter, later to theatre director John Barton. We had all – K, the Bayleys, the Quintons – been to stay with the Bartons at their house near Stratford-upon-Avon, where a succession of famous actors would be invited to eat the extraordinarily rich meals which Anne skilfully prepared. (Anne cooked all her own meals even when in college, scarcely venturing to the High Table for dinner, and believing, by the end accurately but not at all at the beginning, that the other fellows disliked her.)

If she decided to give me the boot, I did not know quite what I'd do for cash, since young A. N., though by now winning prizes for a new novel every couple of years, and writing reviews for the *Spectator* and the *TLS*, scarcely made enough money to keep afloat and was only able to pay for our annual Scottish holiday by marking A-level papers – a job I loved.

A dire indication came one week, via Tosh and Rachel, that Anne had been asking in the faculty whether they could recommend a more scholarly figure than myself to do the medieval teaching at New College, and a week or so later, a chance encounter in the faculty building on Manor Road confirmed my fears that my job was not safe.

Eric Dobson met me and asked me to sit beside him on the bench near the door to the library from which we could see the bust, crafted by Faith Tolkien, of her father-in-law the old professor. Dobson urged on me the need to apply to study for a PhD. He had it in mind that there was some useful research to be done on John Lydgate's *Troy Book*. When I recall this, my friend Peter McKay's phrase about his own avocation as a gossip columnist comes to mind – 'Dirty work, but somebody's got to do it.'

'Lydgate's not much read,' Dobson said.

There are reasons for this state of affairs. Didn't someone once call him a 'voluminous, prosaic and drivelling monk'?

'... but,' Dobson was saying, 'there are interesting things to be done with his *Troy Book*, his debts to Guido delle Colonne and so on. Maybe, if you edited one of the manuscripts ...'

Strangely enough, if you were to ask me now, aged seventy, to revisit medieval versions of the Trojan legends, I'd be rather tempted, but the thought, for a not-quite-thirty-something-year-old man, of ploughing through 30,000 lines of the drivelling monk while trying to keep in Anne Barton's good books, all on an income that was about one third of that of a postman or a charwoman, was not especially appealing.

'You have just won this' – Dobson sounded very sad – 'prize for a novel about a medieval scholar, but we want you to *be* a medieval scholar. Not a novelist. The two things are incompatible and, you know, you are going to have to decide, which of them is it going to be?'

Luckily for me, Fate, that ever-present phenomenon in Old English heroic poetry, took a hand. Shaken by my conversation with Dobson, I wandered home up Parks Road, down Museum Road, through Lamb and Flag Passage, across St Giles'. It was twelve or thirteen years since I had first come to live in this beautiful place of enchantments, of bells and buildings and libraries, of St Hugh's undergraduates in Laura Ashley dresses, cycling to lectures on *Ancrene Wisse*, and churches where the clergy wore Spanish birettas, and all this would forever tug at my heart. This place, however, could never provide me with a suitable line of occupation. There is a sad certainty in your heart when you reach the end of an affair, and so it was, during that afternoon walk, between me and Oxford. Back in the kitchen in Jericho, I flicked on the electric kettle and awaited the end of Emily and Bee's school day. The telephone interrupted my self-pitying reflections.

'It's Alexander Chancellor here.'

(The editor of the *Spectator*.)

'... it's a long shot, I know, and you're probably much too grand ...' There followed what sounded like interference on the line, electronic crackling such as used to emanate from radio sets. I would soon come to recognize this noise as that of Alexander laughing through orifices which in other human beings produce snores. '... but I wonder whether you'd consider becoming our Literary Editor.'

35. Clare

It is nearly forty years since I was sacked from the *Spectator*, after some of the most amusing times of my life, flirting, social climbing and entangling myself in the thorns, which in the Parable symbolize the lures and false enchantments of the world. Almost the only thing to survive from that totally vanished era is my friendship with the deputy Lit Ed, Clare Asquith, who did nearly all the work, while I gadded about enjoying myself.

'You'll get on all right with Clare,' Alexander said, following the observation with one of his interference-on-the-line snorts of mirth. The truest words he ever spoke. Clare had been commissioning me to write reviews for some years by then and was already a friend. Through all the changing scenes of life, four or five different editors, two different proprietors and any number of literary editors, there Clare has remained. She got the job shortly after coming down from Oxford and has remained, like Yeats's daughter in his poem, rooted in one dear perpetual place. Rightly is one of her names Perpetua.

Her film-star beauty, being an intelligent-looking Catherine Deneuve (if that isn't an oxymoron), never fading with the years, was in equal measure intimidating and attractive to all who came into the house and found her sitting beside the window at her desk, filling in the *Times* crossword in her perfect italic hand and smoking a great many cigarettes.

To her left, for she feels the cold, a gas fire would hiss and give out its old-fashioned blasts of heat for most of the year. At the

Clare Asquith at her desk in the Spectator *office.*

other window seat Gina Lewis had her desk, niece of my friend Naomi (she of *Messages* not *Massages*). In those pre-computer and pre-mobile phone days Gina would be the one who answered the phone and put callers through, usually to the editor, sometimes to one of the people upstairs who actually put the paper together, chief among them Patrick Marnham and Peter Ackroyd. Gina, like most of us, mucked in and did a range of jobs, many of which were made more difficult since someone was in the habit of placing on her desk a large crash helmet, encrusted with diamanté.

The owner of the helmet and of the Vespa parked immediately outside the building was then aged sixtyish, a large-voiced, deep-chested figure with dyed auburn hair roped in a piratical pigtail, half-moon specs on her nose, check trousers, motorcycle boots. In the marsupial pouch of her brightly coloured fisherman's tops Jennifer Paterson kept the essentials, a lighter, a packet of Woodbines and a flask of vodka, angostura and ice, to which continual application was made throughout the day until she got home to the large mansion flat, shared with an uncle, near Westminster Cathedral. Once home, she would make the switch from vodka to whisky. 'Sip, sip, sip, like an old dowager,' she would often misquote from *Brideshead Revisited*.

Jennifer Paterson on her scooter, with Clare's son Edward.

Alexander used to say that people who set out to be characters were always embarrassing. There did seem to be times when, as self-appointed court jester, Jennifer saw it as her function in life to embarrass other people. She had been engaged to cook the lunches that happened sometimes once a week or, if the paper were losing even more money than usual, once a fortnight. Those who made their way up the stairs to the dining room at the top to partake of these famous repasts had to run the gauntlet of Jennifer, greeting everyone as if they were her personal guests and hugging those she had never met. 'What are you giving us for lunch?' the Prince of Wales had asked shyly when she had put him down again on the ground. 'Raw fish, Your Majesty!' she had boomed. She had specially devised a way of making gravadlax with halibut. When the Israeli ambassador sat down at the table, he inquired, 'I am very sorry, but is that pork?' as she brought to him a plate with crackling and apple sauce clearly visible on the side of the plate. 'It won't do you any harm, darlin' – just say it's chicken, that's what Anthony Blond says when I give it him.'

Choosing to serve pork to the Israeli ambassador, who of course left rather than be seen by a roomful of journalists to be consuming forbidden meat, was one of the many occasions when Jennifer was sacked, but her tactic on such occasions was to turn up the next day and carry on as if nothing had happened. Alexander was too embarrassed to suggest he really meant the sack; and it was not until he was replaced by Charles Moore that there was an editor who sacked her properly. (She had lost her rag with Charles and thrown a trayful of crockery out of the top-storey window.) By then her fame was spreading and it was not long before she was starring in a TV show called *Two Fat Ladies*. A high point was reached when the show became a hit in Australia and she and the other fat lady, Clarissa Dickson Wright, were paraded round Melbourne on a float, with crowds cheering as they passed. 'I felt like Hitler, darlin'.'

Jennifer believed she was being helpful by opening all my post, a tiresome trick, since so large a part of a lit ed's life consists of unwrapping the parcels. If I did this job with Clare, we could decide which books could be consigned immediately to the Knacker's Yard – a dealer in Chancery Lane who bought review copies for use in public libraries – and which books might conceivably be posted to reviewers. Between us we had built up an impressive team – Anita Brookner regularly doing the fiction, luminaries such as Philip Larkin, Angus Wilson, Isaiah Berlin, Fitzroy Maclean, Enoch Powell, Veronica Wedgwood, Hugh Trevor-Roper also writing for us. Younger writers whom we enlisted included Lucy Hughes-Hallett, now a distinguished biographer, and Nigella Lawson, on whom I formed an embarrassing crush. She was kind about this, and we used to spend hours, sitting in Bertorelli's in Charlotte Street, staring at one another, and in my case unable to eat, while she prodded at a plate of mashed potatoes. We never drank anything stronger than Ribena. In another corner of the restaurant Clive James would be keeping Martin Amis, Julian Barnes and chums in a roar at his jokes. In all the time I knew her well, Nigella, destined to be famed as a gastronomic genius, never ate anything except mashed potato and never mentioned the subject of food.

Tuesday was press day. This was pre-computers. Clare and I would walk down to the press in Saffron Hill. It was a long day, spent quite literally cutting and pasting with a pair of scissors and glue. Clare had an absolutely unerring eye for how to snip an article without the omission showing, and then repasting on the page. It was in this business of snipping that I was to meet my Waterloo.

Apart from our stable of regulars, reviewers fell into two broad categories: those whom we had implored on bended knee for an article, figures such as Isaiah Berlin or Harold Wilson, who had not long since retired as Prime Minister (a completely delightful, polite, humorous man), and those who were themselves the importunate implorers. Two such were a retired headmaster called David Williams, who came into the office about once a week asking for work, and a journalist we all called Belgrano, in real life Bel Mooney, who saw herself as a *littératrice*. David Williams wrote a book. It was not an especially good one, about George Lewes, the life partner of George Eliot.

Clare and I both liked David, who was the father of a more famous writer, Nigel Williams. It so happened that on the day we opened a jiffy bag to find David's Lewes biography, Mooney sailed in, snatched it from my desk and said the book was just up her street.

'Well, please be kind about it,' said Clare.

A few days later, I rang Mooney and said that extra sensitivity was needed, since David Williams had died. Two weeks later, however, she sent in a real stinker of a review. Of course, we should have just binned the article, but I had been lazy and not commissioned enough work for that week, so we somehow felt it had to go in. I got to work, cutting out all the unkind things she had said about David Williams, and leaving in her account of George Lewes, who was a fascinating figure – the first biographer of Goethe, among his other accomplishments.

By the time we were pasting the edited version on to a page, we found it was about eight lines too long. Another cut was needed. She'd begun the piece by explaining who Lewes was, and she did so by making a clumsy comparison between this Victorian man of letters and the Australian broadcaster and writer Clive James. Lewes, she said, had been a polymath, multilingual, witty, and although appallingly ugly, he was a sort of Victorian Clive James. It was only the work of minutes with the scalpel to make Mooney merely say that Lewes, appallingly ugly, was a Victorian Clive James.

Funnily enough, despite Mooney's protests and a formal letter of complaint from James himself, I was not sacked on the spot. It was when, some months later, Alexander had decided he wanted a change of lit eds that he dragged up the Bel Mooney business and said it was a sacking offence. Which it undoubtedly was. I now think my prank was a despicable piece of spite, and I feel doubly cross with myself, since Clare had implored me not to do it. The loss of Clare's companionship was a punishment indeed.

Once we'd put the books pages to bed, we could always look forward to a gentle week. Often, we'd walk to King's Cross together. Those squares between Doughty Street and King's Cross are ones which I still frequent, and my walks there always make me think of happy days with Clare. As often as not we would call at Gavin Stamp's house in St Chad's Street and find him, a tall figure in a double-breasted pinstripe, a glass of whisky invariably in his hand, the room, rather like Catto's at Oxford, filled with those who would continue to be friends for life – Ackroyd, who had known Gavin at Cambridge, Lucy Lambton, whose inspirational photographs and books were celebrations of architectural wonders, Jonathan Meades, Carrie and Glynn Boyd Harte. Gavin was married to one of the most original and hilarious journalists of her generation, Alexandra Artley, whose column about their lives together, Hoorah for the Filth-Packets!, still repays re-reading. They'd managed to buy the little Georgian house for £50,000. No building society would touch them with a bargepole since Gavin made no secret of his ambition never to have a job, but Alex persuaded the manager of Barclays Bank, Redcar, to lend them the cash.

Gavin had taken over the Nooks and Corners column of *Private Eye* from his hero John Betjeman, and the two of them were tireless warriors against the shysters and vandals who wanted to despoil our cities with ugly buildings erected solely to make money. Blessed are the pure in heart. Gavin was perverse, furious much of the time, even a little mad, but good as gold, a person of utter integrity, as is Alex. Paul Foot, another *Private Eye* journalist, had some of the same qualities, though he was much more good-humoured.

Ingrams, the editor of that rather terrifying mag, saw its function not, as it became after he left, mockery of public figures so mild and bland as to flatter their ego but a real determination to expose hypocrisy in high places and to put down the mighty from their seats. Unlike Stamp and Foot, Ingrams was, is, a complicated mixture. Peter McKay, who, with Nigel Dempster, wrote the Grovel column for the *Eye*, says that the beginning and end of Ingrams's character, in his heyday, was envy. With Ingrams coming from the governing or establishment class (his grandfather was Sir James Reid, Queen Victoria's last doctor, and his mother was named Victoria after her – I rather think she was the Queen's god-daughter), McKay's line is that a *bit* of him would like to have been the judge, or the ambassador, or the newspaper baron whose villainies and follies he set out in the *Eye* to unmask. There was plenty of villainy and folly to find, most of which was ignored by the other newspapers, which did not wish to spend their profits settling libel cases. Sometimes what was unleashed by the *Eye* was not strictly speaking journalism but a sort of creative, almost cosmic, malice, never more brilliantly on display than in the Diaries of Auberon Waugh, which I re-read every few years, at each re-perusal more astounded by the fact that anything so scabrous, so cruel, so hilarious (when on form, which was not always), could ever have seen print. It would be quite impossible for them to be reprinted in today's atmosphere. At the time, only Ingrams the Pirate King would have published such stuff. The press, which likes to see itself as Speaking the Truth to Power, that tired old cliché, is for the most part sycophantic towards the Rich, the Privileged, the Established. Reputations, however ill deserved, for brilliance as broadcaster, artist, performer are reinforced by media coverage. Not long after starting work at the *Spectator*, and for about the next seven years, I either saw or spoke to Ingrams most days.

Many of those who wrote for *Private Eye* in those days (Geoffrey Wheatcroft, Patrick Marnham and others) were also stalwarts of the *Spectator*. As well as his Diary for the *Eye*, Auberon Waugh

Richard Ingrams.

did a weekly column for the *Spectator*, and Ingrams wrote a TV
column, my favourite of which was about a play by Angela Huth
that he had not actually watched, but snatches of which he had
heard coming through the wall of a hotel bedroom where he was
trying to get to sleep.

Journalism is of its essence ephemeral. Almost nothing written
for the daily or weekly press is worth re-reading even a few weeks
later. Waugh's writing was different. It had another quality which
makes him sorely missed nowadays. He deliberately said the
unsayable, about half the time simply in order to shock or cause
pain, but often because his Swiftian eye saw a truth which the
majority were too lazy to recognize. The many passages in the
Diary about the Royal Family, in which, while caressing her feet,
or whispering sweet nothings in her ear, he berated the Queen for
allowing her children to marry such trash, are prophecies, truly.

Likewise his defence, in the *Spectator*, of the European Union against the sceptics. His occasional anarchic, lefty moments, as when he had one of his children baptized Biafra and exposed the genocidal policies of the British in that country, sit strangely, but perhaps not so strangely, beside his espousal of the French maverick Archbishop Lefebvre. Bron had his children confirmed by the archbishop, in some garage in Guildford, doubling as a Lefebvrist pro-cathedral. He inherited from his father a contempt for the changes in the Church since Vatican II, but he did not inherit his father's capacity for faith.

Knowing the ecclesiastical preoccupations which from time to time buzzed in my bonnet like mad bees, Ingrams persuaded me to write a series for *Private Eye* on the Anglican bishops. We decided to write about every one in England, but I insisted on omitting Graham Leonard, Bishop of London, since he was a person of total integrity and virtue. The author of the series signed herself Lucy Fer. When she had completed the series, Ingrams remarked that they had published articles exposing the corruptions or incompetence of business people, politicians, head teachers – and it was invariably the case that a little flurry of letters would reach the *Eye*, defending the reprobate or pointing out that the article contained mistakes. From Lucy Fer's entire series we received only two letters of complaint. One was from a girlfriend of Archbishop Runcie. The other was from a bishop himself, Jim Bath and Wells. Lucy Fer had been sent a story about Jim saying that, when he had been Bishop of Stepney, he had sold off a house, church property, at a ludicrously low price to a couple of men as a favour, thereby profoundly impoverishing the Church's resources in this poor part of London. Jim got on to a lawyer who drew the ludicrous inference that Lucy was accusing the bishop of having sexual relations with the two chaps, something which in those days bishops were not meant to do. The article had made it abundantly clear that the bishop had been on the fiddle financially, and it made no mention of his (in fact hetero) emotional preferences. However, rather than take the case to court, the *Eye* settled, for £45,000. Quite a large sum in those days. The bishop claimed he had given every penny to charity, but, as he was often asked by one of Ingrams's importunate stringers, the recipient of these generous charitable donations remained undisclosed and one can only assume that Jim was employing that old-fashioned device, not unknown in ecclesiastical circles, the lie.

I say that Lucy Fer only received two complaints, but the column attracted a large postbag of letters saying that Lucy had not gone far enough in her exposure of the incompetence, or the wetness, or the nastiness, of the bishop under discussion. My own favourite was a letter from a woman who said that she had been prepared to turn a blind eye to her bishop's attentions to her eldest son. She drew the line, however, when he made advances to her second boy and invited the third to play strip poker.

I'd hesitate to put Lucy Fer in the same rank as Langland or Geoffrey Chaucer, but my study of the medieval poets had taught me that disappointment at priestly skulduggery burns most scaldingly in the hearts not of cynics but of believers. Dante was far more anticlerical than Voltaire because, unlike Voltaire, he believed in what the corrupt popes and simoniac abbots had profaned.

Memory doesn't work in a linear progression. Its 'stills' or 'cuts' repeat themselves in no particular order, and this is especially true of *Spectator* memories. The day that Alexander offered me a job on his paper, the whole focus and direction of my life changed. Oxford, although I continued to go back there, was a place to which I returned, not a home where I inwardly resided. London was now where I was in spirit wherever I happened to find myself in body, even though I had not quite reached the position of Nigel Dempster – almost but not quite – of feeling incapacitated by illness when not in London. What had been hopes so short a time before would now, if I still had them, be dreads. There was nothing I should have liked less than to have tenure in an academic job, and the certainty that for the next thirty years I should be teaching the *Ormulum* or the *Peterborough Chronicle* would have been a nightmare.

A new life had truly begun, and from those first intoxicating years of it, snapshots, rather than continuous narratives, remain.

Ingrams taking me down to Robertsbridge in East Sussex to meet the Muggeridges, and thereafter my solo visits to walk with Kitty and Malcolm. We talked of their time in Russia, and of Tolstoy's last writings, which they knew and treasured. *The Kingdom of God Is Within You, A Confession, Resurrection*, Kitty's favourite of the novels. Or I think of old John Stewart Collis, who thought I had never had to struggle, and of our going down, Clare and I, to Abinger, where he lived, and smoking cigarettes in the pub before we went home for lunch because his wife did not like the smell of nicotine. Or I think of Ackroyd in his uproarious, Colony Room prime. (When the Admiral of the Fleet urged the sending of a task force to rescue the invaded Falkland Islands – 'Stupid bitch!') Or I think of my friend Caroline Blackwood, when asked to lunch at the *Spectator*, saying she felt too shy to come on her own – 'Could I bring two friends?' – and she brought Anna Haycraft and Beryl Bainbridge. They arrived at one o'clock and stayed until 7 p.m. and so began, with Beryl, one of the closest friendships of my life. *All the Olympians; a thing never known again.*

I suppose Muggeridge was the last writer, or public broadcaster of any clout, to make a serious effort to defend Christianity. There was no doubt in the 1980s that it was under threat, and beneath all the booziness and play-acting and absurdity at the *Spectator*, there was a feeling among nearly all of us there that we did not want it to go under. Jennifer, court jester though she may have been, was also the most ardent churchgoer. One Ash Wednesday she came back from her uncle's church, St Anselm and St Cecilia in Kingsway, with a little box.

'Darlin', I know you've forgotten to go to mass,' she said, pronouncing 'mass' to rhyme with 'farce', as she opened the box and rubbed ash onto Clare's forehead. Gina Lewis, an agnostic, whose forebears had professed an older version of the Faith than Jennifer's, took exception to the attempt to rub her brow, and said she in any event did not need Jennifer to remind her that she was dust and unto dust would return. Thereupon Jennifer burst into an American number, all too apt for some hearing, 'Ashes to ashes, dust to dust, If the women don't getcha, then the whisky must.' It was striking,

Kitty Muggeridge, me and Malcolm Muggeridge, the best conversationalists I ever knew. They persuaded me to write my Tolstoy book.

however, how many of us allowed ourselves to be ashed by Jennifer. Marnham, Chantal Dawnay (who would later marry him), Suki Marlowe (now Paravicini), all queued up in Clare's office as if at altar rails for the ceremony of ashing to be performed.

Friendship with Clare had intensified, in my quieter moments, my Roman fever. Ever since my marriage, apostasy, return to the C of E, however you define it, my life had been a tale of spiritual confusion, and talking about it all with Roman Catholic friends made me think it would take very little to set it back on track. Monsignor Bartlett, supplier of the ash to his niece Jennifer Paterson, told me he could do it all on the quiet, so that, for example, my wife need not even know. He could secretly legalize my marriage on condition I submitted to Rome. This spooky suggestion, meant kindly by a very nice chap, had an effect which was the opposite of that intended. However ill advised my marriage had been, it was still a marriage. It was legally a marriage, and it had been solemnized in High Anglican ceremony, undertaken with the intention of it being a Christian marriage for life. It seemed preposterous for some

Roman cleric to come along thirteen years after the event and say it had not been a real marriage but that he could make it one with some behind-the-scenes mumbo-jumbo. However disloyal I had been to my wife and however resentful I felt at being trapped in the marriage, I could not subscribe to the canonical and nonsensical claim that the marriage did not exist. Whenever Roman fever sweeps over me, as it does from time to time, the Church's claim that neither of my marriages is really a marriage in canon law makes me glad those marriages led me back to the C of E – a church with a great many faults, but which at least about this matter is honest. It used to be the strictest of all denominations in its interpretation of Christ's teaching on marriage, even sacking the King, in 1936, for marrying a divorced woman. When it slackened its hard line, it did so honestly, however, maintaining that monogamy for life was the Christian ideal but recognizing human frailty. It does not pretend that former marriages are not really marriages.

36. The Green Stick

They'd moved house yet again, Norman and Jean – back to Llansteffan: a pretty cottage on the Green. My aunt died just before the removal, thwarting their wish to confine her in a hellish-sounding care home. Not long after the move, Norman was diagnosed with lung cancer. John Wedgwood – as any fool knows, I mean Doctor John, not John Hamilton – Jos's son, do pay attention – recommended an oncologist, and Norman broke the news to Jeannie and me at a lunch at the Cadogan Hotel, chosen, I suppose, because it was handy for the Royal Marsden Hospital. He had a year to live. The oncologist knew his onions. Norman died more or less exactly a year after that lunch.

Norman had taken enormous delight in my job at the *Spectator*, avidly poring over each week's issue, and striking up pen friendships with some of his favourite columnists, sending regular bottles of vodka to Jeff Bernard. He took exception to only one of the columnists, Auberon Waugh, whose articles I considered the best thing in the magazine but whom Norman deemed spiteful and snobbish. I never had the heart to tell Norman I'd been sacked. Since my reviews and articles continued to be printed in the magazine, there was no reason, in the short time he had left on the planet, to burden him with the truth.

James Knox said that Alexander's friendliness towards me after he had sacked me, and his desire to print more and more of my stuff, reminded him of the behaviour of the senior boys at Eton,

Algy Cluff – patron, hero, friend.

befriending little boys they had beaten with canes. There was something undoubtedly boarding-school kinky about Alexander's expectation that we should form a fast friendship after he had decided to give me the boot.

Algy Cluff, with unforgettable generosity, so disapproved of my sacking that he went on paying my salary even though the *Spectator* continued to lose money hand over fist. He offered me the editorship of *Apollo* magazine, which he also owned, but connoisseurship and the world of art, though always of deep interest to me, were not areas where I would have been competent to move among experts.

Besides, I'd become obsessed by Russia, and learning Russian, and I wanted to write the life of Tolstoy. Algy financed the entire enterprise – trips to Moscow to study at the Tolstoy Institute,

Russian lessons in Oxford, to which, for most of each week, I had returned. I had two tutors: Jennifer Baines, who taught Russian at Reading University and gave me a thorough grounding in grammar, using the Russian course used to train that generation of National Service recruits during the Cold War, and Marina Douglas, an In-Tourist guide in Irkutsk who had lately married a postman from Didcot. Both were superb teachers, and I was soon able to read Tolstoy and to converse fluently. I suppose Marina and I were sort of in love and we did talk about marriage. It would certainly have done wonders for my Russian but rather less for my character, and she had a lucky escape.

In the room where I worked in Oxford there hung a large Scottish landscape in a lumpy gilt frame. The picture had belonged to Grandpa Wilson and came from his house in Worcester. I don't know whether it was painted by his aunt Edith, but it was only hanging there because no one else in the family wanted it. But it was a family object, so associated with Norman.

He, who all his life had been a *malade imaginaire*, spending money he did not possess, bothering specialists in skin, stomach and other supposed disorders, changed his character when real illness struck. He behaved with brio and fortitude, like an old soldier. He had inherited angina pectoris from his father, the owner of the oil painting. This heart condition can be held at bay if you take the pills, which he had been doing for some years. When the cancer was diagnosed, he threw away the heart pills, knowing death to be inevitable. A sudden heart attack was preferable to choking to death with cancer of the lung (hardly surprising that he contracted this after half a century spent smoking sixty cigarettes per diem). He and Jean made all the right provisions. They booked a Macmillan nurse to live at Bute Cottage for the final stage, but he did go to Swansea for some tests to see if he should consider a course of chemotherapy.

It was while he was there, one March morning, that I was sitting in the Oxford house, having seen the children off to school. Just as I had begun my work, the large landscape which had hung there securely for years leapt from the wall and thundered down onto the piano beneath. As soon as I'd recovered from the shock, and propped the painting against a wall, I rang the hospital. I knew beyond any question what had happened. He had died that very moment.

After breakfast, clutching a copy of Michael Holroyd's life of Lytton Strachey, he strode across the ward in his silk dressing gown. It is impossible to doubt that he intended to beard one of the nurses, or perhaps another patient, with some amusing detail he had found in the book. Surely, the pyjama-clad old Welsh farmer in the bed opposite would like to be told that G. E. Moore had been a contemporary at Trinity, Cambridge, of none other than Ralph Wedgwood, father of Veronica and John Hamilton? The farmer might like to hear about John's girlfriends? Or hear about Leith Hill and Ralph Vaughan Williams? But a heart attack instantaneously stopped the word-flow forever.

I scribbled a note to my wife and daughters, and then clambered into the wooden-framed Morris Traveller. I drove to Swansea at breakneck speed, and by the time I reached the hospital I found my sister, consumed by grief, and Jean Dorothy, looking very small and sad. I was taken into the room where the body lay. All the high colour, the pink of the cheeks, had gone. This paper-pale figure from which the moustaches and hair stuck out like grass seized by hoar frost made me see that the soul had indeed flown. There is an enormous dignity in death and in the body we leave behind when we move on, a stateliness, which is what makes the slaughter of battlefields or the deliberate profanation of corpses so shocking. There was also a tremendous pathos about him, during that ten minutes or quarter of an hour we spent together, just the two of us, and I stared at his dead face.

I'd recently been reading Isaiah Berlin's clever (but slightly silly) essay *The Hedgehog and the Fox*. The title derives from a saying by the Greek poet Archilochus: a fox knows many things but a hedgehog knows one big thing. Plato, Dante, Hegel were hedgehogs who had one big idea about the world, whereas the foxes, Shakespeare, Montaigne and others, had many ideas. Tolstoy, Berlin concluded, wanted to be a hedgehog, but he was really a fox and the big simplicities of his later writings were at odds with the foxy achievement of writing *Anna Karenina* and *War and Peace*, which had shared such a multiplicity of sympathies, a capacity to see so many lives, so many viewpoints.

Maybe the game can be extended beyond the literary. With my inconstant heart, and my wavering, superficial mind, I was a fox, with interests and loyalties all over the place, many of them incompatible with one another, but I was the son of a hedgehog whose entire *raison d'être* had consisted in working with and for the Wedgwoods, designing that factory at Barlaston with Keith Murray, producing his own stunning bowls and vases, and throwing his all into his friendship with Uncle Jos. When all that came to an end in 1962, there had stretched ahead over twenty years which had been not merely boring but also without any meaning. Jean had another twenty years to live as a widow. She would be intensely lonely. All her daily bickering and irritation with him were now forgotten, the second he died, and he became the Prince Consort who could do no wrong.

Jeannie drove back to Llansteffan. I took our mother to register the death in a brutalist concrete building quite near the hospital. Then we went home. The funeral, a week later, filled the little church as a hundred people sang 'Cwm Rhondda'. He was carried out into the peaceful churchyard and buried next to his sister among the early daffodils. Everyone came, cousins I'd barely met, Simon Wedgwood, grandson of Jos, friends who had made the arduous journey from Staffordshire. The only notable absentee was my wife. No one mentioned this fact; it was almost as if no one had even expected her to turn up. It would have been unthinkable that my sister-in-law or brother-in-law would not have showed for Norman's funeral. As I drove home to Oxfordshire from Wales, I realized that, although we still lived together, K and I were not really married any longer.

Freud, in *The Interpretation of Dreams*, described the death of a father as 'the most important event, the most poignant loss, of a man's life'. I did not weep at my father's grave, as many did, but many of the symptoms of intense bereavement – sleeplessness, appetite and energy coming and going – for weeks afterwards, these were there. Honesty compels me to say, however, that I also felt relief. To this hour I do not know whether I was relieved for him, that the twenty years of boredom and humiliation were over, or whether the relief was my own.

———

Some weeks after my father's funeral, I was in Moscow. I hired a Lada to drive down to Tolstoy's house and estate at Bright Glade, Yasnaya Polyana, but this vehicle had suffered the fate of many such cars in the Soviet Union. Its wheels and engine had been removed as the car sat innocently in the parking lot of the hotel. No one, least of all the hotel clerk who'd organized the hire, was remotely surprised or dismayed. In my experience the Russians possess a Gogolesque sense of the absurdity of officialdom, and the dismantling of my hire car was *professionalnaya oprasnost*, an occupational hazard. So we went through the whole procedure once more, of filling out forms and my producing *dokumentii*. They asked for *dokumentii* in the Soviet Union wherever you went, my favourite moment being in Novgorod, where I went into the public baths. The procedure was, strip naked, then approach the stout, whiskery babushka at the next door who would give you a very small towel. Before she did so, however, she grinned a toothless grin, looked up and down my white skinny nakedness and, holding out a hand, demanded, '*Dokumentii!*'

While I was waiting for the replacement hire car, I sat in the hotel foyer reading Tolstoy and avoiding the gazes of the bottle-dyed young women who sat there smoking and plying their trade among the foreign *bezneezmin*.

I now loved Russia. Behind the farce of corrupt bureaucracy and the, presumably deliberate, concrete ugliness of all the post-war building, Mother Russia, an idea as much as a political state, a great, suffering, God-bearing monster, survived. Tolstoy used to say that he would not be pessimistic about his country because all Russians read the Gospels, and when we all witnessed, after the collapse of Communism, the speed of the religious revival, the huge number of vocations in the revived monasteries, the crowds of worshippers in the churches, the devotion to the memory of those martyred by the Reds, including their Emperor and Empress, it was hard not to remember that seemingly improbable claim.

Whether they all read the Gospels, the Soviet Russians I met were definitely in one sense people of the book, or at least bookish.

In a small town one winter's day, emerging from my In-Tourist hotel, I saw a long queue in the snow forming outside the general stores. Such queues were usual in the USSR since the shops were always out of stock of something: sugar, shoes, shirts, potatoes. When I returned an hour later, having walked round the town, the queue stretched round the square several hundred people long and rising. 'Why are you queuing?' 'There's a rumour.' 'What sort of rumour?' 'They say some boxes of books are coming.' 'What sort of books?' 'Turgenev is in print again. Had you heard that? Imagine being able to read him.' 'Have you not read him before?' 'My mother had *Fathers and Children*, but we weren't meant to read it. This was the '50s. But under this man' – Gorbachev was mentioned – 'anything could happen.'

I tried to imagine an English provincial town, the people avidly queuing in freezing weather, on the off chance of being able to buy a nineteenth-century novel.

Of course, Russia, vast, suffering Russia, was something largely inside my head, derived from books, not something I knew at first hand. It was the Gulag as described by Solzhenitsyn. It was the queues outside the icebound prisons described by Akhmatova; it was the Red Army holding back the invaders in the 1940s, as described in Alan Clark's masterpiece *Barbarossa*; it was for me, above all, the Russia of Pasternak. *Doctor Zhivago* is for me a sort of bible packed with poems and with truth. It is better, even – give the Red Devils their due – than Alexey Tolstoy's largely forgotten masterpiece *The Road to Calvary*. It conveys the terror and tragedy of the inevitable Revolution, the horrific Civil War and the tyrannous aftermath. Better than any work of literature known to me, it depicts the centrality of love between two people whose spiritual and physical passion for one another seems foreordained: the agony of it, the beauty of it, the cruelty of it to Zhivago's wife, and then, the humiliating fact that he can put it all behind him and slither, in the last section, into a boring second marriage numbed by drunkenness, his poetic talent waning. Lara is lost in the Gulag. Above all, from its first page, when the infant Zhivago follows his mother's open coffin and they all sing the great Russian hymn 'Eternal Memory', it conveys the centrality of soul, of faith, of non-faith. This novel, steeped in Eastern Christianity, is perhaps the best gloss on that fifth Gospel, i.e. the Roman Canon of the mass, which prays *omnibus orthodoxis atque catholicae et apostolicae fidei cultoribus*. Zhivago is a modern agnostic in love with a faith he cannot believe. Lara, his lover, 'was not religious. She did not believe in ritual. But sometimes, to enable her to bear her life, she needed the accompaniment of an inward music, and she could not always compose it for herself. That music was God's word of life, and it was to weep over it, that she went to church.'

In some ways, the central intelligence of the entire book is one of the minor characters who is cut out of David Lean's cinematic version: Zhivago's uncle, a laicized Orthodox priest, a Tolstoyan called Nikolai Nikolayevich Vedenyapin, whose reflections on Christianity filter through the novel, at first from his own lips and then, when he is in exile in Paris, through the printed medium of his books. His great theme is that Jesus liberated the human race from the need to define itself in groups, races, religious denominations. After Jesus we are all individuals, and of course he derives this from his own distinctive reading of Tolstoy. Tolstoy is in a way a co-author of *Doctor Zhivago*, only without Pasternak's poetic gift.

These thoughts swirled through my head as I made my treks, sometimes by train, sometimes in a hired Lada, across Holy Mother Russia. It was the bigness which struck you over and over again, the numberless miles when you saw nothing but silver birch forests and flat, flat land stretching further than the eye could see, dotted with tiny habitations, the pitiless ugliness of collective farms, reproached by the still surviving onion domes of the churches, architecture telling the gut-ripped, bruised, million-times-murdered twentieth-century horror story.

The bigness. Not just the bigness of the fields and skies, but the bigness of the whole experience, which had been in progress, really, since Napoleon's forces were overcome by the snows, by the Fates, by the sheer clever brutality of patient Field Marshal Kutuzov. The whole vastness of their life experience as a nation, the liberation of the serfs, the conflict between Slavophile religious believers and the so-called enlightened Westernisers, the nineteenth-century wars with France and Britain in the Crimea, with Islam in the Caucasus, with Japan in the Far East, and of such bitterness with Germany in the First World War. And out of that war, the fatal German decision to allow Lenin safe passage in the sealed train which arrived at the Finland Station, St Petersburg, in 1917, seven years after Tolstoy's death.

The bigness of Tolstoy matched the bigness of his country and now, at last, having embarked upon my book about him, financed by Algy Cluff, I was on my way to his house at Yasnaya Polyana, 200 kilometres south of Moscow. The house, with its mementoes – the leather sofa on which he was born, the thousands of books, the portrait of Dickens he had in his study – is museumy, less atmospheric, really, than the town house in Moscow, occupied by his communist son and therefore preserved by Stalin.

Stalin was the embodiment of everything Tolstoy struggled against – state control, state violence, warmongering, godlessness. Yet, Georgian though he may have been, a piratical rogue and mass murderer, Stalin was bookish and, much as he dreaded Tolstoy's pacifism (Stalin had trained as a priest and in a corner of his soul he must have always felt wistful for the Gospels he betrayed), he saw that Russia's great writers were almost like the prophets in the story of Israel, figures who, though against the system, were its greatest pride. Stalin decreed that parts of *War and Peace* be reissued in 1941 as a boost to national morale after the Nazi invasions.

The Germans occupied Yasnaya Polyana during the war and, given their destructive record elsewhere, one wonders how much of the house is in fact repro. (The authenticity of the furniture and pictures I do believe, since they were taken into hiding for the duration.) It's outside in the fields and woods that you sense the great man, you remember Levin mowing the hay with his peasants, or Prince

Andrew coming home from Austerlitz to his old father. It was in this place that Tolstoy's enormous life experience was played out, from the motherless childhood through all the subsequent years, as a soldier in the Crimea, as husband and father, as author of *War and Peace*, our modern *Iliad*, a book which is not merely big in page numbers but big, big, big in its scope and makes the English literary achievement in the twentieth century seem a pygmy game by comparison.

One patch of woodland on the estate is Stari Zakaz, the Forest of the Old Order, so called because, since his grandfather's day, it had been forbidden to cut down any of its trees. Tolstoy and his brothers used to play here as children, and it was here that his brother Nikolai had buried a green stick on which, he said, was written the secret of happiness. When humankind understood this secret, then disease and war and social deprivation would come to an end, humanity and God would at last be at one with one another.

Tolstoy's own life and marriage were a battlefield – with himself as well as with his wife. At the end, to escape the rows and tempests at home, the old man set off like a pilgrim, his peasant costume a kind of fancy dress, before collapsing and dying at the railway station at Astapovo. The Church forbade a funeral liturgy, but the coffin was brought back to Yasnaya Polyana and borne by his sons to the place of the green stick. Thousands of people followed it to the grave, singing 'Eternal Memory'. Most of them had never read *War and Peace* but they saw him as a *staretz*, a holy elder, and when they considered his treatment at the hands of the Church they could remember the conclusion of the Beatitudes which the Orthodox love to chant – *Rejoice and be exceeding glad: for great is your reward in heaven: for so persecuted they the prophets which were before you.*

Tolstoy's Western contemporaries had spent the nineteenth century agonizing about whether the Bible was compatible with modern science. Tolstoy, with his bigness, was asking the much more urgent and radical question, are the Gospels morally true? Can we respond to their radical demands? What survives of him in the sheer moral magnitude of his work is this series of searching questions, and the questions will never go away, whether we

Tolstoy's Grave – the Place of the Green Stick.

consciously try to drown them out with trivialities or whether we allow them to puzzle and nag us.

Standing at Tolstoy's unmarked grave cuts any human being down to size. For a minor English writer to stand there in the late twentieth century was to be doubly awestruck in the presence of his life teachings and of his literary achievements, so much larger than anything one could ever manage oneself.

Of course, when I left Russia, and returned to England, the farcical merry-go-round began again, of writings not so good, deeds not so virtuous, as they should have been; books washed down at launch parties by warm white wine. The inconstancy of my heart and the confusion of my mind were as great as ever, when I sat down and began to write my Tolstoy book. Memory of the simple unmarked mound of turf in the Forest of the Old Order, however, reminds even the feeblest of writers why writing and reading play such a vital part in our lives.

FINIS

Index

Note: page numbers followed by an italic *f* indicate figures.

Ackroyd, Peter 20, 36, 37, 256, 283, 287,
    292
Acre, Israel 199–200
Adams, Richard 277–8
alcohol
    drinking culture at St Stephen's
        House 243–4
    drinking culture at *The Spectator* 35–6, 37
    writers and 259–61
Alexander, Sharon 152, 153, 154, 156
Alexander, Thelma 156
Allen, Derek (Nora) 241, 244
Amis, Kingsley 37, 257, 258
Amis, Martin 23, 24*f*, 34–5, 36–7, 285
Angry Young Men 257: *see also* Amis,
    Kingsley; Braine, John; Osborne, John;
    Wilson, Colin
Annan, Gaby 279–80
Antibes Lycée 51
ANWIL Club 113
Apollo magazine 297
Aquinas, Thomas 99–100
Archilochus 298
Ardingly College, Sussex 44–5
Arnold, Matthew 105, 229
Artley, Alexandra 10*f*, 287–8
Aske, Conan 127, 148–9, 150
Asquith, Clare 282, 283*f*, 286, 287, 292,
    293
Austen, Jane 2

Bacon, Francis 256
Bainbridge, Beryl 73–4, 292
Baines, Jennifer 297
Baiss, Jack Llewellyn Rumbold 154–5,
    157–8, 159–60, 188, 195–6
Baker, Janet 161
Bakhtin, Mikhail 252
Bamber, Herbert, SJ 232

Bannerman, Julian 267–8
Bannerman's Bar, Edinburgh 267–8
Barbour-Simpson, Barbara 116, 125, 128,
    130–2, 133–4, 138–9
Barbour-Simpson, Jill 130, 131, 132
Barbour-Simpson, Michael 130–1
Barbour-Simpson, Rudolph 125, 127, 131–3,
    137–8, 148–9
    allegations of anal rape 129–30
Barnes, Julian 35, 37, 275, 285
Barnes, Susan 32–3
Barraclough, Geoffrey 188
Bartlett, Monsignor 293–4
Barton, Anne 271–2, 279–80
Barton, John 280
Bates, RSM 155–6
Bayley, John 8, 194–7, 208, 209, 238, 271,
    275–6
Bayley, Peter 269–70
Belcher, Muriel 256
Bell, Vanessa 64
Belloc, Bar 213–14, 267–8
Bennett, Arnold 38
Berlin, Isaiah 285, 286, 298–9
Bernard, Jeff 296
Berry, Enid 49, 50, 71
Berry, Mrs 49, 50, 71
Best of Young British Novelists 34, 36
Betjeman, John 174, 185, 262, 263–4, 287
    'Myfanwy at Oxford' 16
    'The old Great Western Railway shakes'
        16, 17
Betjeman, Penelope 262–3
Birmingham Oratory 223, 226–7, 228–9,
    230
Blackett-Ord, Mark 215, 219
Blackwell, John 254–7
Blackwood, Caroline 292
Blake, William 68

Blakie (Mrs Blakeman)   94–7, 95f, 98, 107,
    108, 123, 135–6
Blakie/Blakeman, Cyril (Our Cyril)   94, 108
    lupin incident   95–6, 108
Blakie/Blakeman, Vron (Our Vron)   94, 96,
    97, 108
Bloomsbury Group   191
Bowra, Maurice   9, 15
Boyd Harte, Carrie, née Bullock   216, 217, 287
Boyd Harte, Glynn   216, 217, 287
Boys, Thomas Shotter   111
Braine, John   257–9
Bridgewater, Char   218
British Institute, Florence   199
Brooke, Rupert   250
Brookner, Anita   285
Brown, George Mackay   231, 232
Bryan, Arthur   144, 145–6, 147
Bullock, Carrie, see Boyd Harte, Carrie, née
    Bullock
Bullough, Leonora, see Mary Mark, Sister, OP
Bullough, Sebastian, OP   97f, 99, 102
    Roman Catholicism   100–1
Burton, Robert   247

Cadbury's   63, 65
Carpenter, Humphrey   209–10
Carter, Douglas   214
Cary, Joyce   151
Cassidy, Sheila   222
Catacombs, Palermo   227–8
Catholic Worker Movement   99
Catling, Patrick Skene   32
Catto, Jeremy   8, 174, 175, 216–17, 218f,
    239
Cavendish, Elizabeth   174
Cecil, David   210
Chadwick, Henry   29–30, 33
Challoner, John   227
Chancellor, Alexander   37, 281, 282, 284,
    285, 287, 296–7
Channon, Chips   98–9, 101
Chanter, Robin   206
Charles, Prince of Wales   178–9, 284
Chaucer, Geoffrey: The Book of the
    Duchess   204
Cheltenham Ladies' College   47, 50, 76
Christian, Fletcher   48
Christiansen, Eric   212
Clark, Miss (matron)   127
Clenton, Bill   66
Clinton, Bill   242
Cluff, J. G. (Algy)   37, 222, 297, 297f
Cobb, Clarissa   244
Coghill, Nevill   160
Coleridge, Samuel Taylor   48

Collis, John Stewart   292
Conway, Sister (ward sister)   92–3
Cornwell, John   254
Coronavirus pandemic   14–16
Cowper, William   115
Cox, Ka   250
Crookenden, Humphrey   223, 227, 228
Crosland, Anthony   32
Crossman, Richard   161
Crowder, Felix   49, 52, 71, 207
Crowder, Jean Dorothy, see Wilson, Jean
    Dorothy
Crowder, Selena, née Christian   47–9, 53, 69
    death of   70–1
Crowder, Walter Clarence   48–9, 52, 69, 71,
    88, 112–13
    and Lowry   180
Cuddesdon College   240, 241

Daily Express   158, 159
Daily Mail   159
D'Annunzio, Gabriele   98–9
Darwin, Charles   60–1, 81, 122, 191
Davidman, Joy   30
Dawnay, Chantal   293
de Jonge, Alex   212
de Jonge, Judy   212
de Morgan, William   41
de Vere White, Terence   22
Dempster, Nigel   34, 288, 291
Dickens, Charles   133, 134–5
Ditchling Community, Sussex   99
Dobson, Eric J.   278–9, 280–1
Douglas, Marina   297
Duncan, Alan   217, 253
Duncan-Jones, Andrew   240
Duncan-Jones, Dean   240
Duncan-Jones, Katherine   4–5, 7–12, 10f,
    217, 226, 230–1, 254
    dementia   4–5, 7, 9, 10–12, 14–17
    and Francesca Wilson   251–2
    and Hay-on-Wye farmhouse   272–3
    and in-laws   87, 273–4
    and John Braine   258–9
    on Mediterranean cruise   30–2
    on possible fate of Kindly Light   256–7
    and Princess Margaret   173–4
    and quotes   31
    Ungentle Shakespeare   7–8
Duncan-Jones, Mrs   230–1
Duncan-Jones, Richard   250
Duse, Eleonora   98–9, 101
Dyson, Hugo   9, 210

Eliot, George   229
Eliot, T. S.   1, 85, 176

Elizabeth, Queen Mother 173, 176–8
Ellesmere College, Shropshire 44–5, 125
Eustace, Isabel 267–8
Evening Standard 27, 159

Farson, Dan 256
Fascist Beasts' Lunching Club 257
Faulconbridge, Faith 214
Fell, Anna 182
Fell, Sheila 182
Ferryside, Wales 273–4
Fitzgerald, Edward 105
Foot, Paul 251, 288
Forbes-Robertson, Johnston 166–7, 219
Forster, E. M. 261
Freeman, Albert 81, 82
Freud, Sigmund 299–300
Friskie (King Charles spaniel) 116

Galsworthy, John 197
Gardner, Helen 234–6, 252
Gearin-Tosh, Michael 279, 280
Gilbert, Geoffrey 82–3
Gill, Eric 99, 272, 273
Gilling, John 239
Gladstone, William Ewart 64, 229
Glendinning, Victoria 61–2
Glover, Jane 179
Gradon, Pamela 208
Graduate, The (film) 197–8
Grafton Gallery, Mayfair 64
Grant, Duncan 64
Gray, Thomas 105
Greene, Graham 263
Greenlees, Ian 206
Guilding, Ruth 8–9

Hague, William 217
Hale, Emily 85
Halliburton, John 244
Hardy, Thomas 42, 47–8
Harold, Sam 107–8
Harrod, Dominick 219
Harrod, Henry 219
Harrod, Tanya, *see* Ledger, Tanya
Harrowby, Lady 85–6
Haskell, Francis 216
Hassall, Mrs (housekeeper) 73, 75–6, 78, 79
Hastings, Selina 276–8, 277*f*
Haycraft, Anna 292
health issues
    Katherine Duncan-Jones 4–5, 7, 9, 10–12,
        14–17, 245
    Wedgwood family 79
    A. N. Wilson 91–2, 230–1, 255–6, 265–6
    Jean Dorothy Wilson 89, 106, 108–9

Norman Wilson 106, 296, 297–8
Heath, Michael 36, 37
Helliwell, Geoff 157, 158
Herbert, Mr (rector) 90
Hilda-Schule, Koblenz 51–2
Hillstone School, Great Malvern,
    Worcestershire 116, 128–35, 137–9,
        148–52
    abuse at 128–30, 131–3, 138–9
    corporal punishment 129
    journey to 124–7
    letters home 140
    library 133
Hobhouse, Christina 219
Hollinghurst, Alan 216–17
Hollings, Michael 220–3, 238
Hollis, Crispian 222, 239
Hope, David (Ena the Cruel) 244–5, 252
Hope-Wallace, Jacqueline 61
Houlden, Leslie 240
Howard-Johnston, James 173
Huddleston, Trevor 189
Hughes-Hallett, Lucy 285
Hunt, Tristram 146
Hunter, Robert 253
Huth, Angela 173

Independent on Sunday 159
Ingrams, Richard 259, 288, 289, 289*f*, 290,
    292
Inklings 210, 211: *see also* Dyson, Hugo;
    Lewis, C. S.
Inman, Dr 88, 91
Israel 199–200, 203–4
Iveagh, Lord and Lady 98–9

James, Clive 285, 286–7
Jenkins, David 26, 29
John of Gaunt 203–4
Jones, David 272, 273
Josiah Wedgwood and Sons 34, 35*f*, 54,
    117–18
    Etruria Works 53, 64–8, 78
    flotation on stock market 144–6
    Grafton Gallery exhibition 64
    Norman Wilson and 63–4, 66–8, 74, 112,
        117–19, 121
Joyce, James 204

Keeler, Christine 256
Kerr, M. W. G. (Bim) 215–16
Kibbutz Beit Haemek 199–203
Kierkegaard, Søren 13
Knapheis, Baillie 214
Knight, Laura 64
Knox, James 295–6

Korea 21
Kreer, Kate 42

Lambton, Lucy 287
Lancelyn Green, June 30–2, 33
Lancelyn Green, Roger 30–1, 32, 33
Lancing College 44
Larkin, Philip 285
Lavalle, Mark (Father Marcellus) 103–4
Lawson, Alex (LGC) 247
Lawson, Dominic 177
Lawson, Mark 196
Lawson, Nigel 177
Lawson, Nigella 285
Leach, Bernard 41
Leavis, F. R. 190–1
Ledger, Tanya 217–18, 218f, 219, 275
Lee, Donald (Mae West) 242
Lefebvre, Archbishop 290
Leo XIII, pope 99, 223
Lever, Andrew 214
Lewes, George 229, 286–7
Lewis, C. S. 30, 210, 211
Lewis, Dorothy, née Wilson 45, 59
Lewis, Gina 282–3, 292
Lewis, Gordon 59, 91
Lewis, Joan 91
Lewis, Naomi 22
Lewis, Tony 91
Liencourt, Mme de 168–71
Llansteffan 107, 156, 164–6, 172, 181,
    189–90, 219, 273, 295
Lockhart, John Gibson 267
Longford, Lord 27, 242
Lowry, L. S. 180–5
Lowry, Malcolm 160
Lucas, John 207, 208, 245–9, 263
Lunt, Canon 154
Lydgate, John 280–1
Lygon Arms, Broadway 136–7
Lynch, Philip 227
Lyne, Joseph Leycester (Father Ignatius) 273

Macaulay, Rose 225, 239–40
McCarthy, Fiona 99
McEwan, Ian 37
Machin, Arnold 64
McKay, Peter 34, 280, 288
Mackenzie, Christopher 162
Maclean, Allan 10f, 240–1, 245, 254, 267–8
Maclean, Donald 204, 240
Maclean, Fitzroy 285
McMordie, Colin 216, 217
McQuaid, John Charles 103
Maitland, Sara 242
Malvern

moves to 148, 238
train journey to 124–7
Elizabeth Wilson in 164, 167
see also Hillstone School, Great Malvern
Mann, Thomas 40
Manningham-Buller, Eliza 216
Manson, Major 150–1
Margaret, Princess 34, 35f, 119, 173–6
Margrethe, Queen of Denmark 172
Marlowe, Suki 293
Marnham, Patrick 283, 288, 293
Mary Alban, Sister 102, 103
Mary Edith, Sister 100
Mary Mark, Sister, OP 97f, 99, 100–4, 123,
    136, 205
Maugham, Somerset 122
Mavor, Elizabeth 214
Meades, Jonathan 287
Meehan, Miss (teacher) 100, 107f
Menzies, William 267
Merchant Taylors' School, Northwood 252–3
Merton, Thomas: Elected Silence 103
monarchy 172–3
Montgomery, Bernard, Lord Montgomery of
    Alamein 161
Mooney, Bel 286
Moore, Bernard 21, 41, 54
Moore, Charles 26, 285
Moore, G. E. 191
Morris, Edward 154–6
Mosley, Betty (later Dame Betty Ridley) 47
Mount, Ferdinand 22, 37
Muggeridge, Kitty 292, 293f
Muggeridge, Malcolm 28, 252, 292, 293f
Murdoch, Iris 5, 195, 212, 238, 275–6
Murray, Keith 64, 66–7

Naipaul, Jenny 35
Naipaul, Shiva 35–6, 37
Naipaul, Vidia 36, 171
Neale, James 38
Newman, John Henry 223–4, 227, 229, 240
    Apologia 189, 223–4, 229
News of the World 157, 177
Nineham, Dennis 28
North Staffs Infirmary, Stafford 91–2

Oliver, Stephen 178–9
Orkneys 231–3
Orwell, George 143
Osborne, John 255, 257
Osea Island 226, 231
Our Art (Blakie's half-brother) 97

Paisley, Ian 177
Parris, Matthew 172

Pasternak, Boris 301–2
Paterson, Agnes 121
Paterson, Jennifer 283–5, 284f, 292–3
Paul VI, pope: encyclical *Humanae vitae* 196–7, 227
Paula (housekeeper) 110–11
Pease, Helen 119–20, 191
Peterson, Agnes 47–8, 50
Pevsner, Nikolaus 251
Pius X, pope 223
Plantagenets 203–4
Plumb, Jack 120, 190, 191
Pollock, Adam 179
Portuguese friar (in Israel) 203–4
Powell, Alfred 78–9
Powell, Enoch 285
Powell, Louise, née Lessore 78–9
Prayer Book Revisions 60–1
Price, John and Angela 162
Pritchard, Mari 209–10
Private Eye 159
    Lucy Fer articles 290–1

Quennell, Marilyn 263
Quennell, Peter 261–4
Quinton, Marcelle 212–13, 279–80
Quinton, Tony 212–13

Raine, Craig 22, 36
Ramsey, Frank 101
Ramsey, Michael 101
Rapaccini, Luisa 206
Ravilious, Eric 64
Read, Piers Paul 222
religion
    Anglo-Catholicism 44, 224, 239–40, 245–6
    clergy and publicity 27–9
    Joyce and 204
    life after death 5
    in Russia 300–1
    Tolkien and 213–14
    A. N. Wilson and 104–5, 188–90, 191–2, 196, 201, 202–3, 204–5, 219–20, 222–5, 226–7, 238–9
    Norman Wilson and 44, 45, 60, 61, 74–5, 92
Reuter, Ludwig von 232
Rhodesia 188–9
Rich, Miss (art teacher) 141, 150–2
Robinson, John Martin 217
Robson, Frank 248–9
Roesen, Anne/Bobbyann, *see* Barton, Anne
Rosebery, Lord 229
Rossetti, Dante Gabriel 182–3
Rowse, A. L. 8, 259–60, 261f

Rowson, Martin 253–4
Royal College of Art, Kensington 64, 189
Royal Institute of British Architects (RIBA) 178–9
Rugby Advertiser 159
Rugby School 157–63
    Combined Cadet Force 154–5, 161
    The Meteor 157–8, 159
    production of *Volpone* 157, 161f
Rushdie, Salman 23–4, 35
Russia 300–5

St Martin's School of Art 188–9
St Stephen's House 241–4, 252
Sandon, Lord Sandon 86
Sandy (kibbutz volunteer) 201, 202
Schlick, Mr (modern languages teacher) 170
Scott, Peter 137
Scott, Walter 231, 265–7
Seebohm, Freddie 62
Sewell, Brocard 272–3
Shakespeare, William 7–8, 166–7
    Julius Caesar 115
    King Lear 7, 8–9, 12, 14–15
Shaw, George Bernard: *Saint Joan* 104
Simenon, Georges: *Pedigree* 96–7
Skeaping, John 64
Skellern, Victor 63–4
Smith, Logan Pearsall 276
Snow, C. P. 190–1
Snowdon, Lord 22, 34, 35f, 36, 119
Spectator, The 19, 177, 296–7
    drinking culture 35–6, 37
    Literary Editor at 20, 281, 282, 285–7, 291–2
    and Mediterranean cruise 26, 29–30, 224
    sacked from 286–7, 295–6
Spencer, Herbert 81
Spender, Stephen 27
Squire, J. C. 122
Stalin, Joseph 303
Stamp, Gavin 287–8
Stead, Margaret 254
Steane, John 253, 254
Stein, Rick 215
Sterne, Laurence 23
Stewart, Vivien 226, 231, 233
Stockwood, Mervyn 243
Stone, Darwell 247
Stone, Staffordshire 88, 89–90, 116–17
Stopes, Marie 81
Stubbs, George 65
Sunday Telegraph 159
Sunday Times 31–3
Swift, Graham 37

Talbot Kelly, R. B. 185, 186–7
Taylor, A. J. P. 84
Taylor, Elizabeth 112
Taylor, Mr (music teacher) 149
Tennyson, Alfred Lord Tennyson 15, 105
Tennyson, Charles 15
Thatcher, Margaret 143–4
Thompson, Jim 290–1
Tippett, Michael 161
Tolkien, Christopher 31, 118, 195–7, 209–12, 209f, 252
  and Catholicism 213–14
  and finishing *The Silmarillion* 271–2
  relationship with father 212–13
  The Saga of Heidrek the Wise 211
Tolkien, J. R. R. 210, 236
  The Hobbit 160, 210–11
  The Lord of the Rings 159–60, 210–11, 212–13, 214, 226
  The Silmarillion 271–2
  relationship with son 212–13
Tolkien, John 194, 210
Tolkien, Michael 210
Tolkien, Priscilla 210
Tolstoy, Leo 298–9, 300, 302, 303–5
Tosswill, T. D. 160, 161–2, 190, 192–5
Trevor-Roper, Hugh 173, 217, 285
Trickett, Rachel 271, 279, 280
Tudor-Craig, Pamela 61
Tutu, Desmond 224

University of St Andrews 268–70

Vaughan Williams, Ralph 56, 87

Walker, Claude 66
Walker, Sebastian 213, 277
Wall Street Crash 63
Wallace, Dorothy 50
Wallace, Edgar 50
Waugh, Auberon 32, 36, 288–90, 296
Waugh, Evelyn 44, 261
Wedgwood, Alan 67
Wedgwood, Barbara 273–4
Wedgwood, C. V. (Veronica) 59, 61–2, 122, 285
Wedgwood, Dorothy 59
Wedgwood, Frank 54, 55–6, 65
Wedgwood, Hensleigh 110, 144, 273–4
Wedgwood, Iris 59–60, 61, 65
Wedgwood, John 110, 296
Wedgwood, John Hamilton 59–60, 61, 66, 87, 110, 119
Wedgwood, Jos (father of Uncle Jos) 60–1, 65

Wedgwood, Josiah I: 60, 110, 146
Wedgwood, Josiah V (Uncle Jos) 54–7, 62, 63–4, 65, 66, 110–12, 119–20, 143, 144, 250
  annual trip to USA 110
  The Economics of Inheritance 122–3
  marriage breakdown 110–11
  melancholy-madness 79
  and music 76–7
Wedgwood, Ralph 59
Wedgwood, Simon 299
Wedgwood, Tom 66
Wedgwood Museum, Barlaston 66–7, 146
West, Richard 36
West, Timothy 22
Wheatcroft, Geoffrey 288
Wilde, Oscar 21, 152
Wilding, Michael 112
Williams, David 286
Williams, Rowan 196
Williamson, Hugh Ross 104
Wilson, A. N.
  and art 141, 151–3, 180–7, 188, 192
  backpacking in Israel 203–4
  baptism 92–3
  and *Britannia Preserv'd* 178–9
  childhood memories 106–8
  education 97–103, 112–13, 123, 124, 150–1
  evening prayers/hymns 104
  first visit to Paris 152–4
  and Hay-on-Wye farmhouse 272–3
  at Hillstone School 128–35, 137–9, 140–1, 148–52
  holidays in France 168–71
  and journalism 1–2, 157–9
  Literary Editor of *The Spectator* 20, 281, 282, 285–7, 291–2
  and Lowry 180–5
  Lucy Fer articles for *Private Eye* 290–1
  Mediterranean cruise 224
  Merchant Taylors' School, Northwood 252–3
  at Oxford 207–9
  relationship with parents 3–4
  at Rugby 157–63
  and Russia 296–7, 300–1
  sacked from *The Spectator* 286–7, 295–6
  school holidays 135–6
  school photo 107f
  and Shakespeare 166–7
  Somerville love obsession 225, 239
  at Stone 116–17
  surgery for pyloric stenosis 91–2
  teaching at Oxford 271–2, 278–81
  and University of St Andrews 268–70

WORKS
Dante in Love 206, 254
first novel 237
God's Funeral 254
The Healing Art 255, 257
Kindly Light 255–7
The Laird of Abbotsford 266–7, 268
The Life of John Milton 177
The Potter's Hand 110, 254
Scandal 22
Stray 278
The Sweets of Pimlico 254–5
Tolstoy biography 2, 293*f*, 296, 305
Unguarded Hours 254, 255
The Victorians 1–2
Wise Virgin 61, 175, 255, 278
Wilson, Angus 285
Wilson, Beatrice/Bee 171, 245
Wilson, Colin 257
Wilson, Dorothy, *see* Lewis, Dorothy, née
    Wilson
Wilson, Elizabeth 40, 42, 44, 45, 81–2,
    114–15, 219
    death of 296
    at Ferryside 273
    mince pies 114, 164
    and reading 166
    and Shakespeare 166–7
    and Wales 165–6
Wilson, Elizabeth Jean (Jeannie/Jish) 48, 69,
    82, 91
    education 88, 125
Wilson, Emily Rose 171, 225–6, 234–5
Wilson, Francesca 250–2
Wilson, Georgie 189
Wilson, Harold 286
Wilson, James 38
Wilson, Jean Dorothy, née Crowder 13,
    47–53, 58–9, 62, 72–3, 108–10
    and aesthetic sense 77–8
    and Barbour-Simpsons 131–2
    and Bible/quotations 121–2
    and cooking 108, 109
    and German family 69–70
    illnesses/health obsession 89, 106, 108–9
    marriage 68–9, 72, 73–4, 80–1, 86, 87–8,
        111–14
    move back to Llansteffan 296
    move to Stone 89
    moves to Wales 156, 273–4, 296
    and music 76–7
    and religion 74–5, 80–1, 90, 92, 101,
        103, 165
    and smoking 88
    and Stonefield Cottage 89–90

and tennis club 109
writing ambitions 121–2
Wilson, Norman 3, 21, 34, 35*f*, 38–41, 40*f*,
    42–4, 54–7, 58–62, 86–7
    and aesthetic sense 77–8
    annual trip to USA 110
    and Barbour-Simpsons 131–2
    death of 296
    dinghy incident 106–7
    education 44
    emigration to Canada 45–6
    and family business 45, 46
    funeral 299
    gun incident 275
    illness and death 297–8
    illnesses/health obsession 106
    at Josiah Wedgwood and Sons 63–4,
        66–8, 74, 112, 17–19, 121
    marriage 68–9, 80–1, 86, 111–14
    move to Malvern 148, 238
    moves to Wales 156, 164–5, 273–5, 296
    move to Worcester 140, 142–3
    and music 76–7
    post-war return home 85, 87
    post-war service 83–4
    return to Potteries 54–5
    and Royal Horse Artillery 62, 68
    trips abroad 110–11
    and WWII 78, 82
Wilson, Stephen 40*f*, 42–3, 44, 81–2, 91,
    106, 119, 120, 151–3, 154
    and Combined Cadet Force 154–5
    education 88, 124–5
    marriage 154, 156
    in Paris 152–3
Wilson, Stephen James 39–40
Wilson, Stephen Thomas 38
Wilson, Tom 40, 41–3, 46, 111 39–40
Winnicott, Donald 96
Winser, Dorothy 250
Woodard, Nathaniel 44
Woods, G. F. (Eric) 59, 71, 72–3, 75, 207
Woolf, Virginia 264
Wordsworth, William 48, 122
Worsthorne, Peregrine 176, 178
Woudhuysen, Henry 8
Wrenn, C. L. 210
Wright, Clarissa Dickson 285
Wyatt, Woodrow 176, 177, 178

Yates, Dorothy (Dot) 59–60, 61
Yeats, W. B. 8, 31
Young, Gavin 163
Young, Winnie 69
Yturbe, Isabelle de 171–2